ILLUSTRATED
WORLD OF
THE BIBLE
LIBRARY

ILLUSTRATED

WORLD OI

LIBRARY

McGRAW-HILL BOOK COMPANY, INC.

THE BIBLE

4. THE WRITINGS

NEW YORK · TORONTO · LONDON

First published in Jerusalem — Ramat-Gan, Israel,
under the title, VIEWS OF THE BIBLICAL WORLD: Volume 4

Library of Congress Catalogue Card number 59— 43080

41170

PRINTED IN ISRAEL

THE fourth volume of "Illustrated World of the Bible Library", which completes the commentary on the Old Testament books, has been compiled in accordance with the principles underlying the three previous volumes. Like them, it too contains a selection of biblical verses, arranged in the order in which they appear in the Bible, each illustrated by one or two pictures, as the subject matter requires. As in the previous volumes, the Editors have once again carefully chosen the illustrations for their authenticity and their value as visual aids to the understanding of the biblical text.

At the same time, the fourth volume of "Illustrated World of the Bible Library", being devoted to the group of Bible works known as the

"Writings", is of a somewhat different character from its predecessors. The volume containing the "Former Prophets" was a direct and natural continuation of the "Law" (at least as regards the historical and geographical descriptions in it); and the words of the prophets in the volume of the "Latter Prophets" similarly formed a kind of commentary on the historical events of the Monarchy which are described in the "Former Prophets". But in this present volume of the "Writings" the literary material is far more varied and far less homogeneous than in the previous volumes, nor has it, for the most part, any connection with the sequence of historical events.

This volume can be divided into three or four large literary units, each with its own special character. In the first of these come all the psalms, of which the book of Psalms is by far the largest single collection. This book contains not only psalms of praise and thanksgiving, of entreaty and complaint, of lament and repentance, but also hymns in praise of the people of Israel and its king, of Zion the city of God and of the Temple, as well as didactic poems on the theme of Israel's religious law. The poetry of the psalms, like all poetry of the ancient East, follows fixed linguistic patterns suited to the expression of set themes, with the addition of phrases and figures of speech in common use. Parallels to several of the patterns characteristic of the poetry of the Psalms have been found in the painting and sculpture of the ancient East, and examples of this kind have therefore been chosen by the Editors as concrete illustrations of the meaning of various verses in the book of Psalms.

A second self-contained literary unit is formed by the "Wisdom" books— Proverbs, Job, and Ecclesiastes, despite the many differences between them. The Book of Proverbs is composed of a number of anthologies of maxims and didactic sermons, some still bearing the stamp of their popular origins and others having a more polished literary form, but all of them written in verse. Evidences of Egyptian influence, resulting from contact with the literature of Egypt, are particularly numerous in this book, and the Editors have therefore endeavoured to give prominence to this fact in the choice and combined effect of the pictures. To find suitable archaeological illustrations for the Books of Job and Ecclesiastes was a harder task. As regards Job, we were somewhat helped by the ending of the Book with its detailed descriptions of nature's wonders and especially of wild creatures — descriptions which are unique in the Bible and which could be "illustrated" from the painting and sculpture of Mesopotamia and Egypt. But in the case of Ecclesiastes even the historical setting of the Book is still in dispute. We have, therefore, not confined ourselves here to pictures from Greek sources (in the spirit of the theory held by many scholars about the milieu from which it sprang), but have also included Egyptian and Assyrian material illustrative of certain unchanging features of the culture of the ancient East.

The Song of Songs, which contains the ancient love-poetry of Israel, presented a separate problem. In illustrating it, we have had to rely, as usual, mainly on pictures from Egypt, with a few from Assyria, but in doing so it has not been our intention to take any stand with regard to the question of the historical setting of this book. In Lamentations, which is a collection of dirges for the destruction of Jerusalem, we have sought to bring home the full meaning of that catastrophe by pictures of conquest and deportation from Assyrian art. It should be stressed that, in the section of the "Writings" which consists of psalms and wisdom literature, chronological considerations were not decisive in the choice of illustrations (in contrast to the previous volumes). Our main criterion was the extent to which the pictures displayed the characteristic, persistent features of the culture of the ancient East, and consequently we did not hesitate to make use of pictures widely separated in time from the verses which they illustrate.

The last unit in the volume is a historical one, comprising two short books with a historical colouring — Ruth and Esther, and two fully historical works — Ezra-Nehemiah and Chronicles. Ezra-Nehemiah, which Jewish tradition regards as a single book, rounds off the historical writings of the Old Testament with a description of the Return from the Babylonian Exile. The Book of Chronicles, on the other hand, recapitulates the whole of biblical history, from Adam to Cyrus, the Persian king. The main problem in this book, from our point of view, was thus its duplication of the contents of Samuel and Kings. In our selection of suitable illustrations, we had to be careful to avoid simply repeating what had already been offered the reader in volume II. We have therefore used the Book of Chronicles as a framework for a general survey of Israelite history in the biblical period, at the same time trying to give special prominence to those events recorded in the book which have no parallel in Samuel and Kings. In Esther and Ezra-Nehemiah we have made use of pictures illustrating the daily life and history of ancient Persia. In the Book of Daniel, which is the forerunner of the later apocalyptic literature, we have tried to give the reader a clear conception of the meaning of the symbols employed by the author and of the historical background that forms the setting to his apocalyptic vision.

This volume, like all the previous ones, also contains illustrations divorced from any particular historical context, such as pictures of Arab life in our own day, views of the Israeli landscape, and photographs of the country's wild life and vegetation. Pictures of the life of the Arab fellahin are particularly numerous in Ruth, as required by the special contents of this book.

CREDITS

Changes have been made in the composition of the Editorial Board responsible for this volume. Prof. M. Avi-Yonah was once again one of the editors, thus ensuring the continuity of the work of the editorial board, but he was joined this time by Dr. M. Haran and Dr. H. Tadmor, in place of Dr. A. Malamat and Dr. S. Talmon, who were thus able to devote themselves to the speedy completion of Volume III.

The Editors take this opportunity of expressing their gratitude to all those who have helped them in their task.

We are glad to acknowledge our indebtedness to all the members of the Editorial Board, the Editorial Advisory Council, and the Assistants, whose names are listed on the title-page of the Volume. Particular mention should also be made here of the assistance given by Mr. M. Weinfeld in the writing of the commentaries on Proverbs, and of that given by Mr. A. Allon in those on Ruth.

We also thank all those who have helped us in obtaining the reproductions or have given us the benefit of their comments on the actual contents of the volume: Dr. R. D. Barnett of London; Professor A. Parrot and Professor C. F. A. Schaeffer of Paris; Father R. North S.J., of the Pontifical Biblical Institute of Jerusalem; Dr. M. Dothan and Dr. K. Katz, both of Jerusalem.

We again wish to express our appreciation to all those distinguished public figures, both in Israel and abroad, who have given this project their approval and support from the outset, and above all to H.E. the President of Israel, Mr. Izhak Ben-Zvi; the Prime Minister, Mr. David Ben-Gurion; the former Minister of Education and Culture, Mr. Z. Aranne; and the Minister of the Interior, Mr. M. H. Shapira.

It is once more our pleasant duty to thank the Israel Ministry for Foreign Affairs, the Ministry of Education and Culture, the Ministry of Commerce and Industry, the Ministry of Finance, and the Ministry of Defence, as well as the Jewish Agency and "Malben" for their encouragement and ready assistance.

We also express our grateful sense of obligation to all the museums, individuals and photographers who have helped us in obtaining the plates required. Those in Israel include the staff and library of the Archaeology Department of the Hebrew University; the Department of Antiquities (museum and library) of the Ministry of Education and its former director, Prof. S. Yeivin; the National and University Library, Jerusalem; the Bezalel National Museum; the Haaretz Museum, Tel-Aviv; the James de Rothschild Expedition at Hazor; the collection of Mr. J. Leibovitch; the Clark Collection in the Y.M.C.A. building, Jerusalem; the collection of Professor Y. Yadin; the collection of Mr. K. Katz; the collection of the Ben-Zvi Institute for the Study of the Oriental Jewish Communities at the Hebrew University; the Shrine of the Book, Jerusalem; the Tell Qasile Collection, Tel-Aviv; the collection of A. Reifenberg, Jerusalem; Kibbutz Sdot-Yam; the Pontifical Biblical Institute, Jerusalem; the Ethnographical Museum, Tel-Aviv. Contributions from abroad have been provided by: the Metropolitan Museum, New York; the Oriental Institute of the University of Chicago; the collections of the Marburg and Alinari Photographic Institutes; the Museum of Fine Arts, Boston; the University Museum, Philadelphia; the Brooklyn Museum; the British Museum, London; the Hittite Museum, Ankara; the Staatliche Museen, Berlin; the Archaeological Museum, London University; Ny-Carlsberg Glyptothek, Copenhagen;

the Louvre, Paris; the Rijksmuseum, Leiden; the Musées Royaux d'Art et d'Histoire, Brussels, Belgium; the Musée Municipal de l'Eveché, Limoges; the Glasgow Art Galleries; the Museo dell'Arredamento, Florence; the Public Museum, Liverpool; the Museo di Antichita, Turin; the Museo Civico, Bologna; the Bibliothèque Nationale, Paris; the Cincinnati Art Museum; the Fogg Art Gallery, Harvard; the National Museum, Naples.

The Editorial Board also wishes to thank the following authors, editors and publishers for their kind permission to use plates published by them: W. F. Albright, W. Andrae, N. Avigad, D. Baldi, R. D. Barnett, P. Berger, A. M. Blackman, H. Bonnet, E. Douglas van Buren, M. Burrows, E. Chiera, Ch. Chipiez, F. M. Cross, G. Dalman, W. R. Dawson, N. de G. Davies, A. Deimel, J. Dossin, M. Dunand, G. R. Driver, A. Erman, C. S. Fisher, H. Frankfort, A. Furman, S. J. Gadd, K. Galling, A. H. Gardiner, P. C. Gau, A. J. Gayet, H. Gressmann, H. Grimme, L. H. Grollenberg, U. Hölscher, L. Klebs, S. N. Kramer, P. Lemaire, A. Lhote, G. Loud, D. G. Lyon, R. A. S. Macalister, M. J. L. Mallowan, Ch. McCown, B. Meissner, A. Mekhiterian, J. T. Milik, P. Montet, S. Moscati, H. H. Nelson, P. E. Newberry, J. Nougayrol, A. T. Olmstead, M. Oppenheim, M. Pallottino, R. A. Parker, A. Parrot, A. T. Peet, G. Perrot, W. M. Flinders Petrie, K. Pflüger, W. Phillips, H. Ranke, G. A. Reisner, P. Rost, A. Rowe, H. W. P. Saggs, A. H. Sayce, C. F. A. Schaeffer, H. Schmökel, O. Schröder, C. Schumacher, W. Stevenson-Smith, C. Steuernagel, E. L. Sukenik, F. Thureau-Dangin, J. Trever, O. Tufnell, N. H. Tur-Sinai, B. Ubach, C. Watzinger, R. Weill, M. Werbrouck, J. G. Wilkinson, H. E. Winlock, L. Woolley, W. Wreszinski, G. E. Wright;

American Schools of Oriental Research, E. J. Brill, Ltd., British Museum, British School of Archaeology in Iraq, F. A. Brockhaus, Constable & Co., W. de Gruyter & Co., Editions Cahiers d'Art, Editions Ides et Calendes, Egypt Exploration Fund, Egypt Exploration Society, Folkswang Verlag, Fondation égyptologique Reine Elizabeth, M. P. Geuthner, V. Gollancz, Hachette, Harvard University Press, J. C. Hinrichs, Imprimerie nationale, G. Klipper, Marietti, Metropolitan Museum, J. C. B. Mohr-Paul Siebeck, Monestir de Montserrat, John Murray Ltd., Oriental Institute — University of Chicago, Oxford University

Press, Palestine Exploration Fund, Penguin Books, Ltd., Presses universitaires de France, Routledge & Kegan Paul, Ltd., Ferdinand Schöningh, A. Skira, Society of Antiquaries, University Museum — University of Pennsylvania, The Trustees of the Late Sir Henry S. Wellcome, Yale University Press.

In addition we have availed ourselves of the comprehensive studies of R. Lepsius, A. H. Layard and P. E. Botta. The photographs in Israel were taken mainly by Z. Kluger, B. Rotenberg, A. Allon, I. Tal, M. Baram, A. Volk and J. Lister. Use has also been made of photographs from America and various European countries whose owners wish to remain anonymous.

Finally, we express our warm appreciation to the management and workers of the Schwitter A.G., Zürich; to the A. Levin-Epstein Ltd. Press, Bat-Yam; to the Haaretz Press Ltd., Tel-Aviv; to the Hakorech Binders' Cooperative, Holon (supported by "Malben"); and to the Tel-Aviv Bindery, for their devoted care in preparing the plates, setting up the text, and printing and binding this volume.

The English translation·of the biblical text used in this publication is mainly that of the *Revised Standard Version of the Bible,* copyrighted 1946 and 1952 by the Division of Christian Education, National Council of Churches, and used by permission.

At the conclusion of the four volumes treating the Hebrew Scriptures, the Editors may perhaps justifiably feel a sense of pride and satisfaction in having completed them in such a short time for so complicated a task. But they are also keenly aware that the work may, in some places, have fallen short of the high ideal which they set themselves. Nevertheless they hope that this visual commentary on the Book of Books will help to bring the world of the Bible to life for the general reader, and particularly for those of the younger generation.

THE EDITORS

PSALMS

The plate on the right is a reproduction of the illuminated
first page of the Book of Psalms in the Rothschild Manuscript.
The Bezalel National Museum, Jerusalem.

אַשְׁרֵי

הָאִישׁ אֲשֶׁר לֹא הָלַךְ בַּעֲצַת רְשָׁעִים וּבְדֶרֶךְ חַטָּאִים לֹא עָ
מָד וּבְמוֹשַׁב לֵצִים לֹא יָשָׁב : כִּי אִם בְּתוֹרַת יְהֹוָה חֶפְצוֹ וּבְ
וּבְתוֹרָתוֹ יֶהְגֶּה יוֹמָם וָלָיְלָה : וְהָיָה כְּעֵץ שָׁתוּל עַל פַּלְגֵי מָיִם
אֲשֶׁר פִּרְיוֹ יִתֵּן בְּעִתּוֹ וְעָלֵהוּ לֹא יִבּוֹל וְכֹל אֲשֶׁר יַעֲשֶׂה יַצְ
יַצְלִיחַ : לֹא כֵן הָרְשָׁעִים כִּי אִם כַּמֹּץ אֲשֶׁר תִּדְּפֶנּוּ רוּחַ : עַל
כֵּן לֹא יָקֻמוּ רְשָׁעִים בַּמִּשְׁפָּט וְחַטָּאִים בַּעֲדַת צַדִּיקִים :
כִּי יוֹדֵעַ יְהֹוָה דֶּרֶךְ צַדִּיקִים וְדֶרֶךְ רְשָׁעִים תֹּאבֵד :
לָמָּה רָגְשׁוּ גוֹיִם וּלְאֻמִּים יֶהְגּוּ רִיק : יִתְיַצְּבוּ
מַלְכֵי אֶרֶץ וְרוֹזְנִים נוֹסְדוּ יָחַד עַל יְהֹוָה וְעַל מְשִׁיחוֹ : בְּנַתְּ
בְּנַתְּקָה אֶת מוֹסְרוֹתֵימוֹ וְנַשְׁלִיכָה מִמֶּנּוּ עֲבֹתֵימוֹ : יוֹשֵׁב
בַּשָּׁמַיִם יִשְׂחָק יְהֹוָה יִלְעַג לָמוֹ : אָז יְדַבֵּר אֵלֵימוֹ בְאַפּוֹ וּבַחֲ
וּבַחֲרוֹנוֹ יְבַהֲלֵמוֹ : וַאֲנִי נָסַכְתִּי מַלְכִּי עַל צִיּוֹן הַר קָדְשִׁי :
אֲסַפְּרָה אֶל חֹק יְהֹוָה אָמַר אֵלַי בְּנִי אַתָּה אֲנִי הַיּוֹם יְלִדְתִּיךָ :
שְׁאַל מִמֶּנִּי וְאֶתְּנָה גוֹיִם נַחֲלָתֶךָ וַאֲחֻזָּתְךָ אַפְסֵי אָרֶץ :
תְּרֹעֵם בְּשֵׁבֶט בַּרְזֶל כִּכְלִי יוֹצֵר תְּנַפְּצֵם : וְעַתָּה מְלָכִים הַשְׂכִּ

HE is like a tree planted by streams of water, that yields its fruit in its season, and its leaf does not wither. In all that he does, he prospers.   (Psalms 1 : 3)

The first psalm, which sets the good man who flourishes in his righteousness over against the sinner who is like chaff blown away by the wind, provides a fitting opening to the whole Book of Psalms, in which one of the main, constantly repeated, themes is the contrast between the righteous and the wicked. The righteous man is here symbolized by a luxuriant tree growing beside water, which gives fruit in season and is always green and fresh. A similar image is contained in the simile, so typical of the ancient wisdom literature, that has been worked into the prophecy of Jeremiah, (Jer. 17 : 5—8): there too the man who trusts in the Lord is depicted as being "like a tree planted by water, that sends out its roots by the stream ... for its leaves remain green ... and it does not cease to bear fruit." Another close parallel to the simile in our psalm is found in one of the works of Egyptian wisdom literature, the Instruction of Amenemopet (see below, p. 87), where the man of reason and moderation is contrasted with the turbulent hot-head. The former is likened to "a tree growing in a garden" which "flourishes and doubles its yield."
The figure of the tree planted by streams of water, as symbolical of the righteous man, is also rooted in the earliest literary traditions of Mesopotamia. In the Sumerian writings, for example, king Shulgi of the Third Dynasty of Ur is compared to "a date-palm planted by streams of water and a cedar growing by many waters."
In Palestine the trees found on the banks of streams, in marshy ground and in the valley of the Jordan — such as the Jordan tamarisk, the Mesopotamian poplar and the palm — are remarkable for the greenness and luxuriance of their foliage (growing as they do in regions where the annual rainfall is slight), though, for ecological reasons, they are not particularly tall. Photographed here are palms beside the flood-waters of the Jordan.

THE wicked are not so, but are like chaff which the wind drives away.   (Psalms 1 : 4)

In contrast to the righteous man, who is likened to "a tree planted by streams of water" (see the previous page), the sinner is compared to chaff blown away by the wind. This image is employed in the poetry of the Old Testament to depict sudden and complete destruction. Thus, in Ps. 35 : 5, it is said of the enemies of the righteous: "let them be like chaff before the wind"; and the same simile is also found in other books of the Old Testament, always in reference to the wicked (Isa. 17 : 13; 29 : 5; 41 : 15—16; Hos. 13 : 3; cf. Vol. III, p. 220, and elsewhere). In biblical times, the threshing-floor on which corn was winnowed usually stood on top of a rocky hillock from where the wind could blow the chaff far away. The implements used in winnowing were the "shovel" (Heb. *rahath*) and the "fork" *(mizreh)* (see Isa. 30 : 24; Jer. 15 : 7). This was probably the method most commonly employed by the peasants in all the countries of the ancient East.

The illustration is a section of a wall-painting from the tomb of Menna at Thebes (time of the Eighteenth Dynasty, 15th cent. B. C.) depicting the winnowing of corn on a threshing-floor. The three men in the centre are beating the corn to detach the grain from the rest of the ear (cf. Ruth 2 : 17; and below, p. 156), while the three on each side are winnowing the beaten out grain and separating it from the chaff.

Bᴜᴛ thou, O ʟᴏʀᴅ, art a shield about me, my glory, and the lifter of my head. (Psalms 3 : 3)

The psalms are full of poetical images taken from war and the weapons of war. In the verse above God is compared to a shield *(magen)* which protects the worshipper from his foes. This particular figure of speech is very common in the psalms (cf. Ps. 18 : 2, 30; 28 : 7; 33 : 20 and elsewhere; also Prov. 2 : 7; 30 : 5), and a similar usage also occurs in the Pentateuch (Gen. 15 : 1; Deut. 33 : 29). We further find God, or "His will", or "His truth" compared to a large shield *(zinah)* (Ps. 5 : 12; 35 : 2; 91 : 4). See also below, p. 60.

The *zinah* and *magen* were designed as an additional protection for the warrior's body, besides the breast-plate that he wore. The main difference between these two defensive weapons lay in their size. The *zinah* was large enough to cover most of the body, and was therefore often carried by a shield-bearer who kept close to the warrior while the latter employed his offensive weapons. (See below, p. 280). The *magen,* on the other hand, was primarily intended to cover those exposed parts of the body (such as the head) which could hardly be protected by a coat of mail. Though its shape varied from period to period and from nation to nation, it was always carried on the warrior's left arm by means of a special thong attached to its inner side. To make it easy to handle, this small shield was of light construction, usually consisting of a framework of wood or plaited reeds with a piece of leather stretched over it. The leather was apparently oiled before battle (2 Sam. 1 : 21; Isa. 21 : 5). The *magen* was convex in shape (see the illustration — a section of a relief from the palace of Sennacherib at Nineveh) to afford protection for the body from the front and from both sides.

FOR lo, the wicked bend the bow, they have fitted their arrow to the string, to shoot in the dark at the upright in heart.

(Psalms 11 : 2)

Every theme in the Book of Psalms has its stock images and stereotyped figures of speech. Thus, in the out-pourings of personal supplication the sinner is regularly described as drawing his bow and shooting an arrow at the unsuspecting righteous man; while the upright true-believer is portrayed as the hunted worshipper of God. This word-picture is not confined to the verse above, but recurs in other passages dealing with the same theme: "If he does not repent, he will whet his sword; he has bent and strung his bow" (Ps. 7 : 12); "the wicked draw the sword and bend their bows, to bring down the poor and needy" (ibid. 37 : 14); "who . . . aim bitter words like arrows, shooting from ambush at the blameless" (ibid. 64 : 3—4), and elsewhere.

The bowman of antiquity prepared his weapon for action before taking up his position on the battle-field. This he did by fastening the bowstring in place by means of the loops at its ends. First he tied the string to one end of the bow (which was curved over slightly to form a hook shaped like a duck's head), and then he bent the body of the bow so that he could attach the other loop to the opposite end. The next stage was the use of the bow in battle, as described in our verse here. First, the bowman "bent" (Heb. *darakh*) the weapon i. e., pulled back the string, holding the arrow in his right hand. Then he aimed the arrow at the target, steadying its tip with his left thumb.

In the picture here a bowman belonging to the auxiliary forces of Sennacherib's army is seen "bending" his bow and aiming an arrow. In order to show the soldier's body in its entirety, the Assyrian artists sometimes twisted the body, showing the head and the legs in front and the trunk from the back. Therefore it seems as if the bow were being held in the right hand. But a closer examination of the shape of the fist shows that the hand in question is actually the left.

KEEP me as the apple of the eye; hide me in the shadow of thy wings.   (Psalms 17 : 8)

In several of the psalms, the supplicant refers to "the shadow of God's wings" (ibid. 36 : 7; 57 : 1; 63 : 7) or the "shelter of His wings (ibid. 61 : 4), in the sense of a place of hiding and refuge. Similar expressions are also found in Ps. 91 : 1, 4: "in the shelter of the Most High, in the shadow of the Almighty"; "he will cover you with his pinions, and under his wings you will find refuge". This metaphor is hardly found anywhere else in the Old Testament, outside the Book of Psalms, the closest approximations to it being the picture of the eagle hovering with outspread wings over its young in the Song of Moses (Deut. 32 : 11), and the words spoken by Boaz to Ruth (Ruth 2 : 12). In the Psalms this is merely a picturesque figure of speech for the Temple in which the supplicant is standing as he offers up his prayer: "the shadow of God's wings" is "the house" or "the tent" of the Lord which is explicitly mentioned in the same or following verses of the same psalms (Ps. 36 : 8; 61 : 4; cf. 27 : 5; 31 : 20; 32 : 7; and elsewhere). There is no doubt, however, that the origins of this metaphor go back to earlier, non-Israelite thought-patterns. In Israel the expression had already lost its primal meaning and become nothing more than a set phrase.

This metaphor is frequently given plastic form in the art of ancient Egypt, in which wings are a symbol of divinity and the gods are often portrayed as stretching out their wings over the king to protect and shelter him. Reproduced on the left is the dark grey diorite statue of the Pharaoh Chephren (of the Fourth Dynasty, first half of the third millennium, B. C.) which was discovered at Gizeh in the king's Valley Temple. Standing on the back of the throne is the god Horus, in the form of a falcon, with his wings spread out to cover the back of the king's head. On the right — a granite statue of Osiris and Isis from the temple at Karnak (time of the Thirtieth Dynasty, 4th cent. B. C.). Osiris, wearing a crown and holding the symbols of royal power, is standing "in the shadow" of Isis' wings.

HE bowed the heavens, and came down; thick darkness was under his feet.   (Psalms 18 : 9)

The coming of the Lord in answer to the king's cry for help is described in Psalm 18 in a series of vivid word-pictures: the earth shakes, smoke rises from the Lord's nostrils and "devouring fire from His mouth" (verses 7—8); He rides down from the heavens on a cherub and "comes swiftly upon the wings of the wind" (9—10); He is shrouded in a "canopy of thick clouds dark with water", "hailstones and coals of fire" rain down before Him (11—12); He thunders with His voice and shoots arrows from His bow (13—14); and finally, He draws up the supplicant from the mighty waters that threaten to overwhelm him and delivers him from his foes. As used by the Old Testament poet, these expressions are no more than metaphors in the contemporary literary and artistic tradition, their purpose being to heighten the awe-inspring impression of the theophany in answer to the king's appeal. But the origin of this literary tradition goes back to pre-Israelite times. It was apparently taken over by the Israelites from the early Hebrew nomad tribes which, at the beginning of their history, were constantly on the move in Mesopotamia and the regions influenced by its culture. These tribes conceived their gods in similar terms, and for them these anthropomorphisms may well have been far more real.

The influence of this ancient Mesopotamian tradition can still be traced, here and there, in Assyrian works of art from the first millennium B. C. Something of its atmosphere can be found, for example, in the picture reproduced below which is a fragment of a coloured, glazed brick discovered at Ashur, from the reign of Tukulti-Ninurta II (890—884 B. C.). On it the god Ashur is portrayed descending from the heavens, surrounded by tongues of flames, with a drawn bow in his hand. Painted on either side of him are heavy, rain-laden clouds. Underneath the god there was a picture of a chariot, of which all that remains is the head of the man standing in it and the end of the horse's mane.

I pursued my enem[ies]
and overtook the[m],
and did not turn ba[ck]
till they were co[n]
sumed. I thrust the[m]
through, so that the[y]
were not able to ris[e;]
they fell under my fe[et]
(Psalms 18 : 37-3[9)]

The king's battles against his foes are depicted in the psalms as undertaken by
himself alone. In fact, of course, the actual fighting was done by the armed
forces of the nation, under the king's command. It is therefore remarkable that,
in the whole of the Book of Psalms, there is hardly any mention of the army.
Instead, the individual figure of the king is enlarged out of all proportion
and, with complete disregard for reality, the battle and the victory are portrayed
as his single-handed achievement. It is the king himself, as stated in the verses
above, that pursues his foes and thrusts them through till they fall "under
his feet." This grandiose vein continues throughout the rest of the psalm, the
enemy's destruction being drawn in particularly vivid detail: the king himself,
supposedly with his own hands, annihilates his foes, grinds them fine "as
dust before the wind", and tramples upon them "like the mire of the streets"
(Ps. 18 : 39—42, 47).

These characteristic images of the royal psalms are derived, like other
frequently repeated figures of speech in the Book of Psalms, from traditional
stereotyped poetical patterns that were shared by Israel with the other peoples
of the ancient East. These set patterns can also be found in the other branches
of ancient oriental art, especially in painting and sculpture. The most striking
examples are provided by Egyptian wall-paintings and reliefs (cf. below,
pp. 28, 34). Here too the figure of the king is enlarged to more than human
proportions and every one of his victories is portrayed as his own personal
achievement. The relief reproduced above, which belongs to the time of
the Nineteenth Dynasty in Egypt and is from Abu Simbel on the Upper
Nile (Nubia), depicts the victory of Ramses II over the Libyans. The king
is "annihilating" one of his foes, while another is already falling "under his
feet."

SOME boast of chariots, and some of horses; but we boast of the name of the LORD our God.

(Psalms 20 : 7)

The Twentieth Psalm is a prayer for the king's victory in war, uttered in the Temple before the army marched out to battle. In the first part of it (Ps. 20 : 1—5), the worshippers pray that God may help the king in his fight, may remember his sacrifices and "fulfil all his wishes". Then (ibid. 6—8), the tone changes to one of joyful confidence, arising from the assurance that the prayer has been granted and the enemy's doom is already sealed. The psalm ends (ibid. 9) with an entreaty to the Lord to give the king victory at all times.

In the second part of this psalm it is stressed that, whereas the enemy places his trust in chariots and horses, Israel "boasts of the name of the Lord our God". This does not mean, of course, that the king of Israel fought without chariots and horses, but is simply an expression of the profound awareness, so fundamental to Israelite religion, that human destiny is, in the last analysis, decided not by material force, but by divine grace. This idea recurs in other psalms (e. g. 33 : 16—17; 147 : 10—11), in the words of the prophets (e. g. Isa. 31 : 3), and also in biblical narrative (see David's remarks to Goliath, 1 Sam. 17 : 45).

However, something of this reliance on divine favour, rather than on chariots and horses, can also be found in the literary conventions of ancient oriental liturgy. A striking example is the tone of Ramses II's prayer to "his father", Amon-Re, during his battle with the Hittites outside Kedesh-on-the-Orontes. He too, in describing that battle, speaks of the worthlessness of "soldiers and chariots" by themselves and of the help of his god as alone decisive; though he too, of course, continued to make use of those weapons of war. The picture below of Egyptian cavalry and chariots on the banks of the Orontes is taken from one of Ramses II's reliefs (in his temple at Abydos) portraying the battle against the Hittites.

The king's victory over his foes is depicted in this verse, after the regular manner of the psalms, as his personal, single-handed achievement, the part played in the battle by the army being completely ignored. The king's own right hand will find all his enemies, all those that hate him. This conception is also a common motif in the paintings and reliefs of the ancient East, especially in Egypt (see pp. 26, 34). In Egyptian art, the victorious king is portrayed holding the kneeling foe by the hair with his left hand, while he smites him with a blow from his right. This artistic motif was introduced as early as the First Dynasty (the Narmer palette) and persisted throughout almost all of Egypt's long history. Here is an example of it on a painted ostracon from the time of the Twentieth Dynasty (12th cent. B. C.), which was discovered at Thebes: Ramses III is shown smiting his Syro-Canaanite foes with the sword in his right hand, holding them by the hair with his left hand as he does so. This kind of blow may be the "shattering of the head" mentioned in various poetical passages of the Old Testament (Hab. 3 : 13; Ps. 68 : 21; 110 : 5—6. Cf. Vol. II, p. 33).

THE LORD is my shepherd, I shall not want; he makes me lie down in green pastures. He leads me beside still waters. (Psalms 23 : 1-2)

Psalm 23 is one of the hymns in which the psalmist expresses his faith and trust in his God. In it God is likened to a shepherd that devotedly cares for a single lamb (the psalmist himself) which symbolically represents the whole flock. This figurative description of the relationship between the Lord and Israel recurs frequently in the psalms, the Lord being metaphorically referred to in such terms as "the shepherd of Israel" and the Israelites as "the sheep of his pasture" (Ps. 80 : 1; 95 : 7; 100 : 3; and elsewhere). This image was also frequently employed by several of the prophets and received particular poetic elaboration by the author of the consolatory vision of the Return to Zion (Isa. 40 : 11; 49 : 10).

The Lord, as the good shepherd, makes his flock lie down in green meadows and leads it beside still waters (cf. Isa. 49 : 10: "by springs of water he will guide them") — still to this day the two most essential conditions of proper pasturage in Israel. In biblical times, goat- and sheep-rearing in Palestine was based entirely on natural pasture, unsupplemented by stall-feeding (as is customary to-day). The shepherds had thus to keep moving with their flocks from one pasturing-ground to another. The lambs, with their gawky movements, tired quickly and were therefore allowed to rest in the midday heat (Jer. 33 : 12; Song of Sol. 1 : 7; and elsewhere), preferably in pastures beside springs, wells or water-holes where the whole flock could slake its thirst. Since this ground-water is not easily accessible in most regions of Palestine, the flocks were usually watered from cisterns and pools specially dug to collect the rains. At shearing-time, which was the beginning of the summer, it was also customary to dip the flock in water to cleanse the animals' fleeces of the dust stirred up by their feet and thus lighten the work of the shearers (cf. Song of Sol. 4 : 2; 6 : 6).

Above is a photograph of a flock of sheep and goats moving along beside a pool.

THOUGH a host encamp against me, my heart shall not fear; though war arise against me, yet I will be confident. (Psalms 27 : 3)

In the first part of this psalm (Ps. 27 : 1—6), the worshipper gives a highly poetical description of his feelings of trust in his God. All the endeavours of his foes to destroy him are doomed to failure, because God is "his light and his salvation", "the stronghold of his life." The Temple, which is the implied scene of this utterance, is depicted as a place of refuge and concealment for the psalmist "in the day of trouble" (verse 5), and his only wish is that he may remain there "all the days of his life" (verse 4). On this rock-like shelter all the evil designs of his enemies will shatter themselves in vain. In the verse at the head of this page the possible actions of these enemies are described in images taken from warfare.

"War" stands here in poetic parallelism with "camp", since the armed hosts used to form up in an encampment before going out to battle. The shape of this camp was either circular (Hebrew version of 1 Sam. 17 : 20; 26 : 5, 7), or square (like the bivouac of the Israelites in the desert, Nu . chap. 2—3). The illustration below (a bronze relief from Balawat, from the reign of the Assyrian king Shalmaneser III), shows the Assyrian army marching out to battle from a square-shaped camp. In the upper register: Assyrian infantry and cavalry who have just left the camp. Below: Shalmaneser is seen himself leaving the camp, escorted by his bodyguard. The whole is a scene from Shalmaneser's campaign to the sources of the Tigris in 852 B. C.

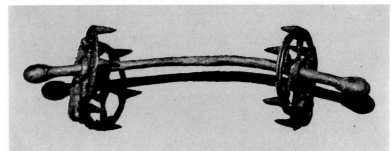

Bᴇ not like a horse or a mule, without understanding, which must be curbed with bit and bridle, else it will not keep with you.   (Psalms 32 : 9)

The last part of Psalm 32 (verses 8-11), which is written in the didactic tone of the wisdom literature, consists of admonition and instruction for the foolish wicked and praise for the righteous. In the verse above, the poet likens the fool to a horse or a mule which, lacking intelligence, needs to have its wildness restrained by the bit and bridle with which its master curbs it. Much the same image is found in one of the sayings in the Book of Proverbs: "A whip for the horse, a bridle for the ass, and a rod for the back of fools" (Prov. 26 : 3); and the use of the bridle and bit .is referred to metaphorically in several other passages of the Bible (Isa. 30 : 28; 37 : 29; and elsewhere). The horse's head-harness, of which the bit and bridle were part, was in antiquity often a work of art and served an aesthestic, no less than a practical, purpose. The upper picture is a reproduction from an Assyrian relief, discovered at Nineveh and dating to the 8th cent. B. C., showing an elaborately groomed horse's head encased in a complete head-harness. For other forms of ornamentation of the heads of horses see below, pp. 131, 193. The lower illustration shows a bit from the Hyksos period (17th—16th cent. B.C.) which was found at Beth Eglayim (Tell el-Ajjul).

_TAKE hold of shield and buckler, and rise for my help! Draw the spear and javelin against my pursuers ...

(Psalms 35 : 2-3)

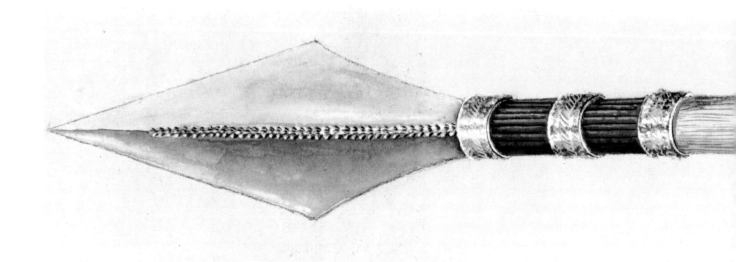

Of the weapons mentioned in these verses, in which the psalmist calls upon the Lord to come to his aid, three are well known: the small shield *(magen)*, the large shield *(zinah)*, and the javelin *(hanith)*. It has generally been assumed that the unknown root of the fourth word in the list, *sgr* (here translated "javelin"), which is joined to the others by the conjunction "and", must also denote some kind of weapon, but its exact meaning has been disputed. Some commentators have conjectured that the reference is to the Scythian *sagaris;* while according to another view, which involves a slight emendation of the text *(sgd* for *sgr),* the weapon in question was something like the Akkadian *shukudu.* Perhaps a better understanding of the meaning of this word can now be obtained from the recently discovered Dead Sea Scrolls, since in one of them — "The War of the Sons of Light against the Sons of Darkness" — the *seger* is mentioned as one of the accessories of the javelin. The description of it runs as follows: "The length of the spear shall be seven cubits, of which the socket and the blade take up half a cubit. On the socket there shall be three rings engraved like a rim of cable work, of gold, silver and copper welded together like a pattern cunningly wrought; and running spiral, the pattern being on both sides of the ring all round, precious stones in ajour work, work of a smith, cunningly wrought, and ear of corn. The socket shall be fluted between the rings like the working of a column, cunningly wrought. The blade shall be of iron tempered in fire, work of a smith, cunningly wrought, and an ear of corn of pure gold in the midst of (or: inlaid in) the blade, the blade being made tapering towards the point."

This description makes it clear (see the reconstruction above) that the *seger* was the metal part by which the blade of the javelin or spear was secured to the wooden shaft, i.e. the socket. In view of its importance, it is quite possible that this small part might be used as a synonym for the whole blade, or even for the whole weapon. The fixing of the *seger* in place was one of the most difficult technical problems involved in the manufacture of a javelin or spear and the methods employed varied from period to period. That described in "The War of the Sons of Light against the Sons of Darkness" seems to have been similar to the one favoured by the Romans.

FOR our soul is bowed down to the dust; our body cleaves to the ground.   (Psalms 44 : 25)

Psalm 44, one of the finest of the outpourings of communal supplication in the whole book, opens with a reference to the wonders wrought by the Lord in ancient times (verses 1—3) and a proclamation that Israel's victory over its foes depends on the Lord's will alone (verses 4—8). Then follows a description of Israel's present defeated and abject condition, with an emphatic assertion that the nation nevertheless remains faithful to the covenant with its God (verses 9—22). The psalm ends with a fervent appeal to the Lord to help Israel in their trouble (verses 23—26). The bitter lament in the last part of the psalm, "for our soul is bowed down to the dust etc.," may be an expression of national grief and despondency similar to the individual's cry of woe in the great didactic Psalm 119: "my soul cleaves to the dust" (Ps. 119 : 25). But it may also contain a reference to the fact that the suppliants have prostrated themselves in worship on the paving of the Temple courts, thereby expressing their self-abasement before their Creator and their complete surrender to His will.

It was customary in the ancient East for anyone presenting an entreaty to go down on his knees, or even to stretch himself full length on the ground. This is well illustrated in the picture above of a group of foreigners pleading with one of the Pharaoh's officials (on a relief from the tomb of Horemheb at Thebes, from the 14th cent. B. C.). Most of the suppliants are Syro-Canaanites; two of them (kneeling, with pointed beards, locks combed down over their foreheads and a feather stuck in their hair) are Libyans; and the one beardless figure is an Ethiopian. The man in the foreground is flat on his stomach, "cleaving to the dust"; while one of the others is stretched out on his back. The expression "(lying) on my belly, on my back, I shall hearken to the king's word" also occurs frequently in the el-Amarna letters.

IN your majesty ride forth victoriously for the cause of truth and
to defend the right; let your right hand teach you dread deeds!
Your arrows are sharp in the heart of the king's enemies; the
peoples fall under you. (Psalms 45 : 4-5)

In this psalm, which is a "love song" for the king's wedding-day, the poet
describes his sovereign in a kaleidoscope of swiftly changing word-pictures
which in rapid succession, portray the beauty of his appearance, the sweetness of
his speech ("grace is poured upon your lips"), the seat of justice on which he
sits, his fragrant robes and so on. Inserted amongst these is the image of the
king as the mighty sword-girt warrior, standing erect in his chariot and shooting
his sharp arrows into the hearts of his foes who fall beneath his feet (ibid. 4—5).
This image is derived from the convention, regularly followed in both the poetry
and art of the ancient East, of enlarging the king's figure to colossal proportions
and portraying his victory as his own single-handed achievement (cf. above,
pp. 26, 28). This convention, which is of non-Israelite origin, finds its most
characteristic expression in the plastic art of ancient Egypt.

In Egyptian reliefs the Pharaoh's victory over his enemies is often depicted in
exactly the same terms as in our psalm. Though his body-guard and cavalry are
shown beside the royal chariot, it is his own figure that dominates the whole
picture and the arrows which he shoots are represented as deciding the fate
of the battle. An example of this artistic convention is given in the illustration
above, which is a reproduction of a relief on one of the walls of the Ramesside
temple at Thebes, (from the time of the Nineteenth Dynasty), portraying the
capture of the Hittite city of Deper by Ramses II. The king is standing erect in
his chariot, while his foes, pierced by his arrows, are falling before him. At the
same time, realistic touches are not entirely lacking, particularly in the representation of the Egyptian storming of the fortified city (at the right). In the bottom row,
under the hooves of the king's horses, it is possible to make out two Egyptian
princes in the act of slaying Hittite soldiers.

HIS holy mountain, beautiful in elevation, is the joy of all the earth, Mount Zion, in the far north, the city of the great king.

(Psalms 48 : 2)

The hymns included in the Book of Psalms contain frequent panegyrical references to the Temple (see Ps. 78 : 68-69 ; 93 : 5 ; 96 : 6 ; and elsewhere, and cf. the psalm in Jer. 17 : 12). There are even cases in which this strain of lyrical praise so dominates the whole psalm as to become its main theme (as in Ps. 84). Sometimes the panegyric is not confined to the Temple, but embraces all the Holy City of Jerusalem (see Ps. 46, 48, 76, 87, 122, 132, and briefer references in the same spirit in other psalms). Hymns of this kind were apparently sung by the caravan-trains of pilgrims wending their way up to the Temple, and perhaps also in the thanksgiving processions round the city-wall. The prophets too, in their occasional ecstatic praises of Jerusalem, also employ the characteristic imagery of the psalmists (Isa. 25 : 1 ; 26 : 2-5 ; Jer. 31 : 23 ; and elsewhere).

In these psalms Zion, "the city of God", is both holy and eternal. It is depicted as a mighty citadel which God "will establish for ever" and against whose towers every hostile onslaught will be shattered. To these two primary motifs of holiness and eternity, a third, aesthetic theme is added : the city is "the perfection of beauty" (Ps. 50 : 2), "the joy of all the earth" (cf. Lam. 2 : 15) ; its palaces and walls are the wonder of all that behold them (Ps. 48 : 12—13). This is the theme which finds expression in the verse at the head of this page.

The photograph is a view of Jerusalem from the east.

BUT I am like a green olive tree in the house of God. I trust in the steadfast love of God for ever and ever.

(Psalms 52 : 8)

The olive-tree, to which the righteous man — i. e. the psalmist himself — is compared here, is one of the most characteristic features of the landscape of Israel. There presumbly were olive-trees growing in the vicinity of the Temple Mount; indeed, the words "in the house of God" may denote the location of the previously mentioned "green olive-tree." A similar comparison of Israel to a green olive-tree is found in one of Jeremiah's prophecies, which was also apparently uttered in the Temple (see Jer. 11 : 15-16).

The olive *(Olea europea L.)*, a typically Mediterranean tree, was one of the "seven species" for which ancient Palestine was famous (Deut. 8 : 8; cf. Vol. I, p. 260). A considerable part of the Israelite peasant's prosperity in Old Testament times came from his cultivation of this tree which does not require much tending. It grows without irrigation, does not need deep soil, but flourishes even in rocky terrain and is therefore common also in the hill regions. It is thus hardly surprising that its oil was regarded as Palestine's export commodity par excellence (1 Kings 5 : 11; Ezek. 27 : 17; Hos. 12 : 1). The olive is also one of the country's most handsome trees. Its foliage retains its greenness in the parched days of summer when its leafy, spreading top is a delight to the heat-weary eye. It is a long-lived tree, sometimes lasting for hundreds of years; its trunk thickens as it grows older, but its vitality is in no way impaired by the passage of the years. Olive-trees of great age are found in various parts of Israel. The one photographed above is a typical specimen in the Shephelah (the southern coastal region).

AND I say, "O that I had wings like a dove! I would fly away and be at rest; yea, I would lodge in the wilderness".

(Psalms 55 : 6-7)

This psalm is one of the outpourings of personal protestation. As usual in such psalms, the worshipper here complains of the treacheries and oppressions of his fellow-men. A prey to every fear and beset by "the terrors of death", he longs to escape from the nightmare of his existence by fleeing far away, like the untrammelled dove, and taking up his abode in the wilderness. This mood recalls the plaint of Jeremiah who also yearned to escape from his people to a "wayfarers' lodging" in the desert (Jer. 9 : 2). The Judean desert was the refuge of the wretched and oppressed (see 1 Sam. 23 : 24; 1 Kings 19 : 4; Job 30 : 3—8), and also of fugitives from war (Jer. 4 : 29).

The sufferer's withdrawal to the desert is here described in terms of the dove's swift flight, a metaphor used by the prophets Isaiah and Hosea to describe the return of Israel to its land (Isa. 60 : 8; Hos. 11 : 11). The bird referred to here must be the wild dove *(Columba livia)* which is very common in Israel and usually breeds in rock-fissures (see Jer. 48 : 28; Song of Sol. 2 : 14), in wadis (Ezek. 7 : 16) and beside water-holes (Song of Sol. 5 : 12). On the domestic dove, which is a descendant of the wild species, see Vol. I, p. 184.

Because of its unusual beauty and grace, the dove was a popular subject in ancient poetry and art. In the wall-painting reproduced above from the western wall of the "Green Room" in the northern palace of Akhenaton at Tell el-Amarna, a dove is shown in a papyrus thicket on the banks of the Nile.

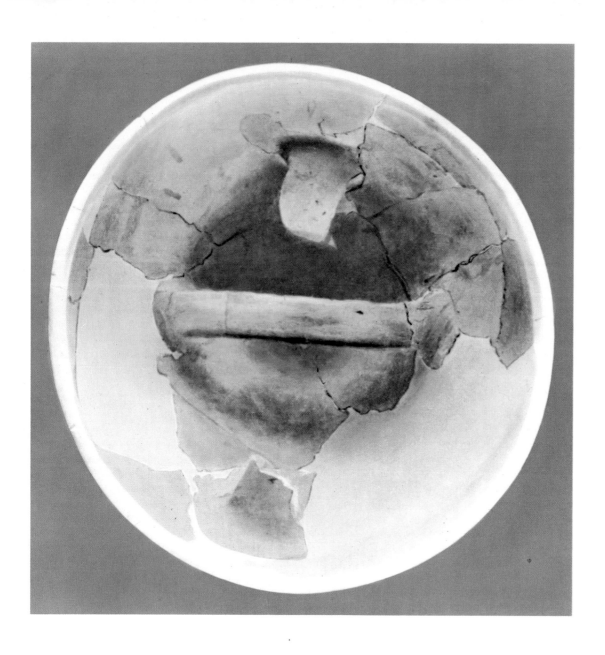

MOAB is my washbasin; upon Edom I cast my shoe; over Philistia I shout in triumph.

(Psalms 60 : 8)

The second half of Psalm 60 contains a divine pronouncement (verse 6 : "God has spoken in his sanctuary"), evidently in reply to the suppliants' entreaties (end of verse 5: "and answer us") or to the king of Israel's prayer. The Lord promises the king of Israel sovereign mastery over all the confines of Palestine and the enslavement of its neighbouring peoples. This same divine response is repeated in Ps. 108 (verses 7-9) which is also apparently a royal psalm. In the verse quoted above, Moab's abject defeat by the king of Israel is vividly depicted by describing the country as Israel's "washbasin".

The ancient pot (Heb. *sir*) had several functions. It was used for both cooking (2 Kings 4 : 38; Ezek. 24 : 3—6; Zech. 14 : 21 and elsewhere) and eating. It served as a receptacle for meat (Ex. 16 : 3, 7) and other foods, such as pottage *(nezid*; 2 Kings 4 : 40), and also for water. The wash-pot mentioned in our verse here was presumably a basin in which the feet were washed: it is immediately followed by a reference to "casting off the shoe" which was a necessary preliminary to washing the feet. The ancients washed their own feet frequently, and this was also one of the courtesies extended to a guest (Gen. 18 : 4; 19 : 2; 24 : 32), as is still done in oriental countries to this day.

The picture above is of a foot-basin from Samaria, from the time of the Israelite Monarchy (9th or 8th cent. B. C.). In the centre of the basin there is a raised ledge on which the feet were placed while being washed. Under the inner side of the lip of the basin there are bosses which served as lifting-handles. The basin is oval in shape, being 24 in. long and 16 in. wide.

I will praise the name of God with a song; I will magnify him with thanksgiving. This will please the LORD more than an ox or a bull with horns and hoofs. (Psalms 69 : 30-31)

Psalm 69, which is another expression of individual protestation, ends, in the regular manner of such psalms, on a hopeful note of reconciliation and gratitude (Ps. 69 : 30—36). In the verses quoted here the worshipper proclaims that his praise of his God with song and thanksgiving will be more acceptable to the Lord than a sacrifice offered on the altar. Similar apparent declarations of the superiority of prayer to sacrifice are found in several other psalms (see ibid. 40 : 6—10; 51 : 15—17). However, the great importance attributed in these passages to prayer is partly a poetic exaggeration, and should not mislead us into thinking that the psalmists intended to belittle the value of sacrifice. On the contrary, they regarded it as the highest form of divine worship; in more than one psalm the suppliant makes a solemn vow to offer sacrifices when he is delivered from his afflictions and to accompany them with a song of thanksgiving (see ibid. 22 : 25-26; 27 : 6; 50 : 23; and frequently elsewhere; also Jonah 2 : 9). Similarly, it is said of the sick who "drew near to the gates of death" that, when their cries to the Lord are answered and they have been saved, they thank Him for His graciousness and "offer sacrifices of thanksgiving and tell of his deeds in songs of joy" (ibid. 107 : 22). Moreover, in one of the psalms which appears to stress the superiority of prayer to sacrifice, the poet ends with the statement that, when Zion is rebuilt, the Lord will again delight "in right sacrifices, in burnt offerings and whole burnt offerings" and that bulls will again be sacrificed on His altar (ibid. 51 : 19).
Prayer, then, was the sacrifice of the poor and, as such, was regarded as of equal worth to a real sacrifice offered on the altar (see the latter part of our psalm, verses 32-33: "Let the oppressed see it and be glad . . . For the Lord hears the needy."). In actual fact, however, the sphere of priestly activity, with its closeness to the altar and the sacrifices, was regarded by the worshippers themselves as of superior sanctity to the Temple precincts in which the popular rites were performed, even though the psalms were uttered there. This recognition of the primacy of the priestly ritual was typical of all the civilizations of the ancient East and has left its mark on their works of art.
In the illustration above, part of a relief from the temple of Ramses II at Abydos (13th cent. B. C.), a sacrificial victim is seen being led to the altar at the dedication ceremony. The animal is a "long-horned" bull of pedigree Nubian stock. The man beside it is carrying a young gazelle on his shoulders.

MAY his foes bow down before him, and his enemies lick the dust! May the kings of Tarshish and of the isles render him tribute, may the kings of Sheba and Seba bring gifts!
(Psalms 72 : 9-10)

Psalm 72 is a royal hymn sung on the accession of a new king. The worshipper or worshippers, who may be one or more members of the royal entourage, invoke three blessings on the new monarch: a reign without end "till the moon be no more" (see verses 5, 7, 17); success in his high office of righteous judge and saviour of the downtrodden (verses 1—4, 6—7; 12 etc.); and dominion over the whole world, "from sea to sea, and from the River to the ends of the earth", with all the nations doing obeisance to him and bringing him tribute and gifts (verses 8—11). This triple invocation originated in the etiquette of the ancient court and its contents recur frequently in the Psalms. For the third motif — the future destiny of the king of David's line to be the ruler of the whole world — cf. Ps. 2 : 8; 89 : 27, 29; and elsewhere.

This formula of address to the reigning monarch is derived from the traditional court-language current in the ancient East. The motif of world-dominion can hardly have been a characteristically Israelite conception, since the actual limits of Israelite sovereignty were always very narrow. It is more in keeping with the large states of the ancient East which from time to time expanded into mighty empires. And indeed, it finds expression in the paintings and reliefs of the great centres of oriental culture, above all in Egypt.

The picture here is part of a wall-painting from the tomb of Menkheperreseneb, the high priest of Amon in the reign of Thutmose III (15th cent. B.C.). The subject of the whole painting is a long procession of foreigners from all parts of the world bringing tribute to the Pharaoh. Four of these figures are seen in the section reproduced here. The first, shown "licking the dust", is portrayed as a Canaanite, even though he bears the caption "the prince of Keftiu (= Crete)". The second, shown kneeling with his arms outstretched, is labelled "the prince of Hatti", though his appearance is not characteristically Hittite. The third, holding a child in his arms (perhaps a hostage), is described as "the prince of Tunip". And the fourth, with dark skin and frizzled hair, is a Cretan.

T HOU didst divide the sea by thy might; thou didst break the heads of the dragons on the waters. Thou didst crush the heads of Leviathan, thou didst give him as food for the creatures of the wilderness.

(Psalms 74 : 13-14)

In this psalm of communal protestation, which is one long dirge for the destruction suffered by the nation at the hands of its foes, the worshippers refer in vivid poetic images to the miraculous deeds performed by the Lord at the beginning of the Creation, when He displayed His omnipotence in overthrowing the primeval monsters — the Sea, the Dragons and the Leviathan — that rose against him. The Lord "divided" the Sea, i. e., reduced it to its component elements; shattered the heads of the Dragons; and crushed the heads of the Leviathan and fed them to the wild beasts of the waters. These images also belong to an ancient poetic tradition which goes back ultimately to pre-Israelite patterns of thought (cf. above, p. 25). Allusions to this literary tradition occur in several other poetical passages of the Bible (Isa. 27 : 1; 51 : 9; Job 7 : 12) and are also found in the Ugaritic epics. In the latter there is frequent mention of the Sea, the Dragon, the Leviathan, the Tortuous Serpent and "Shalyat of the seven heads" as primeval powers that revolted against Baal and were crushed by him. Similar myths about monsters, some of them with seven heads, that sought to overthrow the gods were current amongst the peoples of Mesopotamia. Echoes of them may occasionally have reached the west and become part of later European folklore.

Illustrated below are representations, on Mesopotamian cylinder-seals, of the gods warring against such monsters. In the upper picture (an Assyrian cylinder-seal from the 8th or 7th cent. B. C.) one of the gods is shown driving his sword into the mouth of a horned snake. Behind him are the figures of two other gods. At the tip of the snake's tail and alongside the hindmost figure there are drawings of trees. Below this (on an Akkadian cylinder-seal from the second half of the third millennium B.C.), two gods, one in front and one behind, are fighting a dragon with seven heads. Behind the gods stand their supporters and attendants. Four of the dragon's heads have already been crushed, while the remaining three above them are still viciously alive. Tongues of flame are spurting from the monster's back.

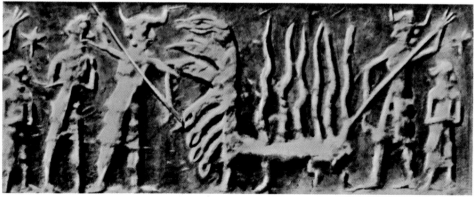

HE cleft rocks in the wilderness, and gave them drink abundantly as from the deep. He made streams come out of the rock, and caused waters to flow down like rivers.

(Psalms 78 : 15-16)

Psalm 78 reviews the history of Israel from the Exodus down to the establishment of David's kingdom. The purpose of this survey is to point a moral to the congregation; hence the poet calls it his "teaching" (ibid. 1). In the course of his review, he recalls many of the miracles and wonders described in the Pentateuch. In our verse here, for example, he refers to the miracle of Massah and Meribah, when Moses struck the rock and water flowed from it and the people drank their fill (Ex. 17 : 1-7; cf. Nu. 20 : 1-11). Making water flow from the rock is mentioned several times in the poetry of the Old Testament as one of the outstanding marvels of the period of the exodus from Egypt. Thus, in Ps. 114 the Lord is described as He "who turns the rock into a pool of water, the flint into a spring of water" (Ps. 114 : 8; cf. ibid. 105 : 41). In Deuteronomy 8 : 15 this miracle is again emphasized as the Lord's distinguishing title: "who brought you water out of the flinty rock". Compare the statements in Isaiah 48 : 21 which are couched in the language of the psalms.

The sources of water in the desert are sparse and poor, and even some of these are excessively saline. Hence the very few that are fit for human use create islands of life all round them — life for man and beast, and also for the soil itself. In the desert of Judea there are several springs that are fed by the rainwater in the Judean hills. On account of the geological fissures by which this region is traversed, the water here spurts out from the hard rock above the steep gorges of the wadis, sometimes falling in impressive cascades (see the photograph) that resemble "rivers".

I relieved your shoulder of the burden; your hands were freed from the basket.　(Psalms 81 : 6)

Set against the background of joyous festal song and music (Ps. 81 : 2—4) described in this psalm, there is a brief historical survey relating the Lord's mercies to Israel from the very beginning of the nation's existence. The survey starts with the slavery of the Israelites in Egypt and their redemption from it, since that was when the festival now being celebrated was made "a decree in Joseph" (verses 4—5). Then follow allusions to the wanderings and miracles in the wilderness (verse 7), and to the theophany and the giving of the Ten Commandments on Mount Sinai (verses 8—10). The survey ends with a rebuke for Israel's wilful backsliding (verses 11—16). This whole historical summary is thus simply a poetical recapitulation of what is related in the Book of Exodus, where the "burdens" of the Israelites in Egypt, referred to in our verse here, are also mentioned (Ex. 1 : 11, 14; 2 : 11; and elsewhere). The slave-labour of the Israelites in Egypt took the form, principally, of "burdens" (Heb. *sebel*, which also means "suffering"), i. e. carrying clay and bricks for the building of Pharaoh's cities. This is confirmed by the frequent representations, in Egyptian pictures of constructional works, of slaves loading a "burden" on to their shoulders, in the form of a basket containing clay or bricks which they hold in place with their two hands. Cf. Vol. I, p. 128.

Reproduced above is a section of a tomb-painting of Rekhmire, from the reign of Thutmose III. One of the slaves is kneading the clay, which is to be made into bricks, with a short-handled hoe. The man on the right is placing a basket full of clay on his shoulders and steadying it with his hands. Another of the slaves is helping him.

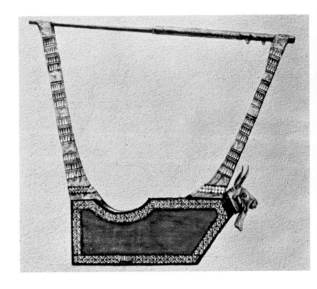

T O declare thy steadfast love in
the morning, and thy faithfulness
by night, to the music of the ten-
stringer and the harp . . .

(Psalms 92 : 2-3)

The string-instruments most common in the world of the Bible were the harp (Heb. *nebel*) and the lyre
(kinnor). The harp had various shapes and sizes, but was always heavier than the lyre. Its Hebrew name
may be connected with the word for a "wine-skin" *(nebel yayin)* and refer to the instrument's bulging shape.
It consisted of a hollow body (to increase the resonance) with, stretched over it, strings which emitted a
sound when plucked. The number of the strings varied according to the size and shape of each particular harp.
Hence, the "ten-stringer" *(asor)* was presumably not a separate kind of instrument, but merely a harp with ten
strings (Ps. 33 : 2; 144 : 9).
Illustrated on the left — a clay plaque from Khafajah in Mesopotamia, from the beginning of the second
millennium B. C.   on which there is a relief of a musician seated on a backless chair and holding a seven-stringed
harp. On the right — a reconstruction of the harp of Ur (from the beginning of the First Dynasty of Ur, 26th
cent. B.C.). It is elongated in shape like a boat, and ends in a bearded bull's head. The instrument itself is
made of wood inlaid with jewels, while the bull's head is of gold inlaid with jewels and shells. As reconstructed,
this harp has eleven strings. It is quite possible that the two kinds of harp illustrated here were not intended to
be carried from place to place. On portable harps see below, pp. 46, 63.

THE righteous flourish like the palm tree, and grow like a cedar in Lebanon. (Psalms 92 : 12)

The problem of the prosperous sinner frequently exercised the authors of the closely related wisdom literature and psalms. The solution most commonly offered by them is embodied in the conception of "the good latter end": the sinner's success is only of short duration, whereas the righteous man is ultimately sure of a lasting reward (cf. Prov. 23 : 18; 24 : 19-20; Job 8 : 7; and elsewhere). In our psalm here this idea is expressed in poetic images: the prosperity of the wicked is like grass which soon withers (Ps. 92 : 7) whereas the righteous man's happiness is like those tall and splendid trees, the palm and the cedar of Lebanon, whose leaves never fall. Similarly, in another psalm it is said of the wicked that "they will soon fade like grass, and wither like the green herb" (Ps. 37 : 2); while the author of Proverbs describes the righteous as "flourishing like a green leaf" (Prov. 11 : 28). This comparison, which is found in other psalms too, of the righteous man to a vigorous tree in full leaf goes back to earlier literary traditions of the ancient East, one of the first known instances of it being from Ur, where one of the city's early Sumerian kings was likened to a palm-tree and a cedar (see above, p. 20). It is quite possible that the worshipper in our psalm here, who identifies himself with the righteous man, was also a king, since he refers to his "horn" (see below, p. 57) and to the "fresh oil" with which he was anointed (Ps. 92 : 10).

Reproduced here is an Egyptian tomb-painting at Deir el-Medineh (from the time of the Nineteenth or Twentieth Dynasty, 13th or 12th cent. B.C.), in which a man is shown kneeling down and doing obeisance under a fruit-laden palm-tree beside a water-channel. In the background there are verses from the Book of the Dead.

SING praises to the LORD with the lyre, with the lyre and the sound of melody.   (Psalms 98 : 5)

In Old Testament times the musical instrument most favoured by the Semitic peoples, including the Israelites, was the lyre *(kinnor)*. It was presumably introduced into Egypt from Western Asia, since it was completely unknown there in the days of the Old Kingdom. The lyre had a wooden body, like the harp (see 1 Kings 10 : 12), and, according to a later Rabbinical tradition, its strings were made from the small intestines of a sheep. But, unlike the harp, the lyre was easy to carry and the musician usually played as he walked (see the picture, and also below, p. 58). The notes were obtained from the lyre by plucking the strings with the bare fingers, whereas for the harp hammers were sometimes used as well (cf. below, p. 63). However, some scholars hold that the hammer served only to beat the time and that the tune was produced by the fingers alone. The music of the lyre, like that of other instruments, was usually accompanied by loud singing. Instrumental music as such, without words, was still relatively uncommon in Old Testament times, as is clear from the verse at the head of this page: "Sing praises to the Lord with the lyre . . ."

The picture reproduced here is part of a relief discovered at Nineveh, from the reign of the Assyrian king Ashurbanipal. The musicians are standing at the entrance to the royal palace, with two of the king's bodyguards in front of them. The first musician in the row is holding a five-stringed lyre, the second a portable harp, while the third, whose hand only is visible, is blowing on a wind instrument.

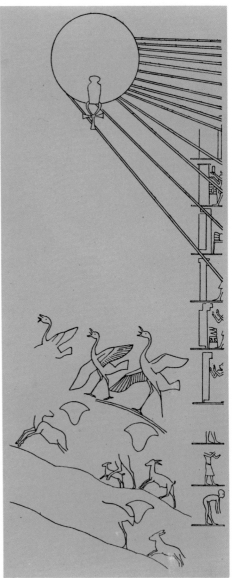

BLESS the LORD, O my soul! O LORD my God, thou art very great! Thou art clothed with honour and majesty, who coverest thyself with light as with a garment, who hast stretched out the heavens like a tent.

(Psalms 104 : 1-2)

Psalm 104, which is a song of praise to the Creator and His works, is in some points similar to the hymn to the sun of the Pharaoh Akhenaton, the Egyptian religious reformer who lived in the 14th cent. B.C. Several verses in the psalm have almost exact equivalents in the hymn. Thus, verses 20-21 of the psalm, "thou makest darkness, and it is night . . . the young lions roar for their prey", are paralleled by "when thou settest in the western horizon, every lion is come forth from his den"; and verse 24, "O Lord, how manifold are thy works!" by "How manifold it is, what thou hast made!" While the biblical psalm was evidently influenced, in these passages, by literary patterns which originated in Egypt, this purely literary resemblance cannot obscure the vital difference between the religious conceptions underlying the two works: the Egyptian god adored by the Pharaoh is the sun (Aton), whereas in the psalm the sun too was created by the God of Israel (verse 19); the Egyptian god is part of nature, whereas the God of Israel is outside nature and above its laws.

A vivid plastic illustration of the above mentioned Egyptian hymn, with its dominant note of sun-worship, is provided by two wall-paintings (from Tell el-Amarna) which are contemporary with Akhenaton's reforms. On the left — "the subjects of Aton", the inhabitants of Egypt and the neighbouring countries, express their adoration of the sun: some of them stand with outstretched arms, others go down on their bended knees, and still others fall upon their faces. Some of the people in the two upper rows are holding banners, and at the very top (on the right) three of them are blowing trumpets. In the other rows there are successive groups of Egyptians, Semites from Syria, Libyans and Nubians. In the picture on the right birds and animals are seen greeting the rising sun. These living creatures are drawn against a background of sloping hills amongst which flowers, or bushes, are painted.

THE trees of the LORD are watered abundantly,
the cedars of Lebanon which he planted.

(Psalms 104 : 16)

Psalm 104 is a magnificent hymn of praise to God as the creator, sustainer and controller of the universe. The poem has two main themes. On the one hand, it emphasizes the unfathomable miracle of the Creation: the nakedness of the world when it was first formed from the primeval chaos (verses 5-6), the confining of the oceans (verse 9), the formation of the springs (verse 10) and the rain (13), the mystery of life and death (29-30). At the same time it extols the largest and mightiest of created things: the cedars of Lebanon (16) and the high mountains (18); the lions that roar for their prey (21), the great and wide ocean (25), the Leviathan which the Lord formed "to sport with" (26), and others. The cedars of Lebanon are figuratively called "the trees of the Lord" which He is said to have planted Himself. This may be an allusion to the story of the Garden of Eden; see Ezek. 31 : 8: "the cedars in the garden of God could not rival it"; ibid. 16 (cf. Vol. III, p. 190). Or it may be no more than a grandiose poetic way of describing trees of great size, such as, for instance, the expression "thy righteousness is like the mountains of God" (Ps. 36 : 6).

The cedar of Lebanon *(Cedrus Libani)* is the most imposing of the trees that grow in the Near East. In ancient times the tops of the Lebanese mountains were covered by extensive cedar-forests of which only a few remnants survive to-day (see the photograph), the largest of them being near Besharre at the source of the river Kadisha. Here there are still several hundred cedars, the tallest of which rises to a height of 115 feet. Something of the striking beauty of the ancient cedar-forests can still be felt to-day even in these sparse remains of their former glory.

THE rocks are a refuge for the coneys.

(Psalms 104 : 18)

The high mountains and their crags are amongst the manifestations of nature's might that powerfully affect the imagination of the author of this psalm (cf. p. 48). His wonder grows all the greater when he beholds that these mountains and rocks, despite their height and inaccessibility, provide a home and shelter for living creatures, such as the wild-goat and the coney. The same contrast was also noted by the wisdom writer in Proverbs 30 : 26: "The coneys are a people not mighty, yet they make their homes in the rocks" (cf. below, p. 95).

The coney found in Israel and the neighbouring countries is the Syrian variety *(Procavia capensis syriacus)*. In Israel itself the animal is found near the Dead Sea (see the photograph) and in Galilee. It makes its lair in rock-fissures where it hides its young and into which it retreats at any sound that frightens it.

THE LORD says to my lord: "Sit at my right hand, till I make your enemies your footstool." (Psalms 110 : 1)

The royal Psalm 110, most of which is addressed to the king apparently by one of his entourage, opens with a message from God. In this introduction, the king is invited to sit at the right hand of the Divine Presence where his foes will be placed as a footstool beneath his feet. The biblical poet uses this image to express his reverent respect for his sovereign "lord", as in the other metaphorical description, also found in the royal psalms, of the king of Israel as God's "son" or "firstborn" (Ps. 2 : 7; 89 : 26-27; cf. 2 Sam. 7 : 14). Rabbinical Judaism (followed by Christianity) understood all these passages as referring to the Messianic king who was to reign "at the end of time"; and that is how our verse here is interpreted in the Midrash to the Book of Psalms and also in the New Testament. But the word-picture itself is derived ultimately from pre-biblical thought-patterns, being one of the liturgical formulae taken over by the Israelites from other cultures (cf. above, p. 24).

This and similar figures of speech seem to have been a regular feature of the official court-language in the main centres of ancient Near Eastern culture. A similar idea is expressed in plastic form in several ancient Egyptian works of art, as in the picture reproduced here (from the tomb of Kenamon at Thebes, belonging to the time of the Eighteenth Dynasty). It shows Amenhotep II resting on the lap of his nurse who is supporting him on her right arm, while "his foes" — portrayed in two rows, one of Nubians and the other of Semites — serve as his footstool. Their hands are bound behind their backs, and round their necks there is a rope the end of which the king is holding in his right hand, together with a sceptre. Above the king's head hovers the sacred goose of Amon, sheltering him in the shadow of its wings (cf. above, p. 24).

THEIR idols are silver and
gold, the work of men's hands.
(Psalms 115 : 4)

The writers of the Old Testament employ two terms of contempt for the statues of gods — "things of nought" (Heb. *elilim)* and "idols" *(azabbim)* — and also frequently identify the gods of the gentiles with their actual images. In their attacks on polytheism, these writers do not enter into a philosophical debate on the truth or falsehood of its doctrinal assumptions, but simply dismiss all the gods of the gentiles as so much silver and gold. This categorical denial of the existence of polytheistic deities is especially common in the Psalms: "For all the gods of the peoples are idols; but the Lord made the heavens" (Ps. 96 : 5). Similarly the section of Ps. 115 (verses 4-6) from which our verse here is taken emphasizes the nothingness of the gentile gods by describing the ineffectiveness of idols. The whole section is repeated in Ps. 135 : 15-18. The same manner of expression is also found in those prophets who use the literary images of the Psalms (Isa. 40 : 18-20; 41 : 7; and elsewhere; Jer. 10 : 3-5; 8-9; Hab. 2 : 18-19). Ultimately, however, this whole mode of thought and expression goes back to Deuteronomy 4 : 28.

Reproduced here is the head of a gilded Egyptian "thing of nought" from the 14th or 13th cent. B.C., which was discovered at Beth-Shan. It is a bronze head of the goddess Hathor overlaid with gold. It probably adorned the top of a military standard.

THEY surrounded me like bees, they blazed like a fire of thorns; in the name of the LORD I cut them off.

(Psalms 118 : 12)

In this psalm of thanksgiving the poet compares his enemies to bees swarming angrily round a man and to the flickering, leaping flames of a fire of thorns. Even so, he does not lose his faith in the Lord's help and, desperate though his plight seems, he knows that his assailants will be destroyed.

The wild bee can indeed be a dangerous insect. Being unaccustomed to the proximity of human beings, it is suspicious, easily angered and extremely pugnacious. Hence its use in the Old Testament as a symbol of vicious aggressiveness. When the Amorites, for example, routed the Israelites at Hormah, it is said that "they chased them as bees do" (Deut. 1 : 44); and Assyria is similarly likened to a bee by the prophet (Isa. 7 : 18). Bees, as is well known, live in colonies (see the photograph) each of which is composed of a "queen", hundreds of males (before the mating season) and tens of thousands of barren females. It is these last that secrete the wax from which they construct the honeycombs (1 Sam. 14 : 27; cf. below, p. 89), and that also manufacture the honey from the nectar of flowers. In Old Testament times, when bee-keeping in hives was still unknown in Palestine, the only honey was that scooped out at random from the nests of wild bees. By the time of the Mishnah, however, bee-keeping had become an important branch of the country's agriculture.

Closely related to the bee is the hornet, another biblical symbol for vicious enmity. On this insect see Vol. I, p. 158.

RESTORE our fortunes, O LORD, like the water-courses in the Negeb.   (Psalms 126 : 4)

Gladness and hope are the twin themes of Psalm 126. The first half (verse 1-3) is an ecstatic utterance of joy at the Return to Zion which was a great and unexpected event both for the Jews themselves who took part in it and for the Gentiles who witnessed it. The second part (verses 4-6) consists of a prayer for a rich harvest. In the verse at the head of this page, with which the prayer opens, the worshippers compare their return (Heb. *shevuth*) — i.e. their deliverance from hardship and their restoration to their former happy state — to "streams in the Negeb."
In Israel the sudden, seasonal flooding of previously dry watercourses is especially characteristic of the rocky barren regions of the Negeb. As soon as there is any rainfall these watercourses become raging torrents, flowing in such spate that they sometimes burst their banks and cause floods that strike fear into man and beast. So great is the force of the water that it uproots and sweeps away even the trees in the beds of the watercourses, let alone any beduin encampments that may have been pitched there. This kind of flash-flood was therefore used in the Old Testament as a symbol for any sudden and terrible disaster (see Isa. 28 : 2; Jer. 47 : 2; Nah. 1 : 8; Ps. 32 : 6; and elsewhere). However, these watercourses dry up again as quickly as they fill. On the "treacherousness" of these wadis see below, p. 107.
Seen in spate in the photograph here is Nahal Besor in the northern Negeb.

THE ploughers ploughed upon my back; they made long their furrows.   (Psalms 129 : 3)

Agriculture was the basis of Israelite economy throughout biblical times. It is therefore only natural that biblical literature should have drawn many of its verbal images from the various aspects of land-work. Such images, especially those taken from ploughing and harvesting, are particularly numerous in the poetry of the Old Testament. Thus, in Psalm 129 Israel's foes are likened to ploughmen who have yoked Israel to their plough (like a team of oxen), and are now driving it down long furrows.

But the Lord, the nation's watchful guardian, brings to nought the insolent designs of Israel's foes, as stated in verse 4: "The Lord is righteous; he has cut the cords of the wicked". Here "the cords" (Heb. *aboth*) are the ropes by which the Israelites were harnessed to the plough (cf. Isa. 5 : 18, where "cart-ropes" occur in parallelism with "cords").

The reproduction is a relief from the tomb of Paheri at el-Kab in Upper Egypt, from the time of the Eighteenth Dynasty (15th-14th cent. B.C.). It shows four slaves yoked to a plough by means of ropes tied over their shoulders. The man with a beard and long hair is guiding the plough, assisted by the man walking behind him who has a bag of seeds in his left hand.

LET them be like the grass on the housetops, which withers before it grows up.　　　　(Psalms 129 : 6)

In the verse above, the enemies of Zion are compared to "grass", i.e. corn, growing on the rooftops which quickly shrivels up at the breath of the east wind. The simile is developed in the following verses of the psalm (7—8): there is not enough of this grass for the reaper to fill his hands with or the binder to hold in his bosom; nor do passers-by ever utter over it the blessing with which the reapers were traditionally greeted by wayfarers: "the blessing of the Lord be upon you" etc., (cf. Boaz's greeting to the reapers, Ruth 2 : 4). Isaiah too similarly likens the inhabitants of the cities overwhelmed by Sennacherib to "grass on the house-tops" (2 Kings 19 : 26; Isa. 37 : 27).

The roofs of houses in the ancient East were constructed of parallel horizontal beams, the spaces between them being filled with planks or reeds and the whole plastered over with a mixture of clay and corn-stalks. A roof of this kind required frequent repair, especially during the rains of winter (see Eccles. 10 : 18). The straw used to reinforce the clay plastering still contained odd grains of corn left over from the threshing, and it was from these, when wetted by the rain, that "grass on the housetops" used to sprout. This sickly corn, its ears mildewed through growing in soil that had no access to the air, was of no use to man or beast. The scene described in our verse can still be seen to this day in the villages of the Near East.

Photographed here is the roof of an Arab house, made of wooden cross-beams and plaster, with "grass" growing out of it.

I will not enter my house or get into my bed ... until I find a place for the LORD, a dwelling place for the Mighty One of Jacob.

(Psalms 132 : 3, 5)

Psalm 132, which is a song of praise to Zion and its king, recalls the foundation of the Davidic dynasty and the sanctification of Zion by the installation of the Ark there. The poet extols David's unsparing devotion to his God which led him to vow that he would deny himself rest in his tent and sleep upon his couch, until a permanent site was found for the temple.

During their wanderings in the wilderness, the Israelites lived in tents. After they had taken possession of Canaan and become settled agriculturalists, most of them built themselves houses, and there remained only small groups, such as the Kenites and Rechabites (Judg. 4 : 11, 18-21; Jer. 35 : 7-10), who continued to live the life of tent-dwellers. In this period the house itself was sometimes still called a "tent", the word having lost its original meaning through constant usage (see 2 Sam. 20 : 1; 1 Kings 12 : 16; Prov. 14 : 11; and elsewhere; cf. the appellation "tent of the Lord" applied to the temple). But the fighting-men naturally continued to camp in tents when preparing for battle (2 Kings 7 : 7, 10; Jer. 37 : 10; cf. 2 Sam. 11 : 11). The verses at the top of this page thus depict the years preceding the installation of the Ark in Jerusalem as a period of constant wandering and fighting in David's life.

The practice of camping in tents in war-time is vouched for both by many representations of Assyrian art and by the written descriptions of the military campaigns of Assyrian and Egyptian kings. Reproduced here is an Assyrian relief from Nineveh, from the reign of Ashurbanipal (middle of the 7th cent. B.C.) portraying a soldiers' tent in a war-camp. The servants of the Assyrian officer (seen entering at the right) are preparing his meal for him and making his bed. Hanging up in the middle of the tent are a water-bottle and weapons. Outside the tent various animals, including two camels, are lying. At the upper edge of the relief can be seen the wall of the camp with its defence-works.

THERE I will make a horn to sprout for David; I have prepared a lamp for my anointed. His enemies I will clothe with shame, but upon himself his crown will shed its lustre.

(Psalms 132 : 17-18)

At the end of Psalm 132 the Lord assures David that his descendants will reign for ever and that they will have absolute dominion over their foes. In the verses before us, this dominion is depicted in the form of a promise "to make a horn sprout" for David when he is seated on the royal throne in Zion. The king's "horn" is referred to in several other psalms, always in connection with his enemies (Ps. 18 : 2; 89 : 24). This horn-symbol was evidently later transferred to the whole people (see Jer. 48 : 25; Ezek. 29 : 21, the same expression as in our psalm; Micah 4 : 13; Ps. 148 : 14; and elsewhere; Deut. 33 : 17 is very similar), and sometimes also to a righteous man other than the king (Ps. 112 : 9; and elsewhere). In the visions of Daniel, however, the horns are still the specific symbols of royalty (Dan. 7 : 7-8, 24; and chap. 8).
This image too, like all the other figures of speech in the language of the psalms, seems to have belonged to the traditional repertoire of ancient oriental symbolism. In the ancient art of the Near East we sometimes find gods, or deified kings, portrayed with horns sprouting from their foreheads. A striking illustration of this is provided by the picture reproduced here which is taken from the stele of Naram-Sin, king of Akkad (23rd cent. B.C.). The king, shown at the head of his army trampling on his foes, is holding in his hands a spear, a bow and an axe and wearing a helmet with two horns.

FOR there our captors required of us songs, and our tormentors, mirth, saying, "Sing us one of the songs of Zion!" How shall we sing the LORD's song in a foreign land?

(Psalms 137 : 3-4)

Psalm 137 is an impassioned, lyrical description of what the Judean exiles suffered in the dreadful aftermath of the destruction of Jerusalem. With a shudder of horror they recall how they sat down and wept "by the waters of Babylon" (meaning the irrigation canals connecting the Euphrates with the Tigris), when they remembered Zion. They had hung their lyres on the willows beside the streams. Their captors wanted to hear them sing "one of the songs of Zion", but how could they sing "the Lord's song", the sacred music which had once echoed through the courts of the Temple, on foreign soil? Instead, they swore never to forget Jerusalem (verses 5—6) and passionately cursed their cruel enemies, the Edomites and "the daughter of Babylon" (7—9).

Amongst the exiles deported from Jerusalem there were no doubt professional male and female singers, skilled in the performance of instrumental and vocal music, such as were formerly found in all ranks and spheres of Judean life and many of whom had taken part in the divine service in the Temple courts. Thus, the Assyrian king Sennacherib (704—681 B. C.) relates on his prism-inscription (see below, p. 285), that Hezekiah, king of Judah, sent him "male and female musicians". The setting of our psalm is well illustrated by a relief from Sennacherib's palace at Nineveh reproduced here. On it three captives are seen playing on their lyres, followed by an Assyrian guard armed with club and a bow. They are moving through mountainous, wooded terrain, beside a river. In appearance and dress these captives recall the figures on another of Sennacherib's reliefs portraying the siege of Lachish (Vol. II, pp. 286—287). They may therefore be Judeans.

T HEY make their tongue sharp as a serpent's, and under their lips is the poison of vipers.

(Psalms 140 : 3)

In this psalm of individual protestation, the worshipper compares the wicked to snakes and spiders whose mouths secrete poison and whose bite is fatal. A similar description of the wicked is found in another psalm of this type: "they have venom like the venom of a serpent, like the deaf adder that stops its ear" (Ps. 58 : 4), i. e. like the adder that pays no attention "to the voice of charmers", but, in accordance with its true nature, bites and injects its poison. That this image refers primarily to the malicious slanders and lying accusations spread by the wicked about the righteous is clear from several other psalms, such as 52 : 2: "Your tongue is like a sharp razor, you worker of treachery". Sometimes this conduct of the wicked is also likened to the poisoned arrows that they seek to shoot at the righteous (ibid. 57 : 4; 64 : 3; cf. 55 : 21). Jeremiah, in his prayers similarly depicts his enemies as saying: "Let us smite him with the tongue" (Jer. 18 : 18), and "Denounce him! Let us denounce him!" (ibid. 20 : 10).

The Hebrew word *(akhshub)*, which is translated "viper" above, occurs only here in the Old Testament. Its use in poetic parallelism with "serpent" *(nahash)* suggests that it must be similar to the latter in its behaviour and reflexes. In the ancient translations (the Septuagint, Vulgate, and others) it was understood as a synonym for *nahash*. But most modern commentators assume, as is indeed more plausible, that it is simply the word for spider *(akabish)* with the order of the letters inverted (similar inversions occur in other words in the Old Testament).

The spider in the photograph here is one of the kind known as a tarantula.

O LORD, my Lord, my strong deliverer, thou hast covered my head in the day of battle.

(Psalms 140 : 7)

In the verse above, the righteous man's trust in his God is described in a metaphor unique in the Old Testament: God provides cover for the head of the true-believer "on the day of weapons", i. e. in battle. This word-picture is derived from the special conditions of ancient warfare. The most vulnerable part of the warrior's body, especially in an attack on a fortified city, was his head. Only the top of it was protected by his helmet while his face, as he looked up to the walls, was completely exposed. Hence the importance of the small hand-shield and the long shield. The former was designed principally for the use of assault troops; while the latter was carried by a special shield-bearer to cover the bodies of the soldiers armed with long-range weapons, who needed both their hands to hold their bows. The top of the long shield, especially of the Assyrian type made of plaited reeds, was curved slightly backwards to provide better protection for the bowman's head (on this shield see below, p. 280).

In the picture here (part of a relief from the palace of Sennacherib at Nineveh, beginning of the 7th cent. B. C.) Assyrian soldiers are seen shielding their heads in an attack on a besieged city. The one in the centre, who is making use of a round hand-shield, is waiting for the archers' fire to pin down the defenders and soften up their resistance, before storming the walls. The soldiers on either side of him, screened by long shields, are standing in pairs, one holding a shield and a sword while the other shoots with his bow.

HE gives to the beasts their food, and to the young ravens
which cry.   (Psalms 147 : 9)

The feature common to the two kinds of living creature mentioned in this verse is that both of them, though dependent on such food as they can find, obtain enough to satisfy all their needs. The "beasts" (Heb. *behemah*) referred to here are the non-domesticated "beasts of the earth" (Deut. 28 : 26; Isa. 18 : 6; Jer. 7 : 33; and elsewhere). The raven is similarly a wild bird. Thus the Lord's omnipotence is revealed also in His providing for these creatures.

The raven (*oreb*) appears in the Old Testament as a bird of prey (Prov. 30 : 17) inhabiting desolate regions and ruins (Isa. 34 : 11). Thus, it is related of Elijah that he was fed by ravens in his refuge by the brook Cherith, east of the Jordan (1 Kings 17 : 4—6). In the story of the Flood we read that the raven sent by Noah out of the ark as soon as the rain stopped flew back and forth, "until the waters were dried up from the earth"; whereas the dove, which is a domestic bird, did not leave the ark until the earth had dried out completely (Gen. 8 : 7—12). The raven's powers of survival are also mentioned as one of the wonders of the creation in the Lord's answer to Job out of the tempest: "Who provides for the raven its prey, when its young ones cry to God, and wander about for lack of food?" (Job 38 : 41).

The Mosaic Law refers to "every raven according to its kind" (Lev. 11 : 15; Deut. 14 : 14); and indeed modern zoology distinguishes several sub-species of the bird such as the black raven, the crow and the rook.

Photographed here is a brood of grey ravens or crows (*Corvus corone*). On the black raven see Vol. I, p. 188.

PRAISE him with trumpet sound; praise him with lute and harp! Praise him with timbrel and dance; praise him with strings and pipe! praise him with sounding cymbals; praise him with loud clashing cymbals!

(Psalms 150 : 3-5)

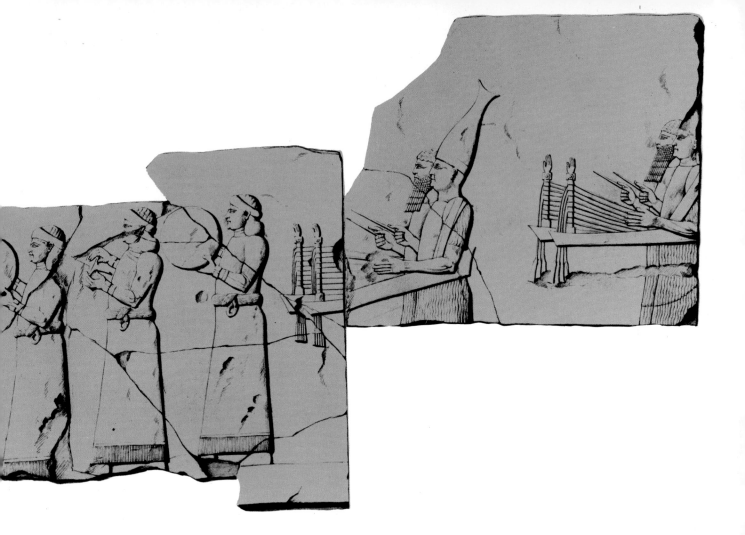

Psalm 150, which closes the Book, is a hymn to the grandeur of God. In impassioned language, the poet exhorts his hearers to praise the Lord with the full volume of all the musical instruments at their command. The psalm thus incidentally provides us with a list of the various instruments that were much used in the Temple courts by the Israelite people to give expression to their religious emotions.

The trumpet (Heb. *shofar*), the wind-instrument most popular with the masses, was made from easily obtainable material — ram's horn (in contrast to the similar *hazozerah* which was hammered out of metal; cf. Vol. I, p. 206). Though primarily used in battle (cf. Vol. II, p. 30), the *shofar* also had a special function in the Temple service. It is therefore mentioned in several other psalms (47 : 5; 81 : 3; 98 : 6), and was probably the instrument on which the "ringing note" *(teruah)*, also frequently referred to in the psalms, was usually blown. The *ugab* (here translated "pipe") was also apparently a wind instrument.

The commonest popular percussion-instrument was the drum or timbrel *(tof)*. This too was used in the Temple courts and is mentioned in other psalms (81 : 2; 149 : 3). The drum was made in various sizes, from the small timbrel to the heavy kettle-drum which was suspended by thongs from the shoulders and beaten on by several people in unison (see the illustrations). It is noteworthy that, in the Old Testament, the drum-players are frequently women (Ex. 15 : 20; Judg. 11 : 34; 1 Sam. 18 : 6; and elsewhere), and in Ps. 68 : 25 there is an explicit reference to "maidens playing timbrels". In all these passages the instrument in question is obviously the popular small timbrel. Percussion-instruments of another type were the cymbals, in Hebrew *zalzalim* (cf. 2 Sam. 6 : 5), or *meziltaim* (Ezra 3 : 10; Neh. 12 : 27; and elsewhere). The distinction made in our psalm here between "sounding cymbals" and "loud clashing cymbals" seems to have been merely one of size, the latter being apparently the larger of the two kinds.

Instrumental music was usually accompanied by loud singing and by dancing, these three forms of rhythmical and emotional expression being inseparable in antiquity. Hence the frequent association of dance and song with musical instruments in the Old Testament. Thus, in our verses here the oft-repeated exhortation "Praise Him!" contains the verbal essence of the song that accompanied the music and dancing.

The pictures illustrate the use of several of the musical instruments characteristic of the ancient East: drums of various sizes (top and p. 62 below), a trumpet (p. 62 below), horizontal, portable harps (top), large cymbals, small cymbals (p. 62 top, second figure from right), a double pipe (p. 62 above). There is also a picture of a dancer (ib.). The originals of the reproductions are as follows: p. 62 above — a limestone relief from Carchemish; below, relief from Nineveh from the time of Sennacherib. Above — a basalt relief from Carchemish, dating to the 9th or 8th cent. B.C.

On the harp and lyre, which are also mentioned in the verses quoted, see above, pp. 44, 46, 58.

PROVERBS

THAT prudence may
be given to the simple,
knowledge and discretion
to the youth . . . to
understand a proverb and
a figure, the words of
the wise and their riddles.
(Proverbs 1 : 4-6)

The wisdom literature of Israel, which finds its most characteristic expression in the Book of Proverbs, apparently originated in and was developed by a school of philosopher-scribes. These were attached to the royal court and sometimes actually attributed the authorship of their work to the king. We learn from the Old Testament that this type of literary composition reached its peak in Solomon's reign, when the sayings of the wise were collected in anthologies to serve as a practical guide in the affairs of life and to provide instruction in the rules of proper conduct. Popular aphorisms are here presented in a polished literary form. There were similar philosopher-scribes in the royal courts of most of the nations of the ancient East, those of Egypt being particularly active and influential.

The wisdom literature of the Old Testament drew its inspiration from the traditional gnomic writings of the whole ancient East, and some of its origins can be traced back to the wisdom of "the people of the East" (1 Kings 4 : 30). But the most noteworthy influence was that of Egypt where wisdom literature first made its appearance in the Old Kingdom (in the middle of the third millennium B.C.) and lasted right down to the Ptolemaic era. From all this long period of time there are extant about a dozen Egyptian wisdom-collections which contain interesting parallels to the biblical wisdom-books. Even in the general atmosphere and special setting of the Book of Proverbs there are, here and there, features reminiscent of Egyptian wisdom, as will be illustrated in the following pages. Moreover, an instructive Egyptian parallel has actually been found to one whole collection of these "proverbs" (see below, p. 87). Nevertheless, in spite of the many points of resemblance, the Book of Proverbs is quite different in spirit and intention from the Egyptian books of instruction. This difference finds expression right at the beginning of the biblical work (Prov. 1 : 1-7). In contrast to Egyptian wisdom, the sole purpose of which was to fit the sons of aristocratic families for high office in the royal service, the gnomic literature of the Old Testament was essentially classless and non-professional: the biblical philosopher-scribe was ready to give instruction to all who asked for it. Compare also what is stated in verse 7 of the introduction: "the fear of the Lord is the beginning of knowledge".

Reproduced here is a statue of an Egyptian scribe from the time of the Fifth Dynasty (second half of the third millennium B.C.) which was discovered at Sakkarah in Egypt. The scribe is squatting on his haunches, legs crossed, ready to write, with a partly unrolled scroll of papyrus spread out on his knees.

For in vain is a net spread in the sight of any bird.   (Proverbs 1 : 17)

This parable vividly describes the folly of the wicked who, though they see the net of sin spread out at their feet, are nevertheless unable to avoid being caught in it — exactly like the bird which thinks that the snare is not there to catch it, until it discovers its mistake too late. The device generally employed in trapping birds in biblical times was the snare, which automatically closed on the bird as soon as the latter entered it (see Amos 3 : 5; Prov. 6 : 5; 7 : 23; Ps. 124 : 7; Eccles. 9 : 12). Our proverb here is exceptional in describing the device as a net instead of a snare.

A visual representation of the use of a net in bird-catching is found in a painting from the tomb of Khnumhotep at Beni Hasan (from the time of the Twelfth Dynasty in Egypt). Khnumhotep is seen in the centre of the painting above the entrance, seated on a chair behind a mat screen and holding a rope with which he closes the net when it is full of birds. Behind him stand his son and one of his clerks. At the left, Khnumhotep is standing in a boat, together with his family, holding in his hand three birds caught in the nearby thicket and flailing at the remainder with a beating-stick. At the right and below he is seen fishing with his servants.

The advantage of the snare was that it closed automatically, whereas the use of the net called for considerable alertness and agility on the part of the hunter. On the other hand, the snare could only catch one bird at a time, while with the net it was possible to trap a large number of birds simultaneously.

LET not loyalty and faithfulness forsake you; bind them about your neck, write them on the tablet of your heart.

(Proverbs 3 : 3)

There are several passages in the Book of Proverbs where wisdom, or conceptions synonymous with it, are described in terms of personal ornaments worn round the neck, or necklaces hanging down from a man's neck on to "the tablet of his heart" (see also Prov. 1 : 9; 3 : 22; 6 : 21; 7 : 3). This figure of speech, like all the other metaphorical descriptions of wisdom in Proverbs, is taken from the actual customs and manners of contemporary life.

The neck-ornaments customarily worn in Israel in Old Testament times, though primarily articles of feminine adornment (Ezek. 16 : 11; Song of Sol. 1 : 10; 4 : 9), were sometimes affected also by men (Ps. 73 : 6; Dan. 5 : 7), especially by high officials and members of the nobility. Of the peoples of the ancient East, the Egyptians were the ones most given, from the time of the Old Kingdom, to wearing all kinds of ornamentation round their necks. In Egypt such ornaments were affected only by men and women of high rank, sometimes as an order of merit in recognition of services rendered to the king (cf. what is related of Joseph, Gen. 41 : 42; and Vol. I, p. 106). It may therefore be presumed that this male wearing of a necklace was one of the customs that found its way into Israel from the Egyptian court. And in fact, it is mentioned in just those passages of the Old Testament which have clear Egyptian affinities: in the story of Joseph, and above all in the Book of Proverbs.

The illustration shows an Egyptian official wearing a typical neck-ornament from the time of the New Kingdom. Necklaces of this kind consisted of a number of rows of beads made of various substances (faience, lapislazuli, malachite). They were usually worn over clothes, but occasionally hung down on to the bare chest (as in the picture here). Sometimes amulets were attached to them.

HONOUR the LORD with your substance and with the
first fruits of all your produce; then your barns will be filled
with plenty, and your vats will be bursting with wine.

(Proverbs 3 : 9-10)

The assurance that human piety will be rewarded by God is one of the
characteristic themes of wisdom literature, particularly in the Book of
Proverbs. Long life, happiness, honour, a large progeny, material plenty —
all these are promised to the righteous man.

According to our verses here, he who gives of his wealth and choice
produce (which is what is meant by "the firstfruits of all your produce";
cf. 1 Sam. 2 : 29; Amos 6 : 6) to the Lord will receive those very same
blessings in return. A similar conception is found in Prov. 11 : 25: "A
liberal man will be enriched and one who waters will himself be watered".
Compare the statement in Deuteronomy — where the theme of reward
also features prominently —: "The Lord will command the blessing upon
you in your barns, and in all that you undertake" (Deut. 28 : 8).

Ancient Israelite storehouses have been excavated mainly in the royal
cities, such as Debir (Tell Beit-Mirsim?), Megiddo, Gezer, Beth-Shemesh
and elsewhere. Private farmers apparently stored their crops chiefly in
granaries (Jer. 50 : 26; Joel 1 : 17).

The picture below is a tomb-painting of Mereruka at Sakkarah in Egypt
(from the time of the Sixth Dynasty). In the top register: men filling
their baskets from piles of fruit. In the middle: store-houses with curved
roofs and doors at the bottom for the removal of the corn. Below (from left
to right): men carrying baskets of grapes to the wine-press, while behind
them others are treading the grapes to the rhythm of music. The two
musicians can be seen at the lower right-hand corner.

The upper picture is a photograph of a Canaanite wine-press found in the
Judean hills near Jerusalem.

SHE is a tree of life to those who lay hold of her; those who hold her fast are called happy.   (Proverbs 3 : 18)

Here wisdom is likened to a tree of life whose fruit endows those who eat it with longevity. The term "tree of life" occurs frequently in the aphorisms of the Book of Proverbs (cf. ibid. 11 : 30; 13 : 12; 15 : 4), being closely akin to "the fountain of life" to which wisdom is also often compared (ibid. 10 : 11; 13 : 14; 14 : 27; 16 : 22). The "tree of life" is first mentioned in the Old Testament in the story of the Garden of Eden, where it is said that whoever eats of its fruit will "live for ever" (see Gen. 3 : 22).

"The tree of life" is a well established expression in the culture of the ancient East. The Babylonians, like the Egyptians, frequently refer to such a tree by whose fruit gods and immortal heroes are nourished (cf. Vol. I, p. 22). It corresponds to another expression, "the elixir of life", which denotes the plant sought by Gilgamesh as the source of immortality. However, in the Book of Proverbs this expression has already lost all its mythological significance. In the biblical collection of gnomic sayings, "the tree of life" is no longer a source of immortality, but merely a literary figure of speech symbolizing health and longevity. Compare this verse with verse 16 which precedes it and which is exactly parallel to it, member for member: "Long life is in her right hand" (corresponding to "She is a tree of life to those who lay hold of her"), "in her left hand are riches and honour" (corresponding to "those who hold her fast are called happy").

The pictures of the tree of life, reproduced above, are taken from a relief dating to the reign of the Assyrian king, Ashurnasirpal (9th cent. B.C.), which was discovered at Nimrud (the modern Calah). The tree is drawn in the form of a palm. Kneeling on either side of the tree in the top register are mythical creatures with a human body, outspread wings, and horned crowns on their heads. Those standing on either side of the tree in the bottom register have a human body and an eagle's head. They are fructifying the tree by sprinkling water on it from the vessels in their left hands, using the male palm-flowers held in their right.

SHE will place on your head
a fair garland; she will bestow
on you a beautiful crown.

(Proverbs 4 : 9)

In the collection of aphorisms contained in Proverbs 1-9, wisdom is twice described as "a fair garland" worn on the head (Prov. 1 : 9; 4 : 9); and in our verse here "a fair garland" is synonymous with "a beautiful crown". A similar image is used by Ecclesiasticus in his description of wisdom: "you shall put her on as a robe of honour, and you shall put her about you as a crown of joy" (Ecclesiasticus 6 : 31). In Old Testament times, the ordinary Israelite usually left his head uncovered, headdress being reserved for festive occasions, or for the upper classes. At wedding-celebrations, the groom wore a "garland" (Heb. *peer*, Isa. 61 : 10), or a crown (Song of Sol. 3 : 11). The priests also wore imposing headdresses, which were regarded as adding to their "honour and glory" (Ex. 28 : 40; 39 : 28). A crown is mentioned as one of the adornments of Job who was "the greatest of all the people of the east" (Job 19 : 9; 31 : 36). The frequent references to it in the Book of Proverbs (12 : 4; 14 : 24; 16 : 31; 17 : 6) are thus an indication of the social background from which the wisdom literature sprang and of the class from which its authors came.

In Egypt various forms of head-ornament were customary from the time of the Old Kingdom onwards. They were regularly worn for adornment by men and women of the upper classes, and sometimes also by female slaves when waiting upon guests at table. They were apparently derived, ultimately, from the lotus-flower wreath, the prototype of the lotus-pattern metal chaplets that were very popular as early as the Old Kingdom. The use of lotus-wreaths was subsequently limited in Egypt to banquets. Isaiah accordingly speaks of the "proud crown" and the "fading flower" (i.e. wreath of flowers) that bedeck the heads of the drunken revellers at their drinking-bouts (Isa. 28 : 1-4). Ezekiel too mentions the "beautiful crown" worn by women during a festive meal (Ezek. 16 : 12; 23 : 42).

The illustration is a relief of a young man from the time of the New Kingdom in Egypt, with his wig enclosed in an ornamental chaplet of lotus-leaf pattern.

SAVE yourself like a gazelle from the hunter, like a bird from the hand of the fowler.

(Proverbs 6 : 5)

The simile above (Prov. 6 : 1—5), like several other passages in the Book of Proverbs (cf. ibid. 11 : 15; 17 : 18; 20 :16; 22 : 26; 27 : 13) contains a warning against striking hands to ratify the giving of a pledge. Here the aphorist is speaking of the man who has already done so and is urging him to try to forestall the probable consequences of his act: if you have gone surety for your fellow, try to free yourself from this guarantee; save yourself at once like a gazelle, i. e. with the utmost swiftness, so as not to fall a prey to the usurer. The gazelle is a remarkably fleet-footed animal, capable of running very fast both on level ground (2 Sam. 2 : 18) and amongst hills (Song of Sol. 2 : 17). Hence its capture, like that of the bird which is frequently coupled with it, calls for great agility and stamina on the part of the huntsman. The Assyrian kings, who (like the Hittite rulers) were famed for their hunting prowess, used frequently to make a proud display of their skill in the pursuit of gazelles and birds. The Hittite relief reproduced here, which was found at Malatya in Asia Minor, shows a fleet animal hunted from a chariot. As usual amongst the Hittites, there are two men standing in the chariot, one handling the horses (only one of which can be seen), while the other shoots with his bow. Running at the horse's side is a hunting-dog.

I have decked my couch with coverings, coloured spreads of Egyptian linen; I have perfumed my bed with myrrh, aloes, and cinnamon.

(Proverbs 7 : 16-17)

The "strange woman" tries to seduce the young man by describing to him her couch spread with "carpets" (Heb. *marbadim*). She further tells him that she has perfumed her couch with spices. Such sophisticated luxury was enjoyed only by the rich. The ordinary Israelite slept on the ground, with only a garment (Ex. 22 : 26; Deut. 24 : 13) or a rug (Judg. 4 : 18) for covering. An Egyptian-style bed was introduced into Israel from the beginning of the Monarchy (cf. Vol. I, p. 119), though as mentioned in the Old Testament it is nearly always used by the king and his entourage, or by wealthy upper-class citizens. To sprinkle one's couch with perfume was the height of effeminate luxury. References to the scenting of clothes are found in the king's wedding hymn (Ps. 45 : 8) and in the descriptions of the beloved in the Song of Solomon (3 : 6; 4 : 11); in the love-poem of the same song there is also an apparent allusion to the perfuming of a bed (1 : 16).

In the picture reproduced here, which is taken from a tomb-painting at Thebes (time of the New Kingdom), an Egyptian waiting-woman is seen making her mistress' bed. On the bed can be seen a head-rest (cf. Vol. I, p. 119), and under it a mirror and containers of perfume.

THEN I was beside him, like a nursling; and I was daily his delight, rejoicing before him always. (Proverbs 8 : 30)

In the poem in Chapter 8 of Proverbs, wisdom is metaphorically depicted (from verse 22 onwards) as an independent entity that existed even before the creation of the world. In language reminiscent of the cosmogonies of the ancient East, wisdom proclaims its own great antiquity: before the creation of the elements — the mountains and the deeps, the heavens and the earth, the sea and "the foundations of the earth" — wisdom was already the "nursling" (Heb. *amon*) of God, i. e. was reared by God like a child in its foster-father's arms and was His constant delight. Later it played on earth, disporting itself with the sons of man who were created after it (verse 31). In Ecclesiasticus and other books of the Apocrypha, this wisdom is identified with the Mosaic Law, which was also believed to have existed before the creation of the world.

It was customary in antiquity for the children of the aristocracy to be placed, soon after their birth, in the charge of nurses and guardians who reared and educated them. The following are mentioned in the Old Testment: the nurse of Jonathan's son Mephibosheth (2 Sam. 4 : 4); Naomi, the nurse of Obed the son of Boaz (Ruth 4 : 16—17); Mordecai, Esther's foster-father (Esth. 2 : 7, 20); the guardians of Ahab's sons (2 Kings 10 : 1, 5). In addition, the term "nurse" or "foster-father" is sometimes used metaphorically (Num. 11 : 12; Isa. 49 : 23; and elsewhere).

In the picture here Senmut, the trusty vizier of Queen Hatshepsut (Eighteenth Dynasty, 15th cent. B. C.), is seen performing his duties as the guardian of the heiress apparent to the throne.

WISDOM has built her house, she has set up her seven pillars.   (Proverbs 9 : 1)

In this poem "Wisdom", the hospitable princess who prepares a magnificent banquet for her guests at which to regale their ears with wise sayings (Prov. 9 : 1-12), is contrasted with the foolish wanton who sits in the doorway of her house calling to honest passers-by to enter, that she may destroy them (ibid. 13-18). A great deal of preparation was necessary for the banquet given by "Wisdom". To accommodate her guests she first built a seven-pillared house; then she set the table and issued her invitations in accordance with the rules of etiquette.

It was customary in the ancient East to build pillared halls (stoa) for ceremonial purposes and for special celebrations. Solomon's "House of the Forest of Lebanon", with its adjoining "Hall of Pillars", contained rows of columns which evidently gave them both an additional solemnity (1 Kings 7 : 2-6). A row of seven columns was presumably of particular ceremonial significance, and may even have had a magical import. Thus, in one of the colonnades in the temple at Luxor, in Egypt, erected by Amenhotep III to the god Amon (see the illustration), we find two parallel rows of seven pillars each. The annual procession of Amon, in which the god's image was carried from Karnak to Luxor, passed between these two rows of pillars.

A son who gathers in summer is prudent, but a son who sleeps in harvest brings shame.

(Proverbs 10 : 5)

This verse is one of many aphorisms in praise of industriousness. "Summer" and "harvest", which are regarded in the Old Testament as synonymous terms (Jer. 8 : 20), were naturally the season for gathering in food (see Prov. 6 : 8). Thus, it is said that a wise son, who is always up and doing, garners provender throughout the summer, whereas a son "that causes shame" (i.e. is idle and undisciplined, cf. Prov. 19 : 26; 29 : 15) falls asleep at harvest-time, when the work in the fields is at its height.

The sayings of the Book of Proverbs present a picture of a people tilling the soil and busily occupied throughout most of the year with the seasonal requirements of agriculture. It is, therefore, natural that the aphorists should have condemned indolence and lauded industriousness, especially where work on the land was concerned (cf. Prov. 12 : 11; 20 : 4; 24 : 30-34; 28 : 19; and elsewhere).

The harvest season, with its various agricultural tasks, is depicted in the most life-like colours in ancient Egyptian paintings. The one reproduced here is from the tomb of Menna (time of the Eighteenth Dynasty, 15th cent. B.C.) at Thebes. In the centre: two labourers carrying a sackful of corn on a pole to the threshing-floor, and two girls who are quarrelling over their gleaning. At the right: two labourers resting under a tree; one is asleep, while the other is drinking beer. Hanging on the tree is a water-bottle made from animal hide.

A false balance is an abomination to
the LORD, but a just weight is his delight
(Proverbs 11 : 1

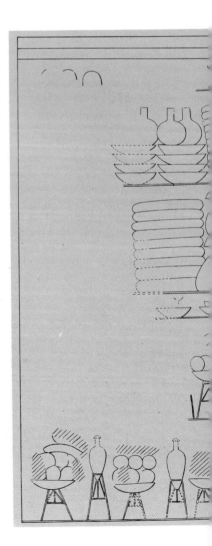

In ancient times, before the introduction of coinage, there was
no possibility of enforcing strict honesty in commercial
transactions, since neither the stones used for weighing, nor
the wet and dry measures, nor even the scales themselves were
sufficiently accurate. It is true that, in periods of orderly
government, stone weights (or at least those authorized by
the king) were subject to control; such a "king's weight" is
mentioned, for example, in the reign of David (2 Sam.
14 : 26) and "stones of the king" occur in the Elephantine
letters. But even these exact weights were not enough to
prevent trickery, since the man holding the scales could, by
a slight movement of his hand, appreciably affect the results
of the weighing. Conditions such as these have persisted in
oriental life down to the present day. It is therefore not at
all surprising that stern admonitions against the deceitful use
of weights and measures recur constantly throughout the Old
Testament, this being a matter in which society could exert
only a limited authority and which depended ultimately on
the individual's sense of honesty. Such admonitions are found
in the Pentateuch (Lev. 19 : 35—36 see Vol. I, p. 194;
Deut. 25 : 13—15 see ibid. p. 285), the Prophets (Ezek. 45 : 10
see Vol. III, p. 202; Hos. 12 : 7; Amos 8 : 4—5; Mic. 6 : 10—
11), and also in the wisdom literature (cf. Prov. 16 : 11;
20 : 10, 23). The Babylonian-Assyrian and Egyptian wisdom
literatures also contain many admonitions of this kind.
The scales photographed here, with a stone weight, are from a
Beduin market in modern Israel.

THE people curse him who holds back grain, but a blessing is on the ·head of him who sells it.

(Proverbs 11 : 26)

The verb *hishbir* used in the Hebrew version of our verse here is applied in the Old Testament to "clean corn" *(bar)*, i.e. corn from which the chaff has been winnowed. This corn was kept in store-houses, mainly as a provision against drought-years. The method of distribution was no doubt copied from that employed by the Egyptian administration. The outstanding example of such a distributor of corn in the Old Testament is Joseph (Gen. 42 : 6) who, in the years of famine, opened his granaries to the people that came from far and near to beg for food. The wise Joseph, the Pharaoh's counsellor, is here the embodiment of generosity and humanity, two of the qualities inculcated by the wisdom literature.

A corn-distributor is portrayed on a relief of the 14th cent. B. C. from the tomb of Mahu, one of the ministers of Akhenaton, at Tell el-Amarna (see the reproduction). Seen in the two top registers are the store-houses, containing jars and other vessels of corn and food. At the right stand Mahu and his servants. In the two bottom registers: villagers bringing food and drink. The building in the centre is the garrison-post, its ground flour occupied by a food-store. On the floor above there is a guard-room where the watchman stands armed. The third storey contains an arms-store.

WHERE there are no oxen, there is no grain; but abundant crops come by the strength of the ox.

(Proverbs 14 : 4)

This aphorism emphasizes that the farmer's chief helpmate is the ox, the work-animal par excellence from ancient times right down to the present day. The ox was used above all for ploughing, which is one of the hardest agricultural tasks.

The evidence in the Old Testament indicates that the ordinary Israelite farmer had at least one ox. To the plough a pair of oxen were usually yoked (Jer. 51 : 23: "I will break in pieces the farmer and his pair"; cf. 1 Kings 19 : 21); hence the common use of the word *zemed* ("pair") in biblical Hebrew as a unit of measurement, meaning the area that would normally be ploughed by a pair of oxen (1 Sam. 14 : 14; cf. 1 Kings 19 : 19; Isa. 5 : 10).

The illustration shows two pairs of oxen from ancient Egypt (wooden models of the Twelfth Dynasty), each being managed by a couple of peasants, one of whom is pressing down on the plough to drive the share deep into the ground, while the other urges on the oxen with the "ox-goad" that he is holding (on this instrument see Vol. II, p. 79).

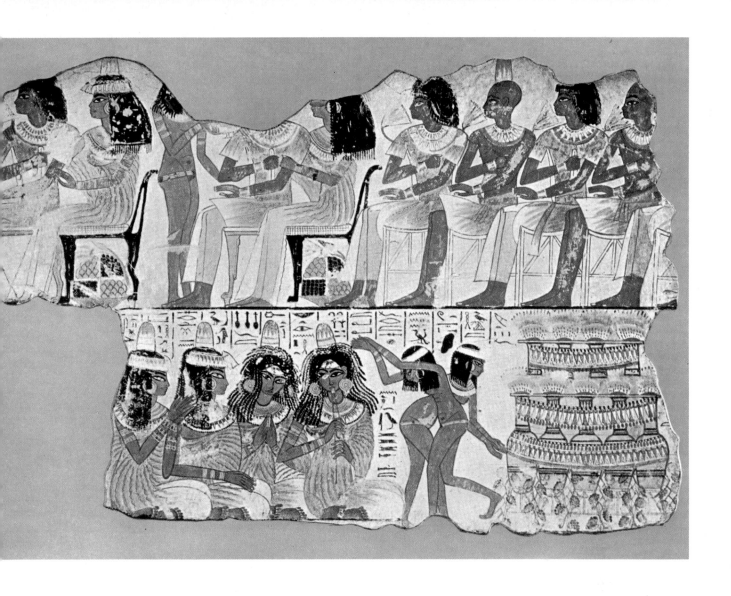

ALL the days of the afflicted are evil, but a cheerful heart has a continual feast.

(Proverbs 15 : 15)

There are various sayings in the Book of Proverbs in praise of wealth as the source of power and honour (ibid. 10 : 15; 13 : 8; 14 : 20; 18 : 11, 23; 19 : 4; and elsewhere), in contrast to poverty which brings nothing but trouble. Ecclesiastes too states that "the poor man's wisdom is despised, and his words are not heard" (Eccles. 9 : 16). What the sages are really praising in these verses is not so much wealth as industriousness, it being axiomatic with them that this is the quality that produces wealth (Prov. 10 : 4; 12 : 24; 13 : 4; 21 : 5). At the same time, they are well aware that wealth is not everything (ibid. 11 : 4); indeed, they stress that it is good only when accompanied by wisdom and integrity (ibid. 28 : 6, 11; cf. 11 : 24; 22 : 16; 23 : 4-5).

The aphorism at the head of the page praises a life of wealth as being "a continual feast", in contrast to a life of poverty which is "evil". An example of a life lived in a continual round of banqueting is provided by the sons of Job in the days of their prosperity, when they used to hold "a feast in the house of each on his day" (Job 1 : 4). Such a feast was accompanied by music and song (see Isa. 5 : 12; 24 : 8-9; Amos 6 : 4-5), sometimes performed by professional "male and female singers" (see Vol. II, p. 190). High living of this style was found in the royal courts and the homes of the wealthy classes, but was presumably almost entirely unknown to the poor.

Banquets are frequently portrayed in the reliefs and paintings of the ancient East, especially those of Egypt. Reproduced here is one such painting from a Theban tomb (time of the Eighteenth Dynasty; second half of the second millennium B.C.). The guests, men and women, are shown seated in the upper register. Underneath some of the chairs there are baskets of fruit, decorated with flowers. At the right: jars of wine. The young women on the left are playing and singing. One of them is playing on double pipes, while two others clap to the rhythm and a third sings a hymn to the Nile floods, excerpts from which are recorded in the hieroglyphic script. The two nude girl slaves are dancing to the tune of the music and song.

A king's wrath is like the growling of a lion, but his favour is like dew upon the grass.

(Proverbs 19 : 12)

This saying, which is repeated with variations in Prov. 20 : 2, is intended to stress the importance of keeping on good terms with the ruling power. The comparison of the king to a lion was a common ancient figure of speech, the lion being regarded as the lord of the animal world; cf. Prov. 30 : 30: "the lion which is mightiest among beasts".

Besides providing biblical literature with an inexhaustible fund of images and symbols, the lion also played an important role in Israelite plastic art: for example, Solomon's throne (1 Kings 10 : 19-20), the stands in Solomon's Temple (ibid 7 : 29), and the walls of the temple seen by Ezekiel in his vision (Ezek. 41 : 19), all had figures of lions sculptured on them. This same motif is also common on archaeological remains excavated in Palestine, such as the Samaria ivories (Vol. II, p. 250), and the seal of Shema, Jeroboam's minister (ibid., p. 278); as also on finds from all the other countries of the Near East. One of the finest Palestinian examples of the use of this motif is the basalt orthostat from one of the temples discovered in the lower Canaanite city at Hazor (14th and 15th cent. B.C.). The lion is shown (see the reproduction) crouching on its hind legs, ready to pounce. Especially noteworthy are the tail, which is curled between the leg and body in northern style (in Egyptian art it is curled above the leg), and the mane with its horn-shaped termination. This lion-relief was one of a pair (the other has disappeared) which flanked the entrance to the temple.

THE sluggard buries his hand in the dish, and will not even bring it back to his mouth.   (Proverbs 19 : 24)

One of the human weaknesses most frequently censured in the wisdom literature is indolence (cf. below, p. 91). In this aphorism, which is repeated with a slight variation in Prov. 26 : 15, it is described with humorous irony: an indolent man who puts his hand into a dish has virtually buried it there, since he is too lazy to lift it to his mouth again.

The "dish" (Heb. *zalahath*) referred to here was apparently a platter large enough to hold the food cooked for a whole group of people. At the end of the meal it was wiped and turned face-downwards (see 2 Kings 21 : 13; Vol. II, p. 292). In 2 Chron. 35 : 13 it is mentioned as one of the vessels used in the Temple. A smaller version of it was the bowl (*zelohith*) which occurs in the story of Elisha (2 Kings 2 : 20). The company helped themselves to food from the large dish with their hands, digging their fingers into the thick stew, as is still done in the East to this day and as can be seen in the Assyrian relief from Nineveh, dating to the reign of Ashurbanipal (7th cent. B. C.), which is reproduced here. Those eating the meal are Elamite captives. The dish, which is relatively flat, may be resting on a pot.

W INE is a mocker, strong drink a brawler; and whoever is led astray by it is not wise.
(Proverbs 20 : 1)

Wine is an ancient beverage and was popular in Israel in biblical times, as is evident from the countless figures of speech and verbal images taken from it in the Old Testament. One of Judah's blessings, for example, is that "he washes his garments in wine" and his eyes are "red" with this liquor (Gen. 49 : 11-12). Again the psalmist, in describing the bounty of the world created by God's grace, includes a mention of "wine to gladden the heart of man" (Ps. 104 : 15). And the Preacher proclaims that "wine gladdens life" (Eccles. 10 : 19). The pilgrims to Jerusalem used also to cheer their spirits with wine as they sat in the Temple courts (see Deut. 14 : 26; 1 Sam. 1 : 13; Isa. 62 : 9; Ps. 116 : 13; cf. below, p. 96).

At the same time, the Old Testament is opposed to over-indulgence and drunkenness. In the Book of Proverbs this opposition is expressed in a typically utilitarian way. In the saying above, the aphorist admonishes his readers that the excessive wine-bibber cannot act wisely. In another passage (Prov. 23 : 20-21) he asserts that the long hours of sleep required by the toper and glutton eventually reduce him to poverty. And elsewhere in this book (ibid. 23 : 29-35) there is a satirical description of drunkards who "tarry long over wine", till in the end they become like "those that lie down in the midst of the sea," bruised and bewildered, and longing to shake off the nauseous effects of their wine — only to return to it again. Such scenes of drunkenness were also common in Egypt, where they likewise provided homiletic material for Egyptian wisdom literature.

Reproduced here is a tomb-painting of Khety at Beni Hasan, from the time of the Twelfth Dynasty. The men being carried by their friends have become intoxicated while treading out grapes in a winepress.

THE glory of young men
is their strength, but the beauty
of old men is their grey hair.
(Proverbs 20 : 29)

The Hebrew word *bahur,* here translated "young man", denotes the fully grown, but still youthful, male, the personification of joyous well-being (Judg. 14 : 10; Lam. 5 : 13; Eccles. 11 : 9) and especially of manly vigour. It is also often used in the Old Testament of a man of military age. Conversely, the Prophets and Psalms contain references to "young men" whose strength could not save them from being killed by the enemy (Jer. 18 : 21; 48 : 15; Ps. 78 : 31, 63; and elsewhere). In 2 Sam. 2 : 14–16 there is a description of a wrestling-match between young men (cf. Vol. II, p. 165) in which the decisive qualities were agility and wiliness.

The illustration here is one scene from a painting on the wall of one of the tombs at Beni Hasan in Egypt, from the time of the Twelfth Dynasty (beginning of the second millennium B.C.). The whole wall-painting depicts various episodes in a contest between two youths, one of them dark-skinned and the other fair, illustrative of the different wrestling-holds. Since the separate episodes form a consecutive sequence, they may well be a complete representation of a wrestling-match from start to finish. Such demonstrations of youthful strength were no doubt a regular feature of life in Egypt (as in other lands of the ancient East).

F OLLY is bound up in the heart of a child, but the rod of discipline drives it far from him.

(Proverbs 22 : 15)

The wisdom literature not only prescribes the contents of education, but also has definite views on the correct method of instruction. The distinguishing feature of this method is "chastisement" (Heb. *musar),* i.e. character-training by punishment. This *musar* has none of the ethical connotation that the word often bears in modern Hebrew, but simply means "discipline" which was one of the bases of this educational system, and indeed was the fundamental tenet of all educators in the ancient East. Thus, in the Words of Ahiqar (see below, p. 88, on Prov. 23 : 13-14) and in Egyptian wisdom literature we find numerous instructions concerning the punishment of children. There are also other aphorisms on this theme in the Book of Proverbs : "He who spares his rod hates his son ; but he who loves him is diligent to discipline him" (ibid. 13 : 24) ; "the rod and reproof give wisdom" (ibid. 29 : 15). The Book of Deuteronomy likewise assumes that parents will "chastise" a wilfully disobedient son, and lays it down that, if he still defies them, he is to be brought before a court of the city-elders (Deut. 21 : 18-21).
The relief reproduced in the upper picture is from the tomb of Hetepharakhti. The overseer of the herd of cattle (on the left) is watching what is either a fight between two youths, or one youth punishing another smaller lad under the overseer's surveillance. The hieroglyphs above the picture represent either the shrieks of the victim or shouts of encouragement to him. The lower picture is a section of a painting (from the tomb of Beket at Beni Hasan, 19th cent. B.C.) in which young people are shown undergoing punishment. At the left, two scribes are recording the penalty. Before them stand a number of people awaiting their punishment (including a woman with a child in her arms), and others being led off to their trial.

INCLINE your ear, and hear the words of the wise, and apply your mind to my knowledge.

(Proverbs 22 : 17)

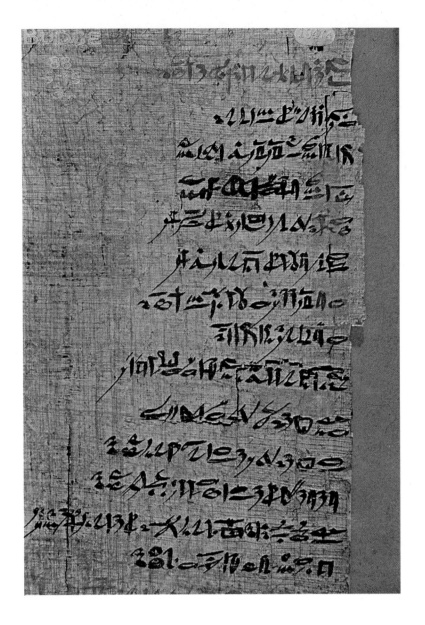

This verse marks the opening of a collection of aphorisms about wisdom (Prov. 22 : 17—24 : 22), entitled "The Words of the Wise", ancient parallels to which have been brought to light by modern discoveries in the field of epigraphy. Thus, the Instruction of Amenemopet, son of Kanakht, the vizier-scribe of the king of Egypt, which was published in 1923, is remarkably similar to this biblical "anthology of wisdom". Indeed, a considerable part of the Egyptian collection of sayings, which is divided into an introduction and thirty chapters, has an almost word-for-word counterpart in the biblical collection. Furthermore the biblical collection too can be seen to fall into an introduction (ibid. 22 : 17-21), followed by thirty aphorisms, as is indeed implied in the opening words (verse 20): "Have I not written for you thirty sayings of admonition and knowledge?" In the same way the Egyptian author concludes his sayings with: "See thou these thirty chapters: they entertain; they instruct."

Though the Israelite scribe-sage thus evidently wrote this collection on originally Egyptian literary patterns, what we have here is, nevertheless, no mere case of mechanical plagiarism. Even the essentially non-Israelite elements have been so well adapted to his people's religion and thought and to the special conditions of their country as to have received a thoroughly Israelite stamp.

Reproduced here is the first column of the papyrus containing the Instruction of Amenemopet in the hieroglyphic script. The exact date of the papyrus is not known, but it is conjectured to have been written in the first half of the first millennium B.C. However, the actual composition of the collection of sayings is earlier and can be assigned to the time of the Twentieth Dynasty or a little later (about the 12th cent. B.C.). Moreover, this particular Egyptian collection incorporates traditional material of even greater antiquity.

IF you beat him with the rod you will save his life from
Sheol.   (Proverbs 23 : 14)

Israelite wisdom literature is supra-national in content and character, and
parallels to it have been found not only in Egypt, but in the other wisdom
literatures of the ancient East as well. In the collection of "The Words of
the Wise" (Prov. 22 : 17—24 : 22; see p. 87), the "Egyptian" section
ends at chap. 23, verse 11. Here begins a new section, opening with the
exhortation: "Apply your mind to instruction, and your ear to words of
knowledge" (23 : 12). The first aphorism in this section is contained in the
verse at the head of this page, to which there is an instructive parallel in
the Words of Ahiqar (see the parts of the papyrus reproduced here, lines 3
and 4 from the top). The parallel passage in the Aramaic work runs as
follows: "Withhold not thy son from the rod, else thou wilt not be able to
save him from wickedness; if I smite thee, my son, thou wilt not die, but
if I leave thee to thine own heart thou wilt not live."
The Words of Ahiqar go back ultimately to an Assyrian book of wisdom (from the beginning of the 7th cent. B.C.), the original of which
has been lost. This book, which has come down to us in translations and
versions in a whole variety of languages (ranging from Syriac and Greek
to Slavic, Turkish, Rumanian and others), was very popular in the first
centuries of the Christian era and in the Middle Ages. In 1906, in the
excavations at Elephantine, the Aramaic version of it was discovered
written on sheets of papyrus from the end of the 5th cent. B. C. (see the
illustration). The version which circulated among the Jews of this military
colony, is of slightly earlier date than the copy preserved on the papyrus
sheets, but is still not the original of this work.

MY son, eat honey, for it is good, and the drippings of the honeycomb are sweet to your taste. Know that wisdom is such to your soul . . .

(Proverbs 24 : 14)

Wisdom and the Law are sometimes compared by the aphorists to sweet-tasting honey. Thus, in Prov. 16 : 24, we find: "Pleasant words are like a honeycomb, sweetness to the soul and health to the body". And in the wisdom psalms it is stated that the Law of the Lord is sweeter than honey and the drippings of the honeycomb (Ps. 19 : 10; 119 : 103).

Honey was one of the seven kinds of natural produce with which the Land of Israel was blessed (Deut. 8 : 8); hence its description as "a land flowing with milk and honey". The honey referred to here was probably obtained both from fruit and from bees. The hot climate and the many nectar-rich flowers of Palestine make the country a suitable habitat for bees. In Old Testament times, before the introduction of bee-keeping in hives, the wild bees used to nest in rock-fissures (Deut. 32 : 13; Isa. 7 : 19; Ps. 81 : 16), in the hollows of trees (1 Sam. 14 : 25-26), and even in carrion (Judg. 14 : 8). Honey was one of the articles exported from ancient Palestine (Ezek. 27 : 17; cf. Gen. 43 : 11). This export honey was apparently made from fruit.

In ancient Egypt bees were kept in clay hives. Then too, as is still the practice to-day, tens and hundreds of hives were placed in a solid mass, one on top of the other, close to the house or to the wall of the courtyard (as shown at the left of the lower picture). Below: a relief from Neuserre's temple of the sun at Abu Gurob, from the time of the Fifth Dynasty. The man at the left is extracting the honey from the hives, while his companion on his right pours it into a large container. The jars are then sealed to preserve the honey. Above: a wild honeycomb.

The reign of Hezekiah was a time of prosperity for the kingdom of Judah (see Vol. II, pp. 286—287). It was, apparently, in his day that there arose a class of philosopher-scribes (cf. Isa. 29 : 14) who played a dominant role in contemporary politics and literature. The political and economic prosperity of Hezekiah's reign has also left its mark on the literary activity of the time. Like the Assyrian king, Ashurbanipal, who formed a library of ancient works in his archive, Hezekiah too made a collection of old wise sayings. The separate collection of aphorisms in chapters 25—29 of Proverbs is stated, in the opening verse, to include parables from Solomon's time which had been copied out by the scribes of Hezekiah. Israelite scribes wrote on sheets either of papyrus, as in Egypt, or of parchment, as in Assyria, which, when written on, were rolled up into a scroll (Isa. 34 : 4; Jer. 36 : 2; and elsewhere). The instruments of their craft were a pen ("the scribe's pen", Jer. 8 : 8; Ps. 45 : 1); a penknife ("the scribe's knife", Jer. 36 : 23), for sharpening the nib, or cutting off the strip of parchment or papyrus; and ink (ibid. 18) which was kept in a special container in the writing-case ("the scribe's case" Ezek. 9 : 2; cf. Vol. III, p. 166). In Assyria and Babylon, however, writing was done not only on parchment, but also on clay tablets on which cuneiform impressions were made with a style.

In the upper picture, which is part of an Assyrian relief from the 7th cent. B. C., two Assyrian scribes are shown at work. Each of them is holding in his left hand two tablets, of bone or ivory, which are joined together and covered with wax to take a rough draft. (More commonly, one of a pair of Assyrian scribes is represented holding a clay tablet and the other a piece of parchment). In his right hand each of the scribes is holding a style with its thicker end upwards. The lower picture, which is part of an Egyptian relief from the time of the New Kingdom, shows a group of Egyptian scribes at work. They are holding the scribe's pen in their right hands, and the scribe's case and a papyrus-scroll in their left.

THESE also are proverbs of Solomon which the men of Hezekiah king of Judah copied.

(Proverbs 25 : 1)

As a door turns on its hinges, so does a sluggard on his bed.
(Proverbs 26 : 14)

Amongst the many aphorisms in the Book of Proverbs condemning indolence (cf. above, pp. 77, 83), there is one group in which the sluggard is depicted as a man who is given to over-sleeping. "Slothfulness casts into a deep sleep" (Prov. 19 : 15). When the sluggard lies late a-bed, he thinks himself to be indulging in only "a little sleep, a little slumber, a little folding of the hands to rest" (ibid. 6 :9-10; 24 : 33). Another lazybones makes fear an excuse for his sloth: "The sluggard says, There is a lion outside! I shall be slain in the streets!" (ibid. 22 : 13; cf. 26 : 13). In our verse here this type of man is likened to a door: just as the door turns on its hinges without moving from its place, so the sluggard merely turns from side to side on his bed, without ever leaving it to get up and work.

The picture on the left is a reconstruction of an ancient door, showing how it was attached to the door frame by means of a pivot or hinge on which it turned. The reconstruction is based on a wooden model of an Egyptian house from the time of the Fifth Dynasty. On the right— a door-pivot, made of basalt and let into a socket, from the Canaanite temple at Hazor. Both this pivot, which was attached to the lower part of the door, and another one above it at the upper end, turned in sockets. Basalt pivots of this type have been discovered in several of the Canaanite buildings at Hazor.

LIKE the glaze covering an earthen vessel are smooth lips with an evil heart. (Proverbs 26 : 23)

As it stands in the Hebrew original, this verse is a little puzzling. "Burning lips" (rendered by the Septuagint translations as "flattering and deceitful words") and "an evil heart" should be compared to a coating of real silver on a clay vessel, not to "silver dross" *(kesef sigim)*, which consists of the impurities left over after the refining of the metal. Moreover, it is doubtful whether clay was ever coated with silver in the ancient East. Hence, it is not surprising that the old commentators were baffled by the meaning of the verse, which now, however, appears to have been elucidated by recent epigraphic discoveries. In the Tale of Aqahat found at Ugarit there is a word *sfsg* which means "glaze" *(zafzag* in Hittite). It may therefore be conjectured that *kesef sigim* in our verse actually conceals a corruption of the biblical equivalent of *sfsg*. The meaning of the verse will then be: "Like a clay vessel overlaid with glaze, so are smooth lips and a wicked heart."

The technique of coating clay with glaze was, in fact, practised in various parts of the ancient East. One such example is the vessel pictured here which was found in one of the graves in stratum V at Alalakh (15th cent. B.C.). It is 7 in. high and is overlaid with bluish-greenish glaze, the composition of which testifies to the influence of Mesopotamian techniques.

Glaze was widely used in the ancient East from the beginning of the second millennium B.C. In Mesopotamia it was known as early as the third millennium B.C. (cf. below, p. 120). Glazed vessels have also been excavated in various places in Palestine; and glass-coated bronze has been discovered at Megiddo (c. 1000 B.C.). The palm-shaped Mesopotamian ornaments reproduced in the picture beside the jar (from the first half of the second millennium B.C.), are covered with a thin coating of glaze.

CRUSH a fool in a mortar with a pestle along with crushed grain, yet his folly will not depart from him.

(Proverbs 27 : 22)

This verse is one of the aphorisms dealing with the incorrigible obstinacy of the fool. Unlike the simpleton who, for all his naivety, is capable of learning and becoming wise (Prov. 1 : 4; 8 : 5; 9 : 4-6; 19 : 25; 21 : 11; Ps. 19 : 7; and elsewhere), the fool is beyond correction, since he hates wisdom. The fool dies a fool (Prov. 10 : 21). Any attempt to give him good advice only results in the mortification of the wise man (ibid. 23 : 9; cf. 9 : 7). Even corporal punishment has no effect on the fool, seeing that "a rebuke goes deeper into a man of understanding than a hundred blows into a fool" (ibid. 17 : 10). There is a similar statement in the Words of Ahiqar, 2 : 40: "A fool, even if thou beat him again and again, will never understand".

This same quality of the fool is metaphorically described in our verse here: even if you place a fool in a mortar and pound him with a pestle, together with "the crushed grain" (i.e. corn that is brayed to remove its husks; cf. 2 Sam. 17 : 19), his stupidity will still not leave him. The pestle and mortar were made of the hardest possible stone. Those reproduced here, belonging to the Israelite period, are of basalt and were discovered in the excavation of one of the tells of Palestine. The pestle was the first grinding instrument invented by man, dating back, in its crudest form, to the Mesolithic Age. One of the first human tools, it is still widely used to-day.

LIKE a roaring lion or a charging bear is a wicked ruler over a poor people.

(Proverbs 28 : 15)

A considerable number of the aphorisms in the Book of Proverbs is devoted to the proper relationships between kings and rulers, on the one hand, and the mass of their subjects on the other. In all of them the authors' sympathy for the poor who are oppressed by a brutal and tyrannous regime is clearly felt; and often they are outspoken in their condemnation of a wicked ruler. Thus, in our verse here, such a tyrant is compared to a roaring lion and a "charging" bear. This same attitude is evident in other sayings too: "when the wicked rule, the people groan" (Prov. 29 : 2), "if a ruler listens to falsehood, all his officials will be wicked" (ibid. 29 : 12). In such sentences it is not only the ruler that is being taken to task, but also his executive ministers who oppress the hapless people. This theme of the tension between oppressive governors and their oppressed subjects is one of the features common to both Israelite and Egyptian wisdom literature (though several of the Egyptian works of this kind do not contain that strong protest against wickedness in a ruler which we find in the wisdom literature of the Old Testament).

Many Egyptian paintings and reliefs show us peasants being brought before officials and judges and condemned to be flogged for not paying their taxes. Thus, in the picture reproduced below, which is taken from the tomb of Mereruka at Sakkarah (time of the Sixth Dynasty, second half of the third millennium B.C.), the heads of the village are being brought before the local officials and condemned to be flogged for such non-payment. The two scribes at the head of the line are taking a record of the proceedings and noting down the evidence. They are seated between pillars (with capitals are shaped like lotus-flowers) representing the hall of one of the government offices.

In addition to didactic aphorisms which teach a moral (and which constitute the greater part of the Book of Proverbs), wisdom literature also contains animal and plant parables, in which close observation of nature serves to provide an exercise in intellectual agility. The Old Testament states that king Solomon "spoke of trees, from the cedar that is in Lebanon even to the hyssop that grows out of the wall", and "also of beasts, and of birds and of reptiles and of fish" (1 Kings 4 : 33; cf. Vol. II, p. 211). However, the only places in the Old Testament where parables of this latter kind, of which there were no doubt originally very many, have been preserved in any quantity are this chapter of Proverbs, (the series of sayings based on numbers in Prov. 30 : 15-33), and the end of Job (chaps. 38—39).

In our parable here there is a description of four different creatures all of which, though small, are intelligent and nimble. The harvest-ant *(Messor semirufus)* (see the photograph) has already featured in the first collection of aphorisms in this book (Prov. 6 : 6—8); and indeed, the whole ant species is regularly used as a symbol of industriousness in the fables of every language, from as early as the time of the el-Amarna Letters (which contain a Canaanite fable about the industriousness of the ant) right down to the present day. On the coney (Heb. *shafan)*, which lives in rock-clefts, see above, p. 49 (on Ps. 104 : 18). For the locust, huge swarms of which migrate over vast distances without any leader, see Vol. III, pp. 220—221 (on Joel 1 : 4). The last creature in the list (Heb. *semamit)* was formerly taken to be a kind of lizard (as translated here), on the basis of the Aramaic translation of the usual Hebrew word for lizard *(letaah)* in Lev. 11 : 30. The species most commonly found in dwellings in Palestine is the house-lizard *(Hemidactylus turcicus)*. To-day, however, scholars are of the opinion that *semamit* means some sort of spider (such as the *Gholcus)* that spins its web even "in kings' palaces".

The photographs show a spider and ants working busily.

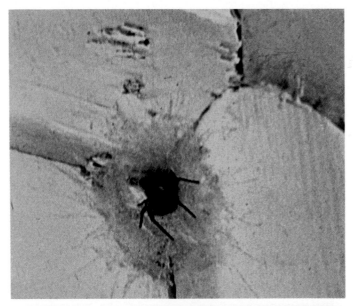

FOUR things on earth are small, but they are exceedingly wise: the ants are a people not strong, yet they provide their food in the summer. The coneys are a people not mighty, yet they make their homes in the rocks; the locusts have no king, yet all of them march in rank; the lizard you can take in your hands, yet it is in kings' palaces.

(Proverbs 30 : 24-28)

I T is not for kings, O Lemuel, it is not for kings to drink wine, or for rulers to desire strong drink.

(Proverbs 31 :4)

In the short poem in Prov. 31 : 1-9 the mother of Lemuel, king of Massa, admonishes her son and instructs him in his duties as a monarch. In the course of this admonition she warns him against drinking wine: it is wrong for kings and princes to take strong drink, since they may forget the established laws and pervert "the rights of all the afflicted". Wine is to be given to the embittered to make them forget their miseries (verses 4-7). This condemnation of wine may be due to the nomadic provenance of the poem, Massa being the name of a desert-tribe of Ishmaelites (Gen. 25 : 14). The Rechabites, who continued to live in tents right down to Jeremiah's time (Jer. 35 : 1-10), had similarly forsworn wine. On the other hand, the whole passage may simply be worded in conventional style, its purpose being to permit the drinking of wine only to "the afflicted". There is a similar plea in the Words of Ahiqar, 189: "Let the hapless man eat his fill of bread, and the soul of the poor be sated with wine".

In actual fact, wine was the daily drink of kings in the ancient East. It was served to the king by a special official bearing the title of "chief butler" (Gen. 40 : 2; 41 : 9; Neh. 2 : 1), one of whose duties was to taste the wine first, in case it had been poisoned. This practice was adopted by princelings and minor rulers as well. On an ivory casket from the time of Seti I, the fragments of which were found in the palace of the Egyptian governor at Tell el-Farah (the ancient Sharuhen) and which is photographed here, we see a lively picture of a scene from the court of this same "princeling". He is seated on his throne, holding a cup in his right hand and a lotus-flower in his left. Before him stands one of his attendants who, after the manner of a "butler", is filling the cup — presumably with wine. Behind this official a naked girl is dancing, and behind her there is a musician playing on a double pipe. Another attendant, in a short tunic, is standing behind the governor.

SHE puts her hands to the distaff, and her hands hold the spindle. (Proverbs 31 : 19)

Spinning in the ancient East was principally done by the woman in her home. Thus, in the description of the making of the tabernacle, it is recounted that all the threads required for it were spun by the women (Ex. 35 : 25—26). For this work the woman used wool, dyed or undyed, and flax (cf. above, verse 13: "she seeks wool and flax and works with willing hands"). Large-scale spinning and weaving were developed in the precincts of the temples where the temple-prostitutes were employed for the purpose; see 2 Kings 23 : 7: "and he broke down the houses of the cult prostitutes ... where the women wove hangings for the Asherah." From the inscriptions found at Ur we learn that one of the temples there employed, at spinning and weaving, one hundred and sixty five women whose output was measured every day and every month.

Reproduced below is a stone relief from Susa on which a woman is portrayed crouching on a chair and spinning. She is holding the spindle in her left hand, while she winds the thread with her right. Behind her stands a servant holding a large fan. In front of her there is a table with carved legs on which fish and round articles of food are laid.

JOB

THERE was a man in the land of Uz, whose name was Job; and that man was blameless and upright, one who feared God, and turned away from evil.

(Job 1 : 1)

The problem of unmerited human suffering is a very old one. Confronted by the harsh facts of a reality which seemed to them to contradict the basic tenets of their religious beliefs, the ancients were often at a loss for an explanation and questioned the justice of God's ways. This questioning finds expression in the wisdom literature, the origins of which go back to the earliest beginnings of Sumerian and Egyptian culture. The true believers, however, were always able to banish such doubts by their firm conviction that God is righteous and His attributes beyond human comprehension.

An example of this characteristic way of thinking is found in a Sumerian work whose origin goes back to the Third Dynasty of Ur, at the end of the third millennium B.C. The tablets on which it is written were discovered in the excavations at Nippur about fifty years ago, but not deciphered until 1954 (see the reproduction; the writing on these tablets dates to the 18th cent. B.C.). Like the biblical Book of Job, this composition — which was entitled "The Sumerian Job" by the scholars who gave its contents to the world — also tells of a righteous man who steadfastly clung to his faith through all the ordeals sent to test him, and was finally delivered from his sufferings and enjoyed a happy old age. There are likewise several subsidiary themes in this work which also find echoes in the biblical Job. Such are the imperviousness of "brothers" and friends to the hero's suffering; the taunts of callow youths; the sufferer's desire to speak directly to God Himself; the complaint that God, who made man, has now abandoned His creature in his misery; and so forth.

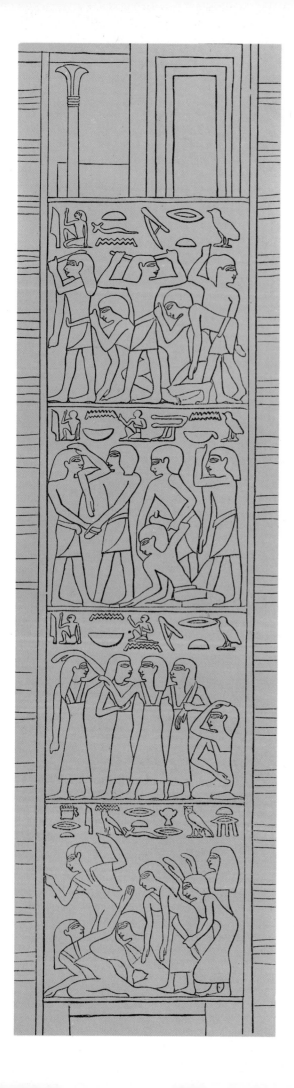

THEN Job arose and rent his robe, and shaved his head, and fell upon the ground, and worshipped.

(Job 1 : 20)

By rending his garment and shaving his head, Job demonstrates his bitter mourning over the disasters that have come upon him. Such tearing of the clothes and shaving of the head is a common sign of grief in the Old Testament (Gen. 37 : 29; 44 : 13, and elsewhere; Isa. 15 : 2; 22 : 12; Jer. 7 : 29; 16 : 6, and elsewhere). This is precisely what Job's friends meant to show when, on seeing him, they "rent their robes and sprinkled dust upon their heads toward heaven" (Job 2 : 12), since covering the head with dust was another of the conventional mourning rites. Job's prostrating himself on the ground, on the other hand, symbolizes his humble resignation to the fate meted out to him by God.

The customary ways of expressing grief and mourning were, in the main, similar throughout most of the ancient East, though there were certain variations from nation to nation. They were also a common theme in ancient reliefs and paintings, especially in Egypt (cf. Vol. I, p. 124; Vol. II, p. 181; Vol. III, pp. 104, 191). The picture on the left is a copy of a relief from the tomb of Edu at Gizeh in Egypt (time of the Sixth Dynasty, the second half of the third millennium B.C.), showing mourning rites. The figures in the two upper registers are men; those in the two lower ones women. It is possible to discern slight differences in the forms of expression given to their mourning by the two sexes.

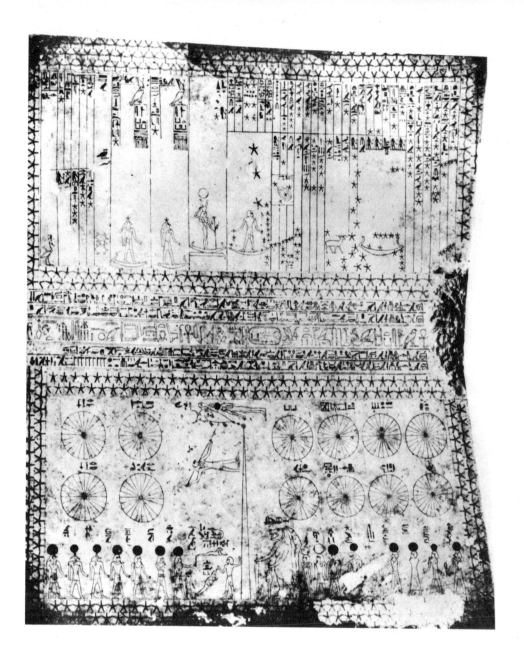

T HAT night — let thick darkness seize it! Let it not rejoice among the days of the year, let it not come into the number of the months.

(Job 3 : 6)

The poetical debate between Job and his friends opens with Job's cursing the day of his birth in a series of powerful images: he begs that the day on which he was born may "perish" from amongst the days of the year, that it may be dark, solitary and wretched (Job 3 : 1-9). The prophet Jeremiah also cursed the day of his birth in similar terms (Jer. 20 : 14-18). In such cursing of a specific day of the year there may be an echo of the archaic conception of the day as an independently existing entity, subject to the laws of change and decay. But in the Old Testament it is essentially no more than a poetic figure of speech, like the image employed by the Psalmist: "Day to day pours forth speech, and night to night declares knowledge" (Ps. 19 : 2). At the same time, such metaphors obviously presuppose the existence of a fixed calendar. Indeed, our verse here actually refers to the tally of "the days of the year" and "the number of the months".

All the peoples of the ancient East had regular systems of calendar reckoning. The most noteworthy were those of the nations of Mesopotamia and the Egyptians, who had considerable achievements to their credit in the field of astronomical calculation. In Israel of the Old Testament period there were two calendars in use: the agricultural calendar of the ordinary people beginning with the autumn (September-October); and the more exact ritual calendar of the priests, according to which the year began in the spring (March-April).

Reproduced here are astronomical drawings from the ceiling of the tomb of Senmut at Deir el-Bahri in Egypt (time of the Eighteenth Dynasty). The signs in the lower part of the picture indicate the months of the civil year.

With kings and counsellors of the earth who rebuilt ruins for themselves.

(Job 3 : 14)

The Hebrew word here translated "ruins" *(horaboth)* is taken by various commentators to mean "pyramids" (cf. the Arabic word for pyramid, *haram,* which is possibly of Egyptian origin). In that case, the verse would contain an allusion to the ancient kings of Egypt who erected these astonishing edifices.

Of the enormous constructional works executed by the kings of Egypt from the Third Dynasty to the Sixth Dynasty (the second half of the third millennium B.C.), the most famous were the pyramids, the largest of which were among the greatest engineering feats of antiquity. They could only have been built at a time when the kings, together with their officials and "advisers", ruled the state with absolute authority and had unlimited means at their disposal. In fact, during this period, much of the strength and skill of Egypt was devoted to these huge structures at which generation after generation of beholders have gazed in wonder, right down to the present day. The large pyramid of Khufu for example, contains more than two million hewn blocks of stone, each one of them weighing more than two tons. And the geometrical accuracy of the construction is still an architectural marvel (cf. Vol. I, p. 53).

Photographed here are pyramids from the time of the Fourth Dynasty (middle of the third millennium B. C.) near Gizeh. The nearest is the pyramid of the Pharaoh Khafre; the second, that of his successor, the Pharaoh Menkaure.

T HERE the wicked cease from troubling, and there the weary are at rest. There the prisoners are at ease together; they hear not the voice of the taskmaster. (Job 3 : 17-18)

The fate of prisoners in antiquity — if they were not flung into the "pit" or into gaol — was one of back-breaking physical toil. They were mercilessly exploited for the most exacting forms of forced labour, their very lives being of no account to their employers. In the Old Testament the prisoner's groan became a symbol of any acute physical suffering; and in the Psalms "prisoner" occurs in parallelism with "those doomed to die" (Ps. 79 : 11; 102 : 20). The forced labour was supervised by "taskmasters" (Heb. *nogesim*), who whipped the prisoners on with shouts and curses. This is what is meant by "the voice of the taskmaster" in our verse here; and also by "the shouts of the driver" mentioned later (Job 39 : 7).

In the ancient East, the great kingdoms of the Euphrates and Nile valleys were able to organize forced labour on a vast scale, owing mainly to the centralized and absolute character of their regimes, which made it possible for masses of human beings to be conscripted into the labour-gangs required for the execution of enormous constructional works. The illustration (a relief from Nineveh) shows "prisoners" hauling a boat containing a large stone (in the continuation of the picture), while the taskmasters (between the registers) drive them on. Cf. below p. 164.

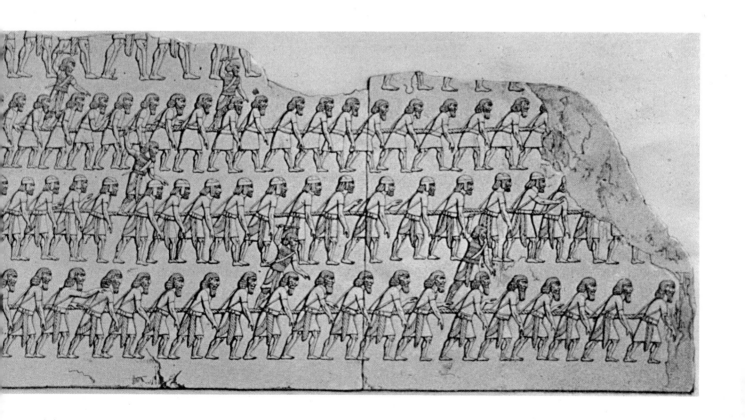

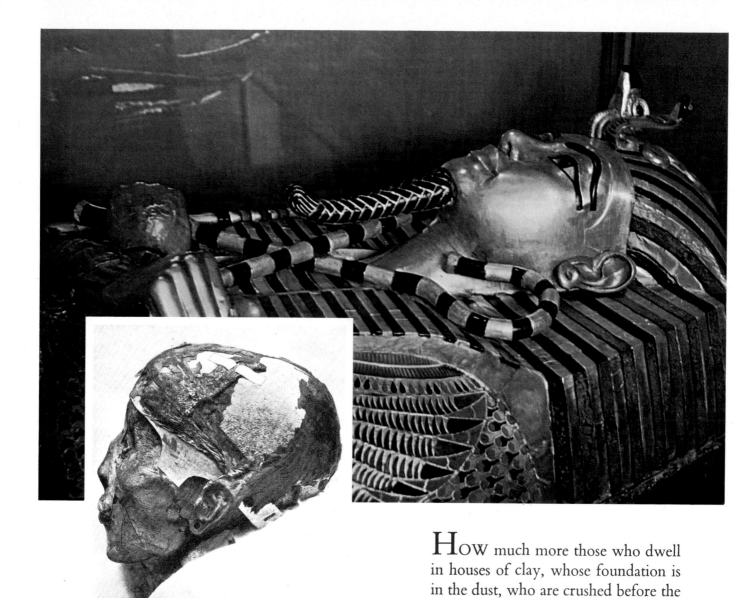

HOW much more those who dwell in houses of clay, whose foundation is in the dust, who are crushed before the moth.   (Job 4 : 19)

Those that dwell in "houses of clay" and in the dust, that can be "crushed" to death even by a moth, are simply mortal men. The general characteristic belief of antiquity was that the human body was made of clay, i.e. dust, this being the perishable part of it which, at death, returned to the earth. Such is the picture drawn in the story of the garden of Eden: God creates man "of dust from the ground" (Gen. 2 : 7), and later, when He drives him out of the garden, He reminds him that he is dust and that to the dust he will return (ibid. 3 : 19). Job too says in one of his speeches: "Remember that thou hast made me of clay; and wilt thou turn me to dust again?" (Job 10 : 9). And Elihu the son of Barachel the Buzite remarks: "All flesh would perish together, and man would turn again to dust" (Job 34 : 15). A similar statement is also found in Ecclesiastes: "and the dust returns to the earth as it was" (Eccles. 12 : 7). See also below, p. 122. This conception of the nature of the human body also finds expression in the traditional creation-myths of the Babylonians, Egyptians, Greeks and many other ancient peoples. It is even evident in the special Hebrew name given to the first human being, "Adam", a word akin to *adamah* (= "earth"). (This etymological affinity is specifically alluded to in the story of the Garden of Eden in Genesis).

One of the most grandiose attempts in human history to arrest physical decay and "immortalize" the body was that made by the ancient Egyptians, whose achievements in the art of embalming were remarkable (see Vol. I, pp. 122-23). The Egyptians took such great pains with their treatment of the dead, because of their belief that the spirit was indissolubly linked to the body in which it continued to dwell even after death; hence their assumption that the dead man's prospects of a life beyond the grave depended on the success with which his body was preserved by embalming. The Israelites did not share this belief (below, p. 122), and therefore did not have recourse to embalming.

Reproduced above is the second of the series of coffins in which was laid the body of the Egyptian king Tutankhamon (14th cent. B.C.). The coffin is a magnificently adorned work of art, portraying the Pharaoh in the likeness of Osiris. At the side — the mummified head of Tutankhamon.

M<small>Y</small> brethren are treacherous as a torrent-bed, as freshets that pass away.

(Job 6 : 15)

The best examples of "treacherous" watercourses are found in southern Israel. Their distinguishing feature, in contrast to the streams in the northern part of the country, is their sudden flooding with torrents of water despite the extreme aridity of the surrounding region. There are several reasons for this: a) The watercourses of the Negeb are the longest in the country and therefore the area drained by them is very extensive indeed. Wadi el-Arish, for example, drains an area as large as the whole of the State of Israel. b) The absence of vegetation that could retard the flow of water in the upper reaches, thus enabling the rainfall to percolate into the ground. c) The rocks of the Negeb, consisting mainly of limestone and marl, are not porous and therefore increase the flow of water in the upper reaches of the watercourse. d) The loess-soil, which covers the beds of the Negeb watercourses, is not porous either. e) The flash downpours of the Negeb are confined to certain limited areas. All these factors together are responsible for the remarkable phenomenon of watercourses, which are so completely dry for most of the year that the Bedouin on their banks almost die of thirst, suddenly filling with a violent spate of water, exactly as described elsewhere in the Old Testament: "You shall not see wind or rain, but that stream-bed shall be filled with water, so that you shall drink, you, your cattle, and your beasts" (2 Kings 3 : 17). But these watercourses dry up again as quickly as they have flooded (cf. above, p. 53). Hence Job compares his "brothers" who have disappointed him to a watercourse in the midst of the desert which suddenly becomes a rushing river, only to be as dry again as before after a short while.

In the photograph — a typical seasonal stream in the Judean desert.

Like a slave who longs for the shadow, and like a hireling who looks for his wages, so I am allotted months of emptiness, and nights of misery are apportioned to me. (Job 7 : 2-3)

In the hot climate of the Near East, shade is what every worker in the fields most longs for. It is therefore readily intelligible that receiving protection, shelter and help from someone should be metaphorically described in the Old Testament by such expressions as "dwelling in his shade" (Ezek. 31 : 6, 17; Hos. 14 : 7; and elsewhere), "taking refuge in his shade" (Judg. 9 : 15; Isa. 30 : 2; and elsewhere) and the like; while, conversely, the "removal" of the shade denotes defencelessness (Nu. 14 : 9, Hebrew version). Outside the city, natural shade was provided by trees (see, e.g., Gen. 18 : 4; 1 Kings 19 : 4-5); where there were no trees, a booth (Heb. *succah*) was sometimes erected, as described by the prophet, "for a shade by day from the heat . . ." (Isa. 4 : 6; cf. Jonah 4 : 5). Occasionally wayfarers, especially in desert regions, even found shelter under a large rock (Isa. 32 : 2). The slave labouring in the field, who had no time to sit in the shade, could only long for the evening with its refreshing shadows and coolness. This is apparently the meaning of the verse illustrated on this page.

Workers resting in the shade of trees are a frequent theme of Egyptian art. In the picture here (a reproduction of a relief from the tomb of Ahhotep at Sakkarah, from the end of the Fifth Dynasty, middle of the third millennium B.C.), a goatherd is seen sitting in the shade of a tree, with his crook in his hand, drinking from a jug. Beside him his goats are nibbling at the tree. One of them (bottom right) is just giving birth. Behind her stands the goatherd's dog. In Egyptian paintings of harvest-scenes there is also often a tree, with food and drink placed beneath it for the refreshment of the reapers during their rest.

CAN papyrus grow where there is no marsh? Can reeds flourish where there is no water? (Job 8 : 11)

The bulrush *(Cyperus papyrus L.)* is a typical marsh-plant which requires an abundant supply of water for its growth (cf. Isa. 35 : 7). The stem is triangular in section; it is ten feet or more high, and ends in wide, tufted heads (see the photograph above).

In antiquity, papyrus grew so thickly along the lower reaches of the Nile that it formed one of the most characteristic features of the scenery of Lower Egypt. The very Hebrew word for bulrush *(gome)* is apparently of Egyptian origin (as also the word *ahu* = "reeds" in the second part of our verse; cf. Gen. 41 : 2). From the stem of the bulrush the Egyptians made papyrus for writing, as well as baskets (see Ex. 2 : 3; Vol. I, p. 131), skiffs (below, p. 110), mats and various containers. The plant features frequently in the reliefs and wall-paintings of ancient Egypt. To-day, however, the papyrus plant has completely disappeared from the whole of Lower Egypt and can only be found on the banks of the Blue and White Niles. In Palestine the papyrus once grew sparsely on the banks of streams and in great profusion in the Huleh marshes. But as a result of the drainage of these marshes, it is gradually disappearing from them too.

The picture on the left (a wall-painting from the tomb of Puyemre at Thebes, 15th cent. B.C.) illustrates the plucking of papyrus plants in the marshes. The man at the extreme right is steering the skiff by means of an oar; the youth at the left is plucking the stems from their roots; while the old man in the centre of the skiff is binding the plucked stems into sheaves, after the removal of their heads. On the right—papyrus plants in the Huleh valley.

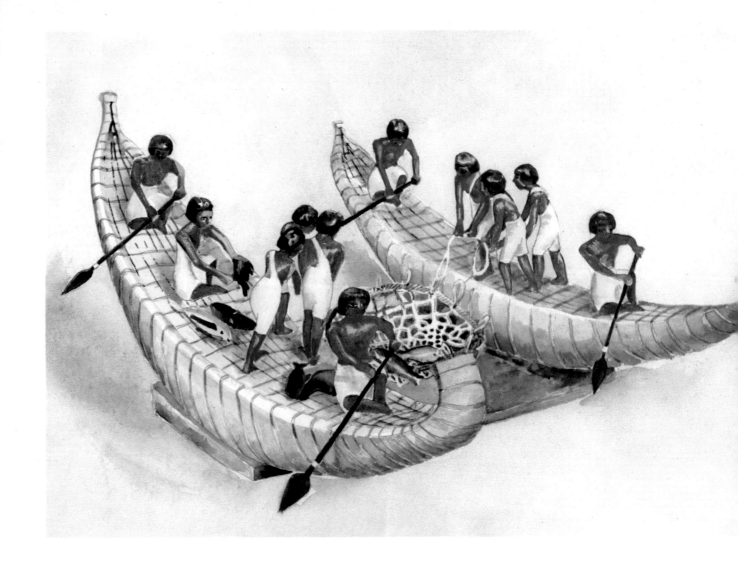

MY days are swifter than a runner; they flee away, they see no good. They go by like skiffs of reed, like an eagle swooping on the prey. (Job 9 : 25-26)

Job complains of life's swift passage, comparing it to the light gliding of reed-boats over the water and the swoop of the eagle on to its prey. In the opinion of most commentators, the otherwise unknown Hebrew word *ebeh* in this verse means the green bulrush, i.e. the papyrus plants from which the ancient Egyptians used to construct their light boats. Hence the translation "skiffs of reed". This reed is called *aba* in Arabic and *apu* in Akkadian. In Job 8 : 12 the reed is described as being "still in its greenness" *(beibo)*. And Isaiah speaks of the distant land "beyond the rivers of Ethiopia" which sends "swift messengers" "in vessels of papyrus upon the waters" (Isa. 18 : 2). The small and easily manoeuvrable skiffs mentioned here were apparently used only on the calm waters of the Nile.

In the picture (wooden models from the tomb of Meketre at Thebes, time of the Eleventh Dynasty, end of the third millennium B.C.) — two Egyptian reed-boats trawling a net. In each of them there are two oarsmen, and three fishermen holding the net which is made of thick cords. Its opening faces the direction in which the boat is travelling.

D<small>IDST</small> thou not pour me out like milk and curdle me like cheese?   (Job 10 : 10)

In the verse above, the poet likens the creation of the human form to the churning of milk and the curdling of cheese. Milk was "poured out" to make it curdle, thus producing what is called in the Old Testament "curds" *(hemah),* or "cheese" *(gebinah* — a word that occurs only here). Thus the biblical maxim states: "For pressing milk produces curds" (Prov. 30 : 33); and, in the story of David's duel with Goliath, mention is made of "cheeses of milk" (1 Sam. 17 : 18).

The method of producing curdled milk has hardly changed in the Near East from ancient times right down to the present day. Even the utensils used in the curdling are almost the same, as shown by the examples illustrated here. Below — a clay vessel from the Chalcolithic Age (fourth millennium B.C.) which was excavated at Horvat Beter, near Beersheba, and has been identified as a churn. Above — a contemporary Arab clay utensil, from Sinai, which is similar in shape to the ancient churn.

A ND if I lift myself up, thou dost hunt me like a lion, and again work wonders against me.
(Job 10 : 16)

The lion usually appears in the Old Testament as a man-eating beast of prey, and there is hardly any mention of lion-hunting as a sport in which the lion is man's victim. In our verse here, however, Job compares himself to such a hunted lion (cf. below, 19 : 6: "and has closed his net about me"). The image here appears to be that of a hunt in which the hunters weary the lion with repeated attacks, until at last it falls under the blows of their arrows and spears, as described in the second half of our verse: "and again thou dost work wonders against me", i.e. you strike me hard again and again.

Although there were lions, in Old Testament times, in the desolate regions of Palestine, neither the people, nor apparently even the royal family, were in the habit of hunting for sport. Elsewhere in the ancient East, especially amongst the peoples of Mesopotamia, the lion-hunt was a popular pastime. Most renowned of all for their hunting prowess were the Assyrian kings, as is testified by many of their reliefs (cf. Vol. III, p. 174). In Assyria this sport, which called for courage, agility and cool-headedness, was a regular part of court-life. The scene reproduced here is part of the series of hunting-reliefs of the Assyrian king Ashurbanipal, from Nineveh. The king is shown shooting at lions with his bow, while standing in a chariot. One already wounded lion charges at the chariot with all its remaining strength, only to be pierced and forced back by the spears of the king's adjutants. The horseman on the right, with a bow in his hand, is also assisting in the hunt.

The stretching out of the hands mentioned in this verse is the characteristic gesture of prayer in the Old Testament, as in the following examples: "When you spread forth your hands, I will hide my eyes from you" (Isa. 1 : 15); "the cry of the daughter of Zion gasping for breath, stretching out her hands" (Jer. 4 : 31); "if we have forgotten the name of our Lord, or spread forth our hands to a strange god" (Ps. 44 : 20; cf. Ex. 9 : 29; 1 Kings 8 : 38; and elsewhere). Similar expressions are: "lifting up the hands" (Lam. 2 : 19; 3 : 41; Ps. 63 : 4; and elsewhere), "spreading forth the hands" (Ps. 88 : 9), "stretching out the hands" (Ps. 143 : 6; Lam. 1 : 17; and elsewhere), "raising the hands" (Lev. 9 : 22; Ps. 28 : 2; and elsewhere). All these slightly different turns of phrase must no doubt have corresponded to certain distinctions in the stance and movements of the worshipper, only the exact details can no longer be ascertained.

This particular gesture of the hands was, essentially, the universal praying posture throughout the ancient East, so much so that it became a characteristic stereotyped motif of Assyrian and Egyptian paintings and reliefs. Signs of this artistic convention can also be seen in the picture here, which is a reproduction of one of the sides of a carved ivory casket found at Hazor and belonging to the period of the Israelite Monarchy. The kneeling man is perhaps stretching out his hands to the tree of life which is carved on another side of the same casket. For another example of this practice of kneeling with outstretched arms see p. 114.

IF you set your heart aright, you will stretch out your hands toward him.　　　(Job 11 : 13)

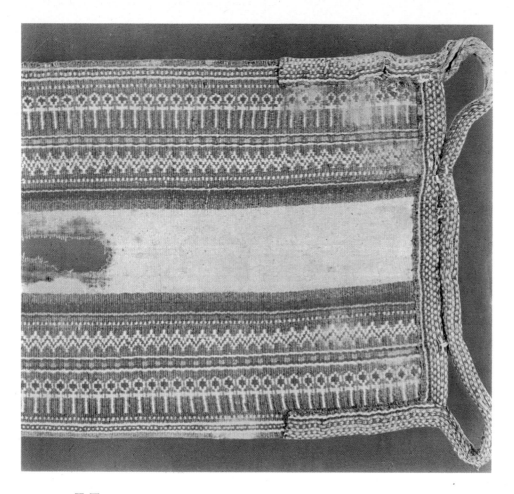

He looses the bonds of kings, and binds a waistcloth on their loins. (Job 12 : 18)

The "girdle" (Heb. *ezor*) was a kind of narrow band tied round the waist. It was a universal article of clothing, worn alike by the common people, by soldiers (Isa. 5 : 27), and even by princes and kings (ibid. 11 : 5). However, the commoners' girdle was made of plain leather (2 Kings 1 : 8) or of linen (Jer. 13 : 1), whereas that worn by princes and kings was an ornate affair which was thought to add both to the appearance and dignity of the wearer. Thus Ezekiel describes the dandified Babylonians as being "girded with belts on their loins" (Ezek. 23 : 15). And, in our verse here, the girdle is similarly referred to as a mark of regal dignity, granted to kings by divine grace in place of the "bond" *(musar)* by which they had formerly been bound. The priestly girdle *(abnet)* (cf. Vol. I, p. 166) also apparently served much the same purpose as the *ezor*, being worn by the members of the royal court as well. Thus Isaiah prophesied to Shebna, "who was over the household", that Eliakim the son of Hilkiah would replace him in his office and wear his robes and *abnet* (Isa. 22 : 21). The *ezor* worn by kings and courtiers was no doubt, like the *abnet*, woven from coloured threads and richly embroidered.

Reproduced above is part of the girdle of Ramses III. It is woven in four colours (blue, red, green and yellow) each of which was obtained from a different plant. Below — an ivory carving discovered at Nimrud (the modern Calah), from the 8th-7th cent. B.C., of a kneeling figure with arms outstretched, wearing a tunic fastened to the body by a coloured girdle. The recesses in the carving appear to have been inlaid with some coloured substance and the whole workmanship shows signs of Egyptian-Canaanite influence.

AS for you, you whitewash with lies; worthless physicians are you all. (Job 13 : 4)

The expression "worthless physicians" *(rophe elil)* is meant to emphasize the total ineffectiveness of human medicine which is unable to bring true healing to the sick. In the view of the Old Testament, God alone is the cause and the cure of all diseases, as stated in the verse: "I will put none of the diseases upon you which I have put upon the Egyptians: for I am the Lord your healer" (Ex. 15 : 26). Hence, in ancient Israel the doctor's functions were entrusted to the priests (cf., e.g., the descriptions of the epidemics in Lev. chaps. 13-14), and also, to some extent, to the prophets. When the sick king Asa "did not seek the Lord, but sought help from physicians", he was regarded as having committed a sin (2 Chron. 16 : 12; cf. below, p. 275). However, from the frequent use of the verb "to heal" *(rippe)* and of its derivate nouns, it may be inferred that there were doctors in Israel nevertheless, and that the ordinary people had frequent recourse to them. Medicaments are also mentioned in the Old Testament, the best known of them being "balm" (Jer. 8 : 22; 46 : 11; 51 : 8).

Magic rites formed such an essential part of medicine in antiquity that priests were amongst its chief practitioners in all the other countries of the ancient East, as well as in Israel. In Gen. 50 : 2, the professional Egyptian embalmers are called "physicians". The peoples of antiquity believed that illness was merely the outward physical symptom of the patient's being possessed by an evil spirit. This is illustrated by the picture here which is a reproduction of one of the scenes on an Assyrian bronze tablet, intended to be used for purposes of exorcism. The priest-doctors, masked as fish, are trying hard to exorcise the evil spirit from the body of a sick man, who is lying on a bed. The lamp on a stand in the left-hand corner is the emblem of the god Nusku. In the right-hand corner two demons are wrestling with each other. The tablet is reproduced in full in Vol. I, p. 273.

BUT the mountain falls and crumbles away, and the rock is removed from its place.   (Job 14 : 18)

The mountain and the rock are Old Testament symbols for unshakeable strength. "Rock" is therefore also metaphorically used of any stronghold or shelter. Thus David says in his poem: "The Lord is my rock, and my fortress, and my deliverer; my God, my rock, in whom I take refuge" (Ps. 18 : 2). But our verse here refers to the downfall of these mighty fastnesses. The second half of the verse is repeated below, 18 : 4. And a similar word picture is also drawn in Job 9 : 5 "He who removes the mountains and they know it not, when he overturns them in his anger",

The shifting and collapse of large rocks is a common phenomenon in desert or semi-desert regions and one which, in Israel, occurs particularly in the Arabah, and in the Negeb mountains. The layers of brittle Nubian sandstone found in these areas are continually being worn down and eroded by the action of wind and water, and by the sharp contrasts of temperature. The layers of hard rock superimposed on them, being thus deprived of their support, then crack and fall. Photographed here is a rock that has been "removed from its place" in the Makhtesh Rammon in the Negeb. This giant, which is composed of limestone strata, split off from its parent cliff when the Nubian sandstone on which it rested crumbled away.

THEY send forth their little ones like a flock, and their children dance. They sing to the tambourine and the lyre, and rejoice to the sound of the pipe.

(Job 21 : 11-12)

In these verses the poet has worked several characteristic details into a composite picture of the happiness of the wicked. There is indeed no more striking evidence of domestic bliss than a large number of offspring all happily playing children's games. Thus, the prophet Zechariah, when foretelling Jerusalem's redemption, says: "And the streets of the city shall be full of boys and girls playing in its streets (Zech. 8 : 5). The boys' games sometimes took the form of contests of physical strength (2 Sam. 2 : 14; Prov. 20 : 29; see Vol. II, p. 165, and this volume, p. 85), while those played by the girls took the form of dances. Thus Jeremiah, in his prophecy of consolation, describes how the maidens of Israel will take up their timbrels and join in "the dance of the merrymakers" (Jer. 31 : 4; cf. ibid. verse 13: "then shall the maidens rejoice in the dance").

The picture — a relief from the tomb of Mereruka at Sakkarah, from the time of the Sixth Dynasty in Egypt (second half of the third millennium B.C.) — shows young girls dancing and playing.

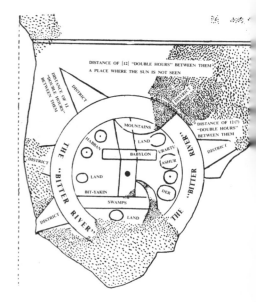

DISTANCE OF [12] "DOUBLE HOURS" BETWEEN THEM
A PLACE WHERE THE SUN IS NOT SEEN

DISTANCE OF 12 "DOUBLE HOURS" BETWEEN THEM

DISTRICT

DISTRICT

DISTANCE OF 12(?) "DOUBLE HOURS" BETWEEN THEM

DISTRICT

MOUNTAINS

HABBAN

LAND

THE "BITTER RIVER"

BABYLON

URARTU

ASHUR

THE "BITTER RIVER"

DISTRICT

LAND

DER

BIT-YAKIN

SWAMPS

DISTRICT

LAND

HE has described a circle upon the face of the waters at the boundary between light and darkness.   (Job 26 : 10)

The ancients believed that the earth was a flat disc floating on the primeval waters, which had covered the whole universe before the creation (cf. Vol. I, p. 153), and completely surrounded by them. All round the earth God had set a limit for the deeps on which the waves of the sea broke and which they could never pass. This is what the Old Testament calls the "decree" (Heb. *hoq*) fixed by divine grace (cf. Jer. 5 : 22; Job 38 : 10-11). There were no angles in this boundary line, since the flat earth, floating over the bottomless deeps, was circular in shape. That is why the noun "circle" is used in the Old Testament to denote the sweep of the earth's horizon. Thus we also find: "It is he who sits above the circle of the earth" (Isa. 40 : 22); "when he drew a circle upon the face of the deep" (Prov. 8 : 27). Beyond the circumference of the earth's horizon lay the everlasting deeps, the dwelling place of perpetual darkness. This is apparently the meaning of the allusion in the second half of our of verse.
The conception of the earth's shape thus expressed in the Old Testament was shared by most of the peoples of the ancient East, being especially widespread in Mesopotamia. A good illustration of this is provided by the reproduction here of an ancient map of the world incised on a clay tablet from southern Babylonia (copied in the 7th cent. B.C.). On it the world is drawn, according to the Babylonian conception, as a circle surrounded by water, with Babylon at its centre (cf. the drawing on the right). The text above the map recounts the conquests of Sargon I, king of Akkad in the 24th cent. B.C.

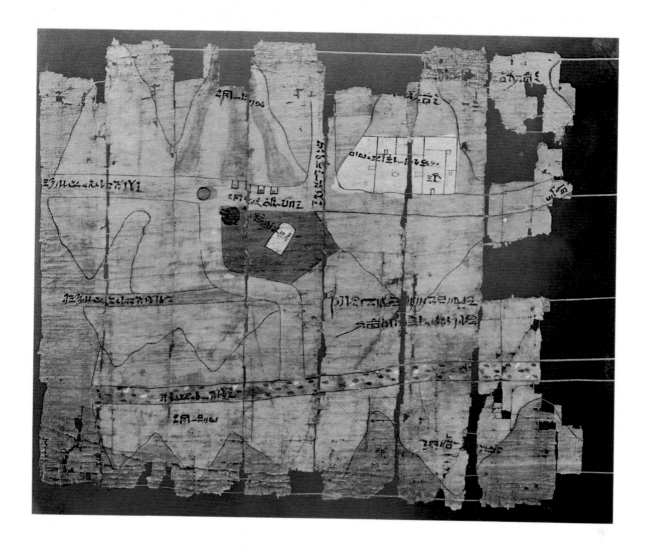

SURELY there is a mine for silver, and a place for gold which they refine. Iron is taken out of the earth, and copper is smelted from the ore.

(Job 28 : 1-2)

Chapter 28 is a song of praise to wisdom whose source man is incapable of discovering either in the bowels of the earth or at the bottom of the sea, and whose value he cannot even begin to estimate. God, and God alone, "knows its place" (Job 28 : 23; cf. Prov. 8 : 22-31) The chapter opens with a description of man's ability to mine precious minerals from the depths of the earth (verses 1-11). Even though wisdom eludes him there too, the poet does at least concede the greatness of man's technical achievements. In those dark subterranean galleries of gold and other mineral wealth, man "searches out to the farthest bound", hewing out passages that no mortal eye has seen, hammering at the flinty rock, levelling mountains, cutting channels through the rock, and laying bare the earth's secrets — "the thing that is hid he brings forth to light".

Precious metals were mined out of the earth in the ancient East as early as the second millennium B.C. But the poet's description here is presumably not taken from local conditions, since the only metals in ancient Palestine were iron and copper (Deut. 8 : 9; cf. Vol. I, pp. 27, 262). The Sinai peninsula was famous for its mines in antiquity. The Egyptians began working these mines as far back as the third millennium B.C., especially in the plain of Serabit el-Khadem and in the nearby Wadi Magharah. There were gold mines in Upper Egypt, and also in regions bordering on Egypt, such as Midian, where the stones containing the ore were detached from the rock by being heated with fire (cf. Job 28 : 5: "and underneath it is turned up as by fire"), or chipped off with picks of stone or bronze. The gold was then refined close to the mine (cf. ibid. verse 1) by being washed in rain-water, which had been collected in cisterns (ibid. 4, 10).

The illustration is an Egyptian map drawn on papyrus (from the 13th cent. B.C.) showing the gold-mines in Wadi Hammamat, in the desert to the east of the Nile.

GOLD and glass cannot equal it, nor can it be exchanged for jewels of fine gold.

(Job 28 : 17)

In this verse, the poet states that wisdom is more precious even than gold and glass, and of greater value than any "vessel of gold". The Hebrew word translated "glass" (*zekhukhith*) occurs only here in the Old Testament, but it is frequently used in Mishnaic Hebrew and is cognate with the Aramaic *zegugita*.

In the ancient East, glass was an article of luxury, like gold with which it is coupled in our verse here. The most famous glassware of antiquity was that made by the Tyrians and Sidonians. In fact, however, the Egyptians produced coloured glass long before the Tyrians, the earliest specimens of their ware going back to the fourth millennium B.C. This early glass, however, was not transparent and was used only as an inlay in jewels, as a substitute for precious stones. It was only some time later that vessels began to be made of glass. See above, p. 92. As late as Talmudic times white, transparent glass was still very valuable. Photographed here is a handsome glass vessel from the 4th or 5th cent. B.C. which may have been used as a cosmetic container.

BUT now they make sport of me, men who are younger than I, whose fathers I would have disdained to set with the dogs of my flock.   (Job 30 : 1)

In this verse Job describes the disastrous reversal of his fortunes in hyperbolical language: formerly he enjoyed the utmost happiness, "when the friendship of God was upon my tent", and dwelt in the midst of his community "like a king among his troops" (Job 29 : 4, 25); whereas now he has become a laughing-stock even to youths who occupy the lowest rung in the social ladder. The youths referred to here may be "the little ones of the flock" (Jer. 49 : 20; 50 : 45; cf. Zech. 13 : 7), i.e. the shepherds' boys, as is also indicated by the mention of "the dogs of my flock" at the end of the verse.

The dog, man's earliest four-footed companion, was domesticated as far back as the dawn of human history, almost with the first beginnings of agriculture. It is interesting to note that rabbinical legend attributes the domestication of the dog to Cain, the first tiller of the soil (Bereshith Rabbah, 24). In the ancient East the dog was used mainly for hunting and shepherding, especially by the Egyptians and Assyrians. The most developed of the several strains found in the ancient East were carefully bred in Egypt, Mesopotamia and Asia Minor. The typical Egyptian dog appears frequently on Egyptian paintings as early as the third millennium B.C., and many skeletal remains have also been found. It was distinguished by its upright ears, long and narrow snout, and curly tail (see the illustration). This breed of dog died out in Egypt long ago. It is to-day found in the islands of Majorca at the western end of the Mediterranean.

The shepherd's boy seen seated behind the dog in the picture here (an Egyptian relief from the time of the Fifth Dynasty) is holding his staff in his hand (cf. 1 Sam. 17 : 43; Zech. 11 : 7). In front of him there is a basket of food and a jug of drink. On the reed-mats at either edge of the picture cf. p. 168.

BEHOLD, I am toward God as you are; I too was formed from a piece of clay.

(Job 33 : 6)

The Old Testament conception is that man was given his likeness by God when He created him from dust (cf. above, p. 106). This is explicitly stated in the story about the Garden of Eden (Gen. 2 : 7); and Job, in one of his speeches, similarly says: "Thy hands fashioned and made me" (Job 10 : 8). This is also the sense underlying the words of Elihu the son of Berachel the Buzite in our verse here, where he seeks to prove that he is Job's equal. Interestingly enough, Babylonian literature also employs exactly the same expression ("formed from a piece of clay") in describing the creation of mortal men by gods. Furthermore, according to the Old Testament, God created man in His own image and likeness (Gen. 1 : 26, 27; 5 : 1; 9 : 6), and breathed into him His own spirit from on high. Thus Job says: "And the spirit of God is in my nostrils" (Job 27 : 3); and Elihu: "The spirit of God has made me, and the breath of the Almighty gives me life" (ibid. 33 : 4; cf. 32 : 8). At death, man's body returns to the dust, but the spirit returns "to God who gave it" (Eccles. 12 : 7; cf. Job 34 : 14-15; Ps. 104 : 29-30; and elsewhere).

This conception of man as created by God in His own image, and of man's soul as containing a divine element, was common to most of the peoples of the ancient East. The relief from the temple at Luxor, from the reign of Amenhotep III (beginning of the 14th cent. B.C.) reproduced here, illustrates the form taken by this conception in Egypt. The ram-headed god Khnum is seen seated on his throne in front of a potter's wheel on which he is fashioning out of clay the figure of Amenhotep III, (with, next to him, his *ka,* the spirit by which the Egyptians believed every man was accompanied). At the other end of the relief sits the goddess Hathor, holding out the *ankh* sign which is the emblem of life.

A<small>ND</small> if they are
bound in fetters and
caught in the cords of
affliction, then he de-
clares to them their
work and their trans-
gressions, that they are
behaving arrogantly.

(Job 36 : 8-9)

In a manner characteristic of wisdom literature, Elihu explains that man is made to suffer for the sake of his own moral improvement. God decrees that human beings should be clamped in fetters and bound in "cords of afflic-tion", in order to remind them of their crimes and thereby chastise them into "returning from iniquity" (Job 36 : 8-10). This same viewpoint is also found in Psalms 107 : 10-12: "Some sat in darkness and gloom, prisoners in affliction and irons, for they had rebelled against the words of God and spurned the counsel of the Most High. Their hearts were bowed down with hard labour . . ." The pure of heart give heed to the true meaning of their misfortunes and return to the Lord in their affliction (Job 36 : 10-12; cf. Ps. 107 : 13); whereas the wicked, who are "godless in heart", "do not cry for help when He binds them" (Job 36 : 13). In antiquity, prisoners' hands were bound in fetters (Heb. *azikim,* cf. Jer. 40 : 1; Ps. 149 : 8), which were clamps made of iron or bronze (cf. Judg. 16 : 21; 2 Kings 25 : 7; and elsewhere). Occasionally, the legs too were fettered (2 Sam. 3 : 34; Ps. 105 : 18). It was also a common practice for prisoners to be marched along in a line with their necks bound to a pole (Isa. 52 : 2; Jer. 27 : 2; and elsewhere).

The picture is part of a relief from the rock temple of Ramses II at Beit el-Wali (13th cent. B.C.), showing three Canaanite prisoners, the first of whom has his hands fettered, guarded by a soldier holding a bow.

HE seals up the hand of every man, that all men may know his work.　　　　(Job 37 : 7)

The slave was the inalienable property of his master who used, therefore, to stamp some mark of ownership on his flesh. Thus the Babylonians, for example, were in the habit of incising the owner's name on the slave's body. It is to some such practice that our verse here probably alludes. Sometimes the mark was placed on the slave's forehead (see Ezek. 9 : 4), as may have been the case with the "mark" of Cain (Gen. 4 : 15). But the more usual place for the owner's sign was apparently the hand. Besides our verse here, there is another allusion to this practice in Isa. 44 : 5: "This one will say, 'I am the Lord's', another will call himself by the name of Jacob, and another will write on his hand, 'The Lord's,' and surname himself by the name of Israel." The custom of piercing the slave's ear may have had a similar purpose (Ex. 21 : 6; Deut. 15 : 17).

The illustration is a relief from the temple of Ramses III at Medinet Habu, from the 12th cent. B.C. On it Egyptian officials are seen branding the shoulders of Philistine captives with a white-hot branding-iron. The iron apparently bears the king's name and its impression on the captives' flesh marks them as the Pharaoh's slaves. On the ground, beside the captives' feet, stands a brazier containing burning coals with the branding-irons stuck into them. At the left two scribes are recording the numbers of the captives.

CAN you, like him, spread out the skies, hard as a molten mirror? (Job 37 : 18)

Elihu wishes to make it clear to Job that he can neither defy the Lord nor vie with Him in strength. There are two possible explanations of the verse above. According to the first, Elihu derisively asks whether Job really thinks that he can soar above the earth and take up his abode in the heights of the heavens like the Lord, whose dwelling is in the skies. The other interpretation of the question (that adopted in the translation here) is: Can Job beat the clouds out flat as the Lord did when He created them — those same clouds that are "hard as a molten mirror?" The ancients envisaged the sky as a kind of flat roof stretched out over the earth. Above this "roof" were the upper waters, "the waters above the heavens", which from time to time descended by God's grace, to fructify the earth (Ps. 104 : 13; 148 : 4; Deut. 28 : 12). Thus a torrential downpour is poetically described as "the windows of the heavens were opened" (Gen. 7 : 11; 8 : 2; cf. 2 Kings 7 : 2). In a similar figure of speech the Psalmist states that, when the Lord rained down manna upon the Israelites in the wilderness, He "opened the doors of heaven" for them (Ps. 78 : 23). Hence in our verse here the skies are described as "a molten mirror", since the mirrors of the ancients consisted of a beaten, polished slab of bronze. In the curse uttered by Moses it is said that the heavens will be tightly closed against the prayers of the Israelites — "the heavens over your head will be brass" (Deut. 28 : 23).

An example of a "molten mirror" from ancient times is shown in the illustration here. This particular mirror, which is Egyptian and belonged to a certain Renseneb, was found in a tomb at Thebes from the reign of Amen-emhet IV (beginning of the 18th cent. B.C.). The reflecting-surface is bronze, while the handle — on which the owner's name and title are engraved — is made of wood partly overlaid with gold.

CAN you bind the chains of the Pleiades, or loose the cords of Orion? Can you lead forth the Mazzaroth in their season, or can you guide the Bear with its children?   (Job 38 : 31-32)

In the opinion of the ancients, the seasonal and daily changes in the weather were directly caused by the stars and the signs of the Zodiac. That is why, in this passage of the Book of Job, the reference to the stars follows immediately on the detailed description of the climatic phenomena of snow, hail, wind, rain, dew and frost (Job 38 : 22-30).

The Pleiades (Heb. *kimah)* and Orion *(kesil)* are mentioned elsewhere in the Old Testament (Isa. 13 : 10; Amos 5 : 8; Job 9 : 9). The ancient translators and commentators took the expressions "chains of the Pleiades" and "cords of Orion" to mean the clusters of stars of which the two constellations are formed. The Bear *(ayish)* is also mentioned again, in Job 9 : 9 (in the form *ash).* Mazzaroth, on the other hand, occurs only in our verse here. Some scholars would identify the word with the *mazzaloth* ("constellations") in 2 Kings 23 : 5 (cf. Vol. II, p. 294), and others take it as the name of one or other of several possible constellations.

These astronomical terms from the Old Testament were no doubt part of the general stock of astronomical lore in the ancient East. The most important contributions to this science were made by the Babylonians and Egyptians, who for generations compiled tables of constellations according to the "regional" division of the skies, the estimated distance between the stars, and the signs of the Zodiac.

Above: pictures of the moon, the Pleiades and the Bull. Below: a picture of Mercury, Virgo and another constellation. These drawings are based on ancient originals, some of which go back to as early as the 12th cent. B.C.

D<small>O</small> you know when the mountain goats bring forth? Do you observe the calving of the hinds?

(Job 39 : 1)

The second part of God's reply to Job contains descriptions of living creatures whose very existence may be regarded as a miracle, or in whose manner of life there is something beyond human understanding. This sequence of word pictures, all in the form of rhetorical questions, presents Job with a panorama of that that transcendental, incomprehensible wisdom out of which the world was created and by which it is controlled. The first in the series of animals is the lion, the king of beasts, which hunts its prey with such amazing ferocity (Job 38 : 39-40). Third in the list, after the raven (cf. above, p. 61), are the mountain-goat and the hind, with the miracle of their reproduction. No human eye can ever behold them in the act of giving birth, since their extreme wariness makes it impossible for man to get near their lairs. But perhaps the poet was even more impressed by the remarkable way in which these two creatures leave their young, immediately after giving birth to them; and that is why he dwells on the fact that, as soon as they have completed their months of carrying and have crouched down and born their offspring, they abandon them — "they go forth and do not return to them" (Job 39 : 1-4). There is another allusion to this strange conduct on the part of hinds in Jer. 14 : 5: "Even the hind in the field forsakes her new-born calf", where, however, this seemingly unmaternal behaviour is explained by the drought. The "mountain goat" (yael), which occurs frequently in the Old Testament, is usually identified with the wild goat (Capra nubiana) found in Arabia, Nubia, the Sinai peninsula, and in small numbers also in Israel. It is a rock-dweller, as described in the Old Testament (cf. 1 Sam. 24 : 3; Ps. 104 : 18). Modern zoological observations of the animal have shown that it has not a particularly well developed family sense. The hind, which is also often mentioned in the Old Testament, belongs to the class of the Cervidae, several kinds of which were once found in and around Israel, but gradually died out with the destruction of the country's forests.

The illustration is a section of a painting from the tomb of Khnumhotep at Beni Hasan in Egypt (19th cent. B.C.). in which an animal of the hind species is portrayed in the act of calving. Such pictures of animals giving birth are very common in Egyptian art, particularly against the background of a hunting-scene. Cf. below, p. 143.

127

WHO has let the wild ass go free? Who has loosed the bonds of the swift ass? (Job 39 : 5)

The remarkable thing about the Syrian wild ass (Heb. *pere* = *Equus hemihippus)* was the lone, untamed existence that it led. Its home was the saline steppes and its food any and every piece of green vegetation that it could find. It "scorned the tumult of the city" and never heard a driver's shouts (Job 39 : 7). It therefore occurs frequently in the Old Testament as a symbol of the wild, utterly uncivilized life of the wilderness (Gen. 16 : 12; Isa. 32 : 14; Jer. 2 : 24; 14 : 6; and elsewhere). No doubt the Syrian ass, despite the harsh conditions in which it lived, was actually a wary and rather timid creature, like the other kinds of wild-ass which still survive in Africa. The Babylonian and Assyrian kings used to hunt it for sport, as we learn from many of their paintings and reliefs. At the beginning of the second millennium, attempts were made to tame the wild ass and use it for pulling war-chariots, but it was soon superseded by the horse.

The reproduction is part of an Assyrian relief from Nineveh portraying an ass-hunt. Two attendants have managed to catch one of the wild-asses in their toils, while the two others escape. The wild-ass was difficult to hunt, because of its strength and speed. This strength is evident in the strong leg-muscles and the thickset, short neck, both of which are emphasized in this picture.

Is the wild ox willing to serve you? Will he spend the night at your crib?

(Job 39 : 9)

Like the wild ass (see the previous page), the wild ox (Heb. *r'em* = *Bos primigenius*) was also an animal of great strength which man rarely managed to tame for his own purposes, and then only with great difficulty. In the poem here, stress is laid on the animal's liking for the freedom of wide open spaces and on man's inability to master it. In the Old Testament the wild ox, and especially its mighty horns, serve as a symbol of strength, courage and dominion (cf. Vol. I, p. 228; and this volume p. 57). In antiquity it was one of the animals (the others being the lion and the wild ass) regularly hunted for sport by the Assyrian kings, as is illustrated by many reliefs. To-day the wild ox is virtually extinct in the Near East, though there may possibly be a few specimens still surviving in the isolated mountainous regions of Kurdistan.

The picture of an ox-hunt reproduced here is from a relief in the palace of Ashurnasirpal II at Calah. The Assyrian soldier, having overtaken the hunted animal, is about to thrust his short spear into it. The second, magnificently accoutred horse, which is being led by the soldier, may have been intended for the king's use. The ox has a thickset body, straight back, short mane, long narrow head, and heavy horns. The spots with which its body is covered apparently represent short, curly hair.

THE wings of the ostrich wave proudly; but are they the
pinions and plumage of love? (Job 39 : 13)

This verse, according to the generally accepted interpretation, marks the beginning of the poet's description of
the ostrich (Heb. *bath-yaanah*). He first describes the strange nature of this bird, which was thought by the ancients
(cf. Lam. 4 : 3) to abandon its eggs immediately after laying them, without the least concern about the danger of
their being trampled on by wild beasts (Job 39 : 14-16). He then refers to the bird's stupidity, and also to the
aerial speed of its run which enables it to outpace every horse (ibid. verse 18). These last two qualities of the
ostrich were also proverbial amongst the Arabs. The bird's great speed along the ground is similarly remarked on,
for example, by the Greek writer Xenophon who accompanied Alexander the Great on his campaigns. He relates
that the Macedonian horsemen tried to hunt down the bird but not one succeeded, because it easily outstripped
them in flight, thanks to its swift legs and sail-like wings.

The ostrich *(Struthio camelus),* the largest of all known winged creatures, is to-day found mainly in the deserts of
Africa. Small numbers have also survived in Arabia and in the desert regions bordering on Palestine. In Egypt
the bird was known already in pre-historic times. Its eggs were used for food at various periods and in various
circles (including the Egyptian court), and its feathers provided adornment for kings, warriors and riding-animals.
In Egypt the ostrich feather was the emblem of the goddess of truth Maat. The ostrich appears on pictures from
the ancient East which portray the hunting of wild animals in the desert, such as the one reproduced here from
the tomb of Kenamon at Thebes (15th cent. B.C.).

Do you give the horse his might? Do you clothe his neck with strength?

(Job 39 : 19)

The most striking quality of the horse, as is stressed by the poet in the passage devoted to this animal (Job 39 : 19-25), is its courage: "his majestic snorting is terrible". The horse prances joyfully into battle, "he laughs at fear and is not dismayed", and is completely unperturbed by the bolts of death whizzing through the air all round him. "With fierceness and rage he swallows the ground"; and when he hears the trumpet sounding the call to battle, he snorts "Aha!" Although courage is one of the qualities that characterize the horse in the Old Testament, it is not usually much esteemed by the biblical writers. Thus, the Psalmist declares that, while the horse may be possessed of "courage" and "great strength", these are "vain" qualities since the Lord does not delight in them (Ps. 33 : 17; 147 : 17; cf. above, p. 27).

The horse's original home was apparently the steppes of central Asia. It was brought from there to the Euphrates valley as early as the end of the third millennium B.C., and was known in Egypt from the beginning of the New Kingdom. By the peoples of the ancient East it was used primarily in warfare and this is the role in which it usually appears in the Old Testament, as in the poetical description here. Its characteristic military function was drawing the iron chariots of the time. Some ancient peoples, however — particularly the Assyrians, Scythians and Persians — also fought on horseback. Similarly, in our verse here the horse appears to be described as a war-animal which is not harnessed to a chariot, but carries a rider.

The cavalry-battle illustrated here is a reproduction of part of a relief from the palace of Tiglath-Pileser III at Calah. An enemy horseman, wearing an unusual type of hat, is surrendering to his Assyrian pursuers. His horse has been wounded by a spear. The horse's head is adorned in Assyrian fashion, but its head-harness is different from that usually employed by the Assyrians.

BEHOLD, Behemoth, which I made as I made you; he eats grass like an ox.
(Job 40 : 15)

In the Lord's second answer to Job out of the storm two creatures are described: Behemoth (Job 40 : 15-24) and Leviathan (see next page). In contrast to the unadorned, naturalistic description of the animals in the first answer, that of these two is coloured with flashes of poetical imagination suggestive of ancient myths. Thus Behemoth is said to be "the first of the works of God" (ibid. verse 19), i.e. the first creature to be created in the world, an expression reminiscent of the cosmogonical speech of wisdom in Prov. 8 : 22: "The Lord created me at the beginning of his work, the first of his acts of old". These mythical overtones become still more pronounced in the subsequent description of Leviathan. But, at the same time, there is no lack of realistic details. The poet dwells on Behemoth's huge strength, its huge bones ("like bars of iron"), its habit of spreading out its bulk amongst the river-willows "under the lotus-plant, in the covert of reeds and in the marsh," and on its power to resist the Jordan which "rushes against his mouth". The commentators assume that the animal thus described is the hippopotamus.

The hippopotamus *(Hippopotamus amphibius)* lives in shallow water, and in antiquity was found in great numbers in the Nile. It was hunted in Egypt from the earliest times down to the Roman period, when it was exterminated because of the damage it caused to cultivation. To-day it survives only in Upper Egypt and a little further south. The hippopotamus was hunted with harpoons having several spiky barbs, each with a long coil of rope attached to it (see the illustration). The hunters surrounded the hippopotamus in their skiffs, plunged their harpoons into it with the aid of long poles, and then kept on tugging at the harpoons with the ropes until the beast's strength had been bled out of it. In the picture reproduced here, — part of a relief in the tomb of Mereruka at Sakkarah (time of the Sixth Dynasty) — the hippopotami are drawn in the setting of "a covert of reeds and a marsh".

CAN you draw out Leviathan with a fishhook, or press down his tongue with a cord?

(Job 41 : 1)

The last beast mentioned in the Lord's answer to Job (Job 41 : 1-34) is, as described, a composite creature — part fiction, part fact. On the one hand, it is called Leviathan, which was the name of the mythical monster that revolted against the Lord and was crushed by Him (Isa. 27 : 1; Ps. 74 : 14; cf. above, p. 41). Indeed, embedded in the first part of the description (Job 41 : 1-5) there are still relics of the story of the crushing of Leviathan, who subsequently became the Lord's "servant for ever" and served for His "sport" (ibid. verse 5: "Will you play with him as with a bird?"; cf. Ps. 104 : 26). Other imaginary poetical details, all bearing an archaic stamp, are the descriptions of the creature's flashing eyes ("like the eyelids of the dawn"), the flames that dart from its mouth, the smoke that issues from its nostrils, its heart "as hard as stone", the terror with which it fills the "gods", its amazing imperviousness to weapons, and so forth (Job 41 : 18-21; 24-30). The whole powerful picture ends with the declaration that "upon earth there is not his like . . . he is king over all the sons of pride" (ibid. verses 33-34). At the same time, there are also certain realistic features in this portrayal, such as the beast's terrifying face and teeth, its armour of scales which cover it like "shields", and its powerful neck (ibid. verses 13-17). These details are assumed by the commentators to indicate that the poet had the crocodile *(tanin)* in mind.

The crocodile (see the photograph) belongs to the lizard family of which there are various kinds and various sizes. The Old Testament makes no mention of crocodiles within the borders of Palestine, but from the works of Roman authors and the reports of travellers it appears that they existed until not so very long ago in the Crocodile River (Nahr ez-Zerqa) which runs into the Mediterranean north of Caesarea. In certain districts of ancient Egypt the crocodile was regarded as a sacred animal and burial grounds of embalmed crocodiles, sometimes whole families of them, have been excavated there. But in other parts of the country the creature was hunted without compunction.

THE
FIVE SCROLLS

SONG OF SOLOMON

O that you would kiss me
with the kisses of your mouth!
For your love is better than
wine.   (Song of Sol. 1 : 2)

The Song of Solomon is a collection of ancient love-poems the authorship of which was attributed to King
Solomon. Written in lyrical vein, with a wealth of poetic imagery, the poems have been acclaimed as gems of
literature by ancients and moderns alike. The collection opens with the yearning of the love-intoxicated mistress
for her beloved, whose passion for her is better than wine. In the first verse she expresses her longing for him,
but does not yet address him directly.
Love-scenes feature prominently in the paintings and reliefs of the ancient East. Reproduced here is a carved
ivory plaque, part of the inlay of a royal bed from the court of the kings of Ugarit (14th cent. B.C.), showing a
couple in a fond embrace. The princess has her left arm around her spouse, while with her right hand she holds
a vial of perfume or stimulant to his nose. This portrait may reflect Egyptian influence, since in the contemporary
reigns of Amenhotep III, and particularly of his son Amenhotep IV (Akhenaton), intimate scenes from the private
life of the royal family became a popular theme of Egyptian art.

DRAW me after you, let us make haste.
The king has brought me into his chambers.
We will exult and rejoice in you ...

(Song of Sol. 1 : 4)

The mistress pictures her beloved as a king and fancifully imagines that he has brought her to the royal chambers and is making love to her there. "His chambers" may refer to the special women's quarters that were often found in the kings' palaces of antiquity. We know from archaeological and literary evidence that, in biblical times, there were no sealed off harems in Israel, not even in the palaces of the nobility and the royal courts. Separate living-quarters were, it is true, sometimes set apart for women (Judg. 15 : 1), and for the daughter of Pharaoh whom Solomon married a special house was built (1 Kings 7 : 8); but, even in these instances, the women appear to have been free to go where they pleased and were not secluded from society.

Reproduced here is a section of a relief from the royal palace at el-Amarna in Egypt (14th cent. B.C.) showing the women's house at the Pharaoh's court. The house has two stories, each with an entrance leading into a hall the roof of which is supported by pillars. In the upper hall women, apparently of Syrian origin, are seen engaged in various activities: one is eating, another is being helped in some work by a maidservant, while the rest are dancing to the music played by one of their number. There is music and dancing in the hall below too. (On the women's house at the court of the Persian kings see below, p. 185).

I compare you, my love, to a mare of Pharaoh's chariots. Your cheeks are comely with circlets, your neck with strings of jewels.   (Song of Sol. 1 : 9-10)

In praising his mistress, the beloved portrays her charms in poetic images taken from the life of the royal court at Jerusalem. In one of these he compares his mistress to a stately mare in the magnificent chariot of Pharaoh. This simile is very appropriate for the period of the Israelite Monarchy, and particularly for the reign of Solomon, when Egyptian chariots were renowned in Israel and constituted an important item of the trade plied by the Israelites as middlemen between Egypt and the Hittite kingdoms in Syria (1 Kings 10 : 28-29; 2 Chron. 1 : 16-17; and below, pp. 262-263).

These chariots and their horses were distinguished by their gorgeous colouring and regal accoutrements. In our verse here, where the mistress is compared to a mare, she is described as being adorned with circlets on her cheeks and "strings of jewels" on her neck. Such, apparently, were the ornaments with which it was customary to bedeck horses in antiquity. The Hebrew word here translated "circlets" *(torim)* is also found in a Ugaritic text dealing with chariot-parts and horse-harnesses. There it is explicitly used of the horse's head-harness. The art of the ancient East gives us a clear picture of the appearance of these ornaments. Thus the section of the relief from Khorsabad (from the reign of the Assyrian king Sargon II), which is reproduced here, shows two horses with "circlets" fastened on to their chaps. The "circlets" are inlaid with jewels and precious metals.

WHILE the king was on his couch, my nard gave forth its fragrance. (Song of Sol. 1 : 12)

The gorgeously attired mistress, fragrant with myrrh and perfume, fancies that she sees the "king" sitting at a feast with his companions and attendants, eating and drinking to his heart's content, and making merry. Although she herself is not there, the scent of her nard reaches his nostrils and stirs his desire for her.
Royal banquets, with a full measure of food, wine, laughter and song, are depicted in the art of the ancient East. In the reproduction here — part of a relief from Nineveh, from the reign of the Assyrian king Ashurbanipal — a royal feast is shown being held in the king's garden. The king, reclining on a divan with a flower in his left hand, is drinking from a cup, as is the queen, who is seated on a high throne beside the divan. Behind the royal pair stand attendants holding fans. (The relief is reproduced in full on p. 167).

MY beloved is to me a cluster of henna blossoms in the vineyards of En-Gedi.
(Song of Sol. 1 : 14)

Though many of the places mentioned in the Song of Solomon (e.g. Lebanon, Tirzah, Gilead) are in the northern part of Palestine or in Trans-Jordan, there are also passing references to such typically Judean scenes as Jerusalem (frequently, Song of Sol. 2 : 7; 3 : 5; 5 : 8; 6 : 4), the Judean desert (ibid. 3 : 6), and the vineyards of En-Gedi on the western shore of the Dead Sea.

En-Gedi, with its fertile soil and copious spring, already had a settled population at the time of the Israelite conquest and occupation of Canaan (Josh. 15 : 62). The strongholds of En-Gedi and the wilderness of En-Gedi are known to us from the stories about David's flight from Saul (1 Sam. 23 : 29; 24 : 1, 2). Three forts of the period of the Judean monarchy have been excavated on the site: one on top of Tell el-Jurn, another near the spring, and a third on the cliffs overlooking En-Gedi. The henna-bushes, spices, and perhaps also dates, probably supported the local population as early as the time of the First Temple. During the Second Temple the oasis of En-Gedi was famed for the richness of its produce, especially for its palm- and balsam-trees. Ecclesiasticus makes wisdom boast: "I have grown high like a palm-tree at En-Gedi". Pliny, the Roman author, relates that En-Gedi was second in fertility only to Jerusalem.

The spring of En-Gedi, with the green shrubs that flourish all round it, is seen in the photograph above.

The beloved rouses his mistress with a description of nature in spring: "The flowers appear on the earth... and the voice of the turtle-dove is heard in our land. The tree puts forth its figs, and the vines are in blossom; they give forth fragrance" (Song of Sol. 2 : 12-13).

Here the poet singles out for special mention, amongst the sights of spring, the remarkable phenomenon of the blossoming (Heb. *semadar*) of the vine *(Vitis vinifera L.)* When the flower of the vine opens (see the upper picture) its five petals separate from the base of the flower and are carried upwards by the growing stamens. This unit of petals covers the flower like a little cap. At blossom time thousands of such little green caps can be found under the flowering vines. The lovers are attracted by this unusual sight: "Let us go out early to the vineyards, and see whether... the grape blossoms have opened" (ibid. 7 : 12).

The Hebrew word *semadar* seems also to have been used of a certain kind of wine or fermentation of grapes, to judge from the inscription, "for Pekah, *semadar*" incised on a fragment of a jar found at Hazor (see the lower picture). The sherd was excavated in an Israelite fortress dating to the reign of Pekah the son of Remaliah. The word "Pekah" may indicate that the jar contained wine belonging to the troops of the royal garrison.

THE vines are in blossom, they give forth fragrance...
(Song of Sol. 2 : 13)

BE like a gazelle, or a young stag . . .
(Song of Sol. 2 : 17)

As she waits for her beloved, the mistress sees him in her fancy hastening to her, "leaping upon the mountains, bounding over the hills" (Song of Sol. 2 : 8), like a gazelle or a fleet-footed young stag (2 Sam. 2 : 18; Hab. 3 : 19). This image of the stag bounding over the ravine-cleft mountains ("the rugged mountains", Song of Sol. 2 : 17) is meant to suggest the strength and high spirits of youth. The gazelle *(Gazella)* and the stag *(Cervus)* were once typical features of the Palestinian landscape. The former is still found in open plains and in wadis, whereas the latter, which formerly inhabited wooded terrain, has been exterminated in the present century. Because of their special characteristics, both these animals were used in the Bible as symbols of swiftness, grace and charm (cf. p. 127).

The young of the stag or gazelle comes into the world fully developed and can stand on its own legs within a few hours of its birth, unlike the young of beasts of prey which are born blind and helpless. The young stag's grey-brown body is speckled with white dots which have the effect of camouflaging it, because of their resemblance to the flecks of sunlight on the trees that form the animal's natural background.

A newly born stag, still curled up in the position in which its mother had deposited it on the ground, is here seen (below) in an Egyptian wall-painting from the Eighteenth Dynasty, and (above) in a photograph from life.

ALL girt with swords and expert in war, each with his sword at his thigh... (Song of Sol. 3 : 8)

Amongst the love-poems collected together in the Song of Solomon, a special place is occupied by the verses depicting the splendour of King Solomon and his bodyguard of sixty warriors. Some scholars consider these verses to be a poetical description of the king's nuptials. The king's palanquin is guarded by sixty mighty men prepared to spring to their royal master's defence. Everything is ready for the wedding and the daughters of Jerusalem eagerly jostle each other to obtain a view of the magnificent regal spectacle (Song of Sol. 3 : 11).

This description probably preserves an echo from the time of David whose thirty picked warriors were famed for their heroic military exploits (2 Sam. 23 : 8-39; cf. Vol. II, p. 197). Here it is said of the sixty members of Solomon's bodyguard (twice the number of David's heroes) that they were "expert in war" and "girt with swords". The sword was a particularly suitable weapon for a royal bodyguard, since it was the most convenient, both for defence and attack, in hand-to-hand fighting. The straight sword, which was the one in common use in the first millennium B.C., was carried in a sheath fastened to the fighting man's hip (cf. 2 Sam. 20 : 8). In time of need, he could quickly draw his sword by clasping the hilt which protruded from the sheath.

This description of the picked royal troops, sword on hip, ready for action, is provided with a visual illustration by a relief from Arslan Tash in Syria, from the time of the Assyrian king Tiglath-Pileser III (see the reproduction). Two members of the king's bodyguard are seen here with their left hands on the hilts of their swords, which are fastened to their hips, and a mace-like staff in their right.

KING Solomon made himself a palanquin from the wood of Lebanon. He made its posts of silver, its back of gold, its seat of purple . . .   (Song of Sol. 3 : 9-10)

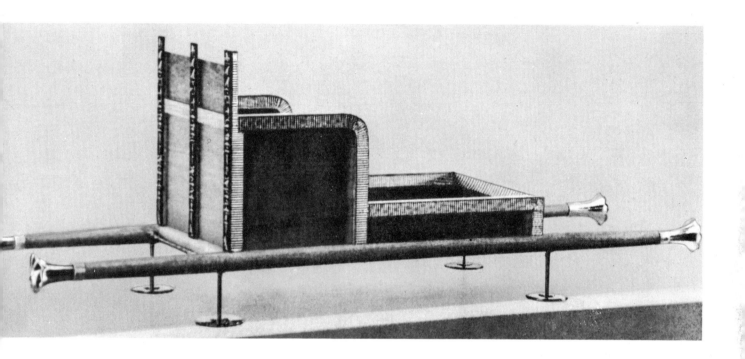

Solomon is here described as a mighty monarch arrayed in all his glory (Song of Sol. 1 : 9,12). The brilliant preparations for his wedding and his glorious crown arouse the eager curiosity of the daughters of Zion (ibid. 3 : 11). The poet dwells with particular pride on the details of Solomon's cedar-wood palanquin, with its silver posts, its coverings and gilt-work, and its high seat spread with purple stuffs. A litter of such magnificence was in keeping with the general splendour of Solomon's palace and its priceless fittings, as described in 1 Kings 10 : 12, 21, the most striking of which was the great ivory throne, overlaid with gold (ibid. 18-20; cf. below, p. 267). Only the aristocracy appear to have made use of litters in Israel. At a later period, in Greece, and even more so in Rome, distinguished citizens were carried through the city streets in splendid palanquins. In Egypt the litter was known as early as the third millennium B.C., as is testified by the one belonging to Queen Hetepheres, the mother of the Pharaoh Khufu (Cheops), which was found at Gizeh. This litter is made of wood and inlaid in various places with gold decorations. Its total length is 6 ft. 10 in., and the length of the seat inside is 3 ft. 3 in. An inscription on the litter, of gold set in ebony, lists the queen's titles.

Y OUR neck is like the tower of David, built for an arsenal, whereon hang a thousand bucklers, all of them shields of warriors.   (Song of Sol. 4 : 4)

One of the many physical charms that the beloved finds in his mistress (Song of Sol. 4 : 1-4), is her long neck which, with its stately poise, reminds him of the lofty tower of David. Just as this tower is hung all round with shields placed there by mighty men of valour, so is his mistress' neck adorned with chains and strings of jewels (cf. ibid. 1 : 10; 4 : 9). The art of the ancient East often shows us the shields that were, in time of war, set in position on the towers of city walls, so that the defenders could safely fire arrows and hurl stones while standing upright behind them (cf. Ezek. 27 : 11).

In the reproduction on the right — part of Sennacherib's relief of the siege of Lachish — it can be seen that the towers are covered by a wooden structure, of the kind described in 2 Chron. 26 : 15 (see below, p. 283) as "invented by skilful men", on which the shields of the embattled defenders are prominently displayed. On the left is an ivory from Calah (9th cent. B.C.), executed in a mixed Syro-Mesopotamian style, which illustrates the metaphor in our verse here: the lady's neck is adorned with an ornament to which are attached small shield-shaped pendants, apparently of precious metal. These two illustrations show in what precise detail the poetical images used by the author of the Song of Solomon reflect the customs of his time.

I arose to open to my beloved, and my hands dripped with myrrh, my fingers with liquid myrrh, upon the handles of the bolt. (Song of Sol. 5 : 5)

The whole setting of the Song of Solomon — with all the lovers' longing for nature, for the trees, the villages and the fields (ibid. 7 : 12) — breathes the atmosphere of an ancient city. Here is Jerusalem with its towers, markets, busy streets (ibid. 3 : 2; 4 : 4), and the watchmen on its walls (ibid. 5 : 7). The mistress decks herself out like a typical daughter of Jerusalem (cf. Isa. 3 : 15-24; and Vol. III, p. 23): her necklace is studded with jewels (Song of Sol. 4 : 9), the perfume of her oils and raiment is like the scent of Lebanon (ibid. 4 : 10,11), and in her bosom she always carries a bag of perfumes, including myrrh, the choicest of them all (ibid. 1 : 13). While the mistress is asleep, dreaming that her beloved is knocking at her door and that she rises to open it for him, myrrh drips from her hands and "liquid myrrh" from her fingers, since she had perfumed her body before lying down on her couch, as did the women of the city. In those times myrrh was evidently one of the most important cosmetics commonly used by women (Esther 2 : 12; Prov. 7 : 17; cf. above, p. 74).
Reproduced here is a section of the sarcophagus of Queen Kawit of the Eleventh Dynasty (21st cent. B.C.) which was found at Deir el-Bahri in Egypt. The queen is seated on her throne, holding a lotus-flower in her left hand and, with two of her right fingers, taking a little cosmetic cream or perfume from a pot held by her waiting-woman. Her personal ornaments are shown at the side of the relief.

To see . . . whether the pomegranates were in bloom.   (Song of Sol. 6 : 11)

The beloved continues to descant upon his mistress' beauties — her hair, teeth, cheeks and veil — in a series of vivid natural images (Song of Sol. 6 : 4-7). In these verses nature not only provides the metaphors for the mistress' striking looks, but is also the setting of the whole romantic scene. The lover who from afar beholds his mistress shining forth like the dawn, with its miracle of cosmic rebirth, also goes down into the garden in the heart of spring to feast his eyes on the trees which are burgeoning again after the winter rains. Nature's spring, with all its primal joy, is here a fitting symbol for youth, the springtime of life.

The pomegranate blossom mentioned here is a prominent feature of the Israel landscape in spring. The pomegranate *(Punica Granatum L.)* is one of the oldest of the cultivated trees found in the Middle East. It sheds its leaves at the beginning of winter and sprouts in late spring. When the buds first open, the young foliage is reddish in colour, so that an orchard of budding pomegranate trees seem to have a thin red veil spread over them. It is not till the early summer that there appear the characteristic large red flowers which catch the eye from afar with their intense, flaming colour (see the photograph). Because of the countless seeds of which its round fruit is composed, the pomegranate was regarded by the peoples of the East as a fertility emblem.

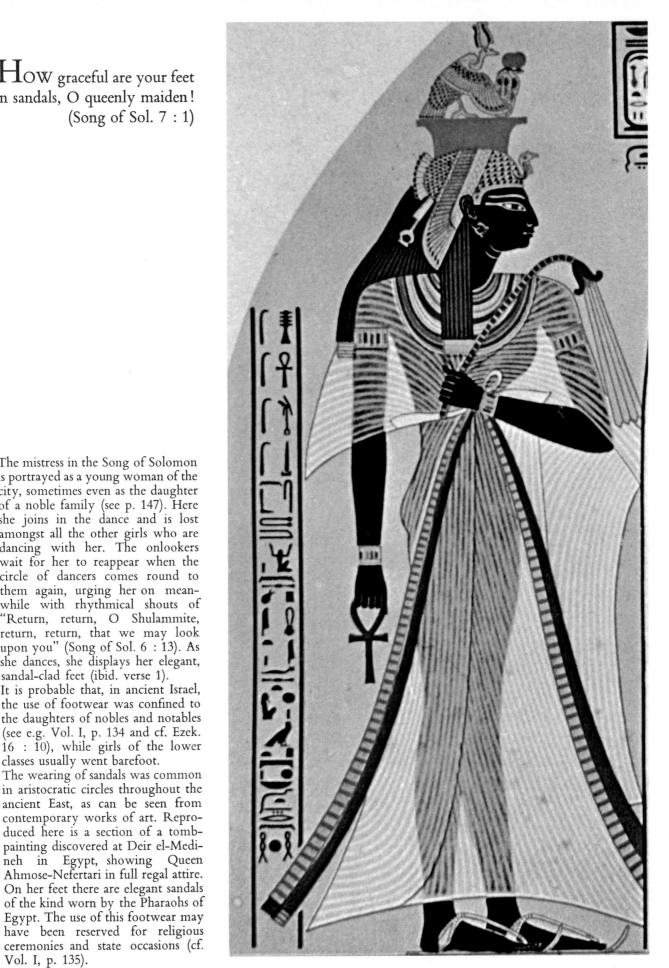

How graceful are your feet
in sandals, O queenly maiden!
(Song of Sol. 7 : 1)

The mistress in the Song of Solomon is portrayed as a young woman of the city, sometimes even as the daughter of a noble family (see p. 147). Here she joins in the dance and is lost amongst all the other girls who are dancing with her. The onlookers wait for her to reappear when the circle of dancers comes round to them again, urging her on meanwhile with rhythmical shouts of "Return, return, O Shulammite, return, return, that we may look upon you" (Song of Sol. 6 : 13). As she dances, she displays her elegant, sandal-clad feet (ibid. verse 1).

It is probable that, in ancient Israel, the use of footwear was confined to the daughters of nobles and notables (see e.g. Vol. I, p. 134 and cf. Ezek. 16 : 10), while girls of the lower classes usually went barefoot.

The wearing of sandals was common in aristocratic circles throughout the ancient East, as can be seen from contemporary works of art. Reproduced here is a section of a tomb-painting discovered at Deir el-Medineh in Egypt, showing Queen Ahmose-Nefertari in full regal attire. On her feet there are elegant sandals of the kind worn by the Pharaohs of Egypt. The use of this footwear may have been reserved for religious ceremonies and state occasions (cf. Vol. I, p. 135).

I say I will climb the palm tree and lay hold of its branches . . .
(Song of Sol. 7 : 8)

In this passage, the lover depicts the sensual delights of passion in images from plant life. His mistress is as tall and stately as a palm-tree, the scent of her breath is sweet as apples, and the roof of her mouth is like good wine. The lover expresses his desire to climb the palm-tree and take hold of its upper branches. A palm-tree is usually climbed either to pick the fruit, or to dust the female flowers with pollen from the male flowers. In the palm the female and the male flowers are to be found separately on different trees. In order, therefore, to obtain a better yield and to accelerate the process of pollination, the date-grower himself transfers pollen from the male trees to the flowers on the female trees. That this method of artificial pollination was known already to the ancients is clear from the evidence of Mesopotamian art. In the picture here — a reproduction of one of the reliefs from Gozan (Tell Halaf), dating to the 9th cent. B.C. — a man is shown climbing up a palm-tree on a wooden ladder, with his hands stretched out to take hold of its top branches. This exactly illustrates the metaphor from the Song of Solomon, though it is not clear whether here the climber's purpose is to pollinate the flowers or to pick the fruit from the tree.

RUTH

A certain man of Bethlehem in Judah went to sojourn in the country of Moab...

(Ruth 1 : 1)

The Book of Ruth tells the story of a pure friendship between two women, against the background of the ancient Israelite's closely knit family-life and deep attachment to his inherited plot of land. It also gives us glimpses of an ancient tradition concerning the relations between Bethlehem in Judah and Moab, and of the constant comings and goings between the two countries, despite the age-long enmity that divided them. In times of famine, Israelites would migrate to Moab, or Philistia (Gen. 26 : 1; 2 Kings 8 : 2-3), or Sidon (1 Kings 17 : 8-9), and return to their homeland when the famine had passed. This is exactly what Naomi, the widow who had lost both her sons (Ruth 1 : 6), did: she returned to Bethlehem, where the kinsfolk of her late husband, Elimelech, who was considered to be descended from the Ephrathite family, had resided for so long (cf. 1 Chron. 4 : 4).
Bethlehem, the scene of the story of Ruth, dominates a fertile valley on the fringe of the Judean desert, near the road running along the watershed from Jerusalem to Hebron. In biblical times it was one of the most important cities in the northern part of the territory of Judah; and, according to the Book of Judges (19 : 1), it was already well known before the establishment of the Monarchy. Its great claim to distinction, however, was that it was the birthplace of David the son of Jesse, one of the descendants of Ruth and Boaz (Ruth 4 : 18-22).
The photograph is a view of Bethlehem as it appears to-day, with the Hebron hills in the background.

A ND they came to Bethlehem at the beginning of barley harvest. (Ruth 1 : 22)

The whole action of the story, redolent as it is of the open fields, takes place during the barley and wheat harvests (Ruth 2 : 23). It is in the harvest-field that Ruth first meets Boaz, and it is to the barley threshing-floor that she comes to ask him to spread his skirt over her (see p. 156).

The barley harvest, which begins in the Hebrew month of Nisan (March-April), is closely connected with the Passover festival and the ritual offering of the sheaf (omer) (Lev. 23 : 9-14; and elsewhere). The harvest was altogether a joyful, happy time (Isa. 9 : 3; 16 : 9), and was made even more so by the festival of Pentecost (Shavuoth) which falls at the beginning of the wheat harvest (Ex. 23 : 16; 34 : 22). This gladness is explicitly enjoined by the Mosaic Law: "Then you shall keep the feast of weeks to the Lord your God . . . and you shall rejoice . . . you and your son" (Deut. 16 : 10-11). The harvest was also a clearly defined season in the Israelite agricultural calendar, distinguished, by contrast, from seedtime (Gen. 8 : 22) and ploughing (Gen. 45 : 6; Ex. 34 : 21). "Harvest" also occurs in poetic parallelism with "summer" (Prov. 26 : 1). Cf. the expression "the month of harvest" in the Gezer Calendar, Vol. I, p. 198.

To this day, the harvest is a very special occasion in the life of the Arab fellahin. This is the season when not a soul remains indoors, but the whole family, from toddlers to grey-haired elders, go out to the fields (note the two children at the right of the photograph) and everyone works as best he can. The corn is either reaped with a sickle (Heb. maggal, Arabic minjal), or pulled up by hand. The single ears are bound together into sheaves which are then carried to the threshing-floor. The head of the family, and sometimes the whole household, sleep on this floor till the end of the threshing, to guard their crop from theft.

Above is a photograph of barley being harvested in the Valley of Jezreel.

ND Ruth the Moabitess said to Naomi, "Let me go to the field, and glean among the ears of grain after him in whose sight I shall find favour." And she said to her, "Go, my daughter."

(Ruth 2 : 2)

Naomi had, of course, inherited the land belonging to her husband and sons in Bethlehem. Nevertheless, when she returned destitute from the country of Moab, her economic plight was such that she had no choice but to sell her inheritance (Ruth 4 : 3) and send out her daughter-in-law to glean ears of corn behind the reapers. It was Ruth's good fortune to find a "saviour" in the person of Boaz who took her under his protection, permitted her to attach herself to his maidservants, let her drink and eat together with the other workers, and even accorded her the special privilege of gleaning between the sheaves and of picking up ears that had been deliberately dropped "from the bundles", i.e. from the collection of ears gathered up under the reaper's arm before being tied into sheaves (Ruth 2 : 8-9; 14-16).

The Mosaic Law forbade the owner of a field to glean the ears that fell behind the reapers, just as it forbade him to harvest his field right up to the corners or to go back for a sheaf that had been forgotten in the field (Lev. 19 : 9; 23 : 22; Deut. 24 : 19). In all these cases the reason given for the prohibition is the same: "you shall leave them for the poor and for the sojourner" (Lev. 19 : 10). Even so, gleaning was no easy task for an unaccompanied and destitute woman, since she was likely to be abused and molested by the labourers (Ruth 2 : 9-10, 16, 22), all the more so if, like Ruth, she was a foreigner who had not yet been accepted in her new surroundings.

In the tomb-painting of Ramose at Deir el-Medineh in Egypt, from the time of the Nineteenth Dynasty (13th cent. B.C.), which is reproduced above, the deceased is shown reaping his field with a sickle (cf. Vol. III, p. 228), while, behind him, his wife is gathering up the fallen ears into a basket made of plaited reeds. In ancient times, the harvesting was done in a hurry, for fear of its being suddenly interrupted by human agency or natural forces. As a result, many uncut stalks and loose, ungathered ears were left behind. This is the agricultural background to the Israelite law against the gleaning of what has been forgotten and of the corner of the field.

S{O} she gleaned in the field until evening; then she beat out what she had gleaned, and it was about an ephah of barley.

(Ruth 2 : 17)

After gleaning all day in Boaz's field, Ruth had by the evening gathered enough corn for her own and her mother-in-law's sustenance (see p. 154). When she had finished gleaning, she beat out the ears in the field, so as to bring Naomi the grains ready for use, — "and it was about an ephah of barley" (Ruth 2 : 17). The usual method of detaching the grains of corn from the straw and chaff was by first threshing the crop, either with a "sledge" or by letting farm animals trample on the ears (see Vol. I, p. 284; and below, in this volume, p. 255). The mixed grain, chaff and straw were then separated out from each other by winnowing (on this process see p. 156). However, when the peasant had only a few ears of corn, or when he was unable to do his threshing in the open on the threshing-floor, he beat out his crop by hand, as follows. The corn was first arranged in sheaves or bundles, with all the ears pointing in the same direction. The ears were then struck repeatedly with a stick, or with a special "beater" consisting of two sticks joined together by a leather thong; the longer of the two was held in the hand and jerked to and fro while the shorter struck the ears. The grains and chaff were thus knocked off their straw stems which were left in the hand, ready to be used for roofing and all kinds of plaited work. It is related of Gideon that he used to beat out wheat in the wine-press (in order to keep it hidden from the Midianites; Judg. 6 : 11). In Ruth's case, having beaten out what she had gleaned, she carried home only the grains of barley, because it was only these that she required as food for herself and Naomi, and not the straw.

The photograph below shows how corn is still beaten out by Arab villagers to-day. The sheaf of ears is held in the left hand and beaten out with a stick held in the right.

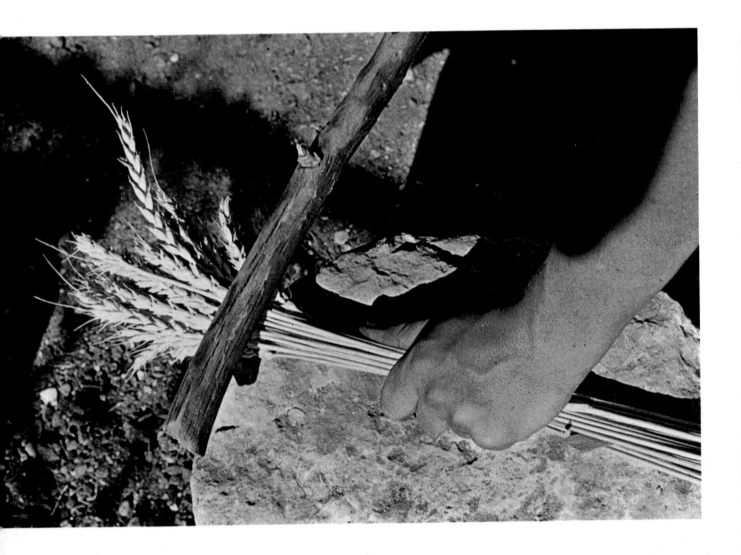

SEE, he is winnowing barley tonight at the threshing floor.   (Ruth 3 : 2)

Naomi urges Ruth to go by night to the threshing-floor where Boaz, their acquaintance and kinsman, was winnowing barley, and there beg him to redeem Naomi's land and thus restore her dead husband's name to his inheritance. Boaz, though an estate owner in Bethlehem, takes an active part in the working of his land side by side with his servants (Ruth 2 : 4, 9, 15-16). Towards evening, when a west wind gets up, Boaz, as was customary in those times, comes to the threshing-floor to winnow his barley (cf. Hos. 13 : 3; Ps. 1 : 4; cf. Vol. III, pp. 220, 244, and this volume, p. 21). The threshing-floor always stood on a spot exposed to the winds, usually at the lower end of the village which was itself generally situated on the top of a hill. Hence, apparently, the expression used in the story here: "so she went down to the threshing-floor" (Ruth 3 : 6).
Reproduced here is a stele from the time of the New Kingdom in Egypt, showing how corn was winnowed in antiquity. At the top right a man is beating out the ears in order to detach the grains from them (see p. 155). The men on the left are winnowing the threshed crop by throwing it up into the north wind with an implement shaped like a shovel. Since this is very dusty work, the labourers have to slake their thirst from time to time. Hence the man at the extreme right is handing his companions water from a jug which can be seen at the edge of the stele. In the lower register, the threshing-floor is seen after the winnowing has been completed. The winnowing-implements are now laid, together with other agricultural tools, on top of the pile of corn, and two labourers are scooping the winnowed grain into buckets. After the winnowing, with the crop safely gathered in heaps, the farmer could relax in the knowledge that his labours had been successful, as described in the Book of Ruth: "And Boaz ate and drank, and his heart was merry" (Ruth 3 : 7).

LAMENTATIONS

H<small>OW</small> lonely sits the city that was full of people! How like a widow has she become... (Lamentations 1 : 1)

The subject of the Book of Lamentations is the destruction of the kingdom of Judah and of Jerusalem, its capital, with the exile of its people and all their consequent physical and spiritual sufferings. The book is a collection of five separate dirges, through each of which runs the same dominant theme: desolate and despised as she is, Zion's only hope in her desperate plight is to throw herself upon God's abundant mercies. Already in ancient times there was a tradition current that Jeremiah, who uttered a lament over the dead Josiah (2 Chron. 35 : 25), had also composed the Book of Lamentations (as is explicitly stated in the short introduction prefixed to the Greek translation of the book and also in the Babylonian Talmud, Baba Bathra 15a). These dirges are indeed steeped in the dark atmosphere of that time of grim destruction and anguished soul-searching. They were therefore presumably written soon after the terrible events described in them, when the full horror of the national disaster was still deeply imprinted on the hearts of those who had lived through it. The verbal images with which Lamentations is studded became the standard metaphors for the destruction of Jerusalem. Thus, many generations later, when Jerusalem was razed for the second time by a foreign foe (70 A.D.), it was again likened, both in IV Esdras and in Rabbinical *aggadah* to a deserted and lonely woman sobbing over the tragedy of her widowhood. On the coin struck by Vespasian to commemorate his capture of Jerusalem in the year 70 (bearing the legend *Judaea Capta,* i.e. "Judah the captured", see the reproduction above), Judea is also symbolically depicted as a deeply sorrowing widow. The only remaining relic of the twice destroyed Temple, the so-called Wailing Wall, is a section of the western wall of the Temple Mount. This Wailing Wall was for centuries a place of pilgrimage for pious Jews who used to make their way to it from all the lands of the Diaspora, in order to pour out their prayers and lamentations before it and kiss its sacred stones, which were for them the sole surviving symbol of the ravaged glories of the First and Second Temples and a visible reminder of their destruction. The five lowest courses of the wall (on the right of the photograph) are undoubtedly from the time of the Second Temple. Beneath the ground-level there are another nineteen courses of masonry, all of them apparently from the same period.

HER princes have become like harts that find no pasture...   (Lamentations 1 : 6)

The author of Lamentations compares the princes of Judah at the time of Jerusalem's destruction to deer that are eagerly pursued by huntsmen for their tasty flesh and their valuable hide and antlers. In the poetry of the Old Testament, the deer and the hind are symbols of agility and fleetness of foot (2 Sam. 22 : 34; Ps. 18 : 33; see also p. 127); but even the deer's swift, sure legs fail it, when it has been exhausted by a long, unavailing search for pasture. That is the hunter's chance to catch it easily. So, here, the princes of Judah are depicted as being suddenly set upon by their foes, like these deer, just at the moment when their powers are exhausted and they would rest: "they fled without strength before the pursuer".

The prophet Jeremiah similarly describes the hind's exhaustion in a time of drought, when it searches in vain for fresh grass and is in the end compelled to abandon its newly born young (Jer. 14 : 5); and the Psalmist compares his yearning for God to the longing of a thirsty stag for streams of water (Ps. 42 : 1).

Another strikingly beautiful and swift-footed creature which is sometimes coupled with the deer in the Old Testament (Deut. 12 : 15; Song of Sol. 2 : 9, 17; cf. p. 143), is the gazelle. It is also used as a simile of flight, when the inhabitants of Babylon are described as fleeing from their city at the time of its downfall "like a hunted gazelle" (Isa. 13 : 14).

Reproduced here is a section from the hunting reliefs of the Assyrian king Ashurbanipal, showing gazelles with their young crossing a wide plain in search of pasture or water. Their bodies are tensed and their necks stretched out eagerly. The protruding ribs of the leading animals indicate their thin, half-starved condition. The last gazelle on the right has its head turned back, as if scenting the approach of danger.

THE enemy has stretched out his hands over all her precious
things; yea, she has seen the nations invade her sanctuary...
(Lamentations 1 : 10)

When the Babylonians captured Jerusalem, they looted the Temple treasuries and stripped the shrine of its precious
fittings. After breaking in pieces the bronze pillars, the stands and the bronze sea, the troops of Nebuzaradan, the
captain of the bodyguard, "carried the bronze to Babylon" (2 Kings 25 : 13). They also removed all the bronze
appurtenances: pots, shovels, snuffers, incense-dishes and the like. Nothing of value escaped their depredations:
"What was of gold the captain of the guard took away as gold, and what was of silver, as silver" (ibid. verse 15).
Such pillage was in no way exceptional: conquerors had always behaved like that. Jerusalem, as well as other
Judean cities, had already suffered similar ordeals, such as the pillaging of the cities of Judah by the armies of the
Assyrian king Sennacherib, in 701 B.C. (see Vol. II, pp. 286-287; and this volume, p. 285).
In the picture reproduced here (part of Sennacherib's reliefs of the siege of Lachish), Assyrian troops are seen
bearing away the plunder from the captured city. The first two are carrying two incense-stands, the next a chair;
a third soldier is holding the shaft of a chariot, and next to him there is another carrying several spears. A noteworthy feature of the relief is that it contains the only extant picture of a Judean chariot. In design, this chariot
resembles the Assyrian model of the 8th cent. "Precious things" like these were amongst the spoil taken from
Jerusalem at the time of the city's destruction.

To crush under foot all the prisoners of the earth. (Lamentations 3 : 34)

"The prisoners of the earth" are captives taken in war. (So the prophet says of the king of Assyria: "he did not let his prisoners go home", Isa. 14 : 17). The poet is inveighing here against the practice adopted by victorious monarchs of treading upon the prostrate bodies of their vanquished foes, to demonstrate the latter's abject surrender. This custom, which was widely followed by the rulers of the ancient East, from the Pharaohs and the Egyptian governor of Canaan (cf. Vol. I, p. 297, and Vol. II, p. 196) to the kings of Assyria and Babylon, is vividly illustrated by a relief from the time of Tiglath-Pileser III at Calah (reproduced below). The Assyrian monarch is seen at the right with his foot on the neck of a prostrate king who has either surrendered or been captured, and who has been dragged into the royal presence by two ministers of the court (at the left). Behind the Assyrian king stands another official holding a fan to keep off the flies. Owing to the damaged condition of the relief, it is impossible to identify the captured king. The action portrayed here gives some indication of the attitude of the Assyrian rulers to those of their enemies who surrendered to them, including kings and princes begging for their lives. Only a few of them were pardoned, while the rest were tortured and killed (see p. 163). There is no reason to suppose that the Babylonians who razed Jerusalem treated their captives any differently.

PRINCES are hung up by their hands; no respect is shown to the elders.

(Lamentations 5 : 12)

Chapter 5 of Lamentations describes in detail the physical suffering and spiritual anguish of what was left of the nation in war-ravaged Judah, after the downfall of the kingdom. "Our inheritance has been turned over to strangers, our homes to foreigners" (Lam. 5 : 2); "slaves rule over us; there is none to deliver us from their hand" (ibid. verse 8). The victorious enemy troops gave free rein to their savage brutality, showing no compassion for women and old men and no respect for princes and dignitaries. The Assyrians' cruelty to the nations that unsuccessfully tried to shake off their rule was a byword in antiquity, and the Babylonians apparently took over the methods of torture which the Assyrians had been in the habit of employing on their conquered foes. (Cf. the vengeance wreaked by Nebuchadnezzar on Zedekiah, king of Judah, and his sons, 2 Kings 25 : 7).

So far from attempting to gloss over the atrocities committed by their kings against conquered peoples, the Assyrian artists proudly commemorated them in stone. Reproduced above, for example, is a section of the reliefs in the palace of Ashurbanipal at Nineveh, on which Assyrian soldiers, acting on the king's orders, are seen subjecting captives to a horrible series of systematically planned tortures. In the upper register captives pegged to the ground are being flayed alive. Below a captive is writhing in agony while soldiers maim him with an iron bar; another (at the bottom) is having his tongue torn out of his mouth by two soldiers. The author of Lamentations may have been poetically referring to tortures of this kind, when he wrote: "He has made my flesh and my skin waste away, and broken my bones" (Lam. 3 : 4).

163

YOUNG men are compelled to grind at the mill; and boys stagger under loads of wood.

(Lamentations 5 : 13)

While the princes and elders of Judah were being subjected to torture (see p. 163), the rest of the nation was carried off into exile. As usual in antiquity, the captives, especially the young men and boys amongst them, were put to work in the royal labour gangs. There is no means of knowing exactly what kind of forced labour is referred to in the second part of our verse here, but it was probably transporting wood and stones for constructional works. The two pictures reproduced here — both sections from Sennacherib's reliefs at Nineveh — illustrate this kind of forced labour very clearly. Below: a row of men, no doubt captives, carrying beams on their shoulders, closely watched by special supervisors, two of whom are beating some of the captives with a stick to make them work faster. (Cf. Vol. I, p. 133). Above: captives making a fill or an embankment; tied to their backs are baskets full of small stones and gravel prepared for the rubble filling. Both groups of captives are being given no respite (cf. above, p. 105).

ECCLESIASTES

I made myself gardens and parks, and planted in them all kinds of fruit trees. I made myself pools from which to water the forest of growing trees. (Ecclesiastes 2 : 5-6)

The "Preacher", who calls himself the son of David and declares that he once ruled in Jerusalem (Eccles. 1 : 1; 1 : 12), was, according to his own words, one of the sages who taught the people wisdom and composed many maxims for them (ibid. 12 : 9, 11). Jewish tradition identified the Preacher with King Solomon who was wiser "than all other men" (1 Kings 4 : 29-34).

The Preacher, who in his later years came to the conclusion that "everything that is done under the sun" was merely "vanity and a striving after wind" (ibid. 1 : 14), had in his younger days lived the life of an aristocrat and enjoyed its pleasures to the full. Like all the nobles and rulers of antiquity, the Preacher had displayed his greatness by lavishly indulging in the delights of the senses, by building himself magnificent residences and by laying out pleasure-grounds for his rest and recreation. One of his many undertakings that he mentions was the planting of gardens and orchards and the making of artificial ponds "from which to water the forest of growing trees", after the manner of the potentates and great landowners of antiquity. The kings and courtiers of the ancient East used to lay out gardens round their houses, both for aesthetic reasons and to increase their prestige (see Vol. II, p. 246). Shady pleasances of this kind are represented in Egyptian and Assyrian art (see Vol. III, p. 127). The practice of making artificial pools to provide the gardens with water, as well as adding to their charm, is also known to us from the art of ancient Egypt. As early as the second millennium B.C. the kings and princes of Egypt had the courtyards of their houses fitted with pools of water in which they could bathe and wash during the hot summer days, and which also lent a restful, calm atmosphere to the surroundings. Such pleasure-pools for the sole use of the king and court were rare in Israel, and are in fact not mentioned anywhere in the Bible outside the Book of Ecclesiastes.

The upper picture on p. 167 is a relief from the palace of Ashurbanipal at Nineveh, showing a banquet in the royal garden (a section of this relief will be found above, p. 140). The king is reclining on a couch with the queen beside him. A long line of slaves and attendants is bringing a rich assortment of foods to the king, while behind them stand musicians playing soft strains on their instruments (cf. above, pp. 62-63). Below is the varied vegetation of the garden — ornamental and fruit trees, palms and vines. Walking amongst the trees are princes belonging to the royal entourage. The reproduction at the top of the opposite page is an ancient model of the courtyard of an aristocratic Egyptian residence from the 20th cent. B.C., in which the pillared entrance can be clearly seen, and also the high-walled courtyard in front of the house. In this courtyard there is a garden of fruit-trees with a pool in the centre of it.

The lower picture on the left-hand page is an Egyptian wall-painting (from the end of the 15th or the beginning of the 14th cent. B.C.) of an artificial pond in a garden. In the pond itself there are water-plants, fish and ducks, and round its sides palms and pomegranate — trees.

I bought male and female slaves, and had slaves who were born in my house . . .

(Ecclesiastes 2 : 7)

The Preacher loved life and denied himself none of its good things: gold and silver, the treasures of kings, male and female singers, and sensual pleasures (Eccles. 2 : 8). Like most of the great landowners of his time, the Preacher had fruit orchards, cattle and sheep, but he himself lived in Jerusalem (Eccles. 2 : 7, 9). His fields, residences and gardens were left to the care of male and female slaves, in addition to whom there were also "homeborn" slaves, i.e. those born in their master's house, on his estates. Slavery, or forced labour, played an important part in the agriculture of the ancient world. The wealth and greatness of feudal lords like the Preacher in the Persian and Hellenistic periods was based on the toil of slaves or enslaved tenants. From the picture given us by ancient art of the conditions of agricultural labour in those days, we can see that they have actually not changed much in the course of the centuries. Reproduced above is a painted Attic cup from the second half of the 6th cent. B.C., portraying work in the field in ancient Greece, in the ploughing and sowing season. The man on the right is turning the soil with his plough. Next to him there are two other men, one naked and the other clothed. In the mule-drawn cart at the left, there are two jars containing agricultural produce. The figure at the extreme left, holding a staff, is a foreman. The man standing between him and the cart, with a whip in his hand, is either a taskmaster or the estate-owner. The farm-labourers thus subjected to the harsh domination of their taskmasters, the foremen and supervisors, are apparently slaves or "slaves born in the house".

A time to mourn, and a time to dance.   (Ecclesiastes 3 : 4)

The Preacher doubts man's ability ever to comprehend the purpose of the things that are done under the sun. He is of the opinion that everything has been pre-determined by divine decree and that nothing can ever be changed. "For everything there is a season and a time for every matter": the constantly shifting kaleidoscope of events is largely beyond man's control, since God has already determined all that can happen from the beginning to the end of time. The Stoic school of Greek philosophy also taught that man should live in accordance with nature's laws and patiently accept the ceaselessly changing flux of events, since they too thought that man was powerless to change his fate. In his list of the human activities that have pre-ordained times, the Preacher mentions mourning and dancing. The pictures above illustrate ancient forms of these two expressions of human emotion. On the right—both sides of an Attic vase, probably from the last quarter of the 5th cent. B.C., decorated with the figures of fourteen mourners, seven men and seven women. The men's arms are stretched out in front of them, while the women are beating on their shorn heads, in Egyptian fashion (see Vol. I, p. 124; Vol. II, p. 168; and Vol. III, pp. 104, 191). At the left — a Greek statuette of a dancing girl, from the beginning of the 3rd cent. B.C. She is swaying rhythmically, with her arms raised and head thrown back.

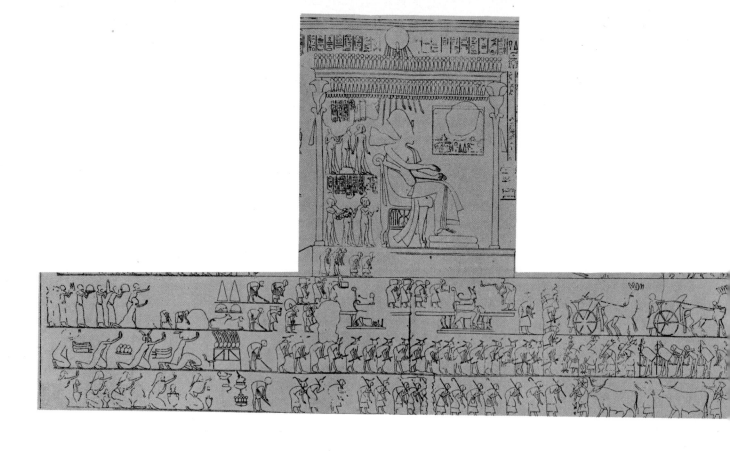

FOR the high official is watched by a higher, and there are yet higher ones over them.

(Ecclesiastes 5 : 8)

Though the Preacher's philosophical reflections are concerned mainly with the fate of the individual, he does not ignore the social injustice of his own day and of all the preceding generations. Sometimes, when he mentions the misery of the downtrodden, a note of bitterness and protest can be heard in his words: "Again I saw all the oppressions that are practised under the sun. And behold the tears of the oppressed, and they had no one to comfort them" (Eccles. 4 : 1). The ancient system of government created a sprawling bureaucratic hierarchy of "high official above high official", resting on an equally hierarchic social system at the top of which stood the all-powerful monarch who was usually far removed from the affairs of the common people. The oppressive weight of this social structure reduced the ordinary citizen to a helpless cipher. It was a regime of this kind that the Preacher had in mind, when he remarked: "If you see in a province the poor oppressed and justice and right violently taken away, do not be amazed at the matter; for the high official is watched by a higher". This description is particularly appropriate to the monarchies of the ancient East which enjoyed absolute, unchecked power and had an elaborate bureaucratic machine at their disposal.

The picture above — part of a drawing made from a tomb-relief at el-Amarna in Egypt, dating to the 14th cent. B.C. — illustrates this kind of royal administration. King Amenhotep IV (Akhenaton) is seated on his throne on a raised dais, with the queen, who is almost entirely hidden behind his figure, beside him and the royal princesses standing behind. The registers below are filled with the king's ministers, the members of the royal guard, senior Egyptian officials, and representatives of conquered peoples — amongst them Canaanites, Libyans and Ethiopians — presenting tribute. All of them are doing obeisance to the king who, in the usual style of Egyptian art, is drawn on a far larger scale than all his ministers and underlings.

BEHOLD, what I have seen to be good and to be fitting is to eat and drink and find enjoyment in all the toil with which one toils under the sun ...   (Ecclesiastes 5 : 18)

The positive essence of the Preacher's philosophy, contained in this verse, is repeated, for emphasis, several times in his book (2 : 24; 3 : 12; 11 : 9): the best thing for a man is to enjoy to the full the material blessings that he has acquired in the course of his life. "Toil" (Heb. *amal)* here really means its product — wealth; and the expression "under the sun" denotes everything that happens in the world and in human society (which is also its meaning in the Phoenician inscriptions). The Preacher arrived at this conclusion, after it had been brought home to him that practical talents and wealth are all too short-lived (Eccles. 2 : 21), and that a man's possessions do not follow him to the grave (ibid. 5 : 15). Hence, the Preacher declares that it is better to live for the moment, "to eat and drink and find enjoyment in all one's toil". Not everyone, however, is fortunate enough to be able to do this: some rich men are incapable of taking proper advantage of their riches because of their innate miserliness (ibid. 6 : 2); and altogether, the correct management of wealth so as to ensure its full enjoyment "is the gift of God" (ibid. 5 : 19).

The Preacher, like the other members of the ruling, land-owning classes of antiquity, had a full share of the good things of life, and partook freely of the pleasures of eating and drinking and the delightful sensation of hearty laughter (ibid. 2 : 2).

In the relief reproduced below from a sarcophagus, which apparently comes from Cyprus and dates to the second half of the 5th cent. B.C., there is a representation of the kind of feasting common among the nobility of Syria and Palestine in those days. The men are reclining on high couches, and being served with food and drink by women who are seated beside them. The solitary male on the couch at the extreme right (the host) is handing a slave a cup to be refilled with wine. In the centre stands a musician who is playing on the pipe to provide music for the revellers' pleasure.

I say that an untimely birth is better off than he. For it comes into vanity and goes into darkness, and in darkness its name is covered. (Ecclesiastes 6 : 3-4)

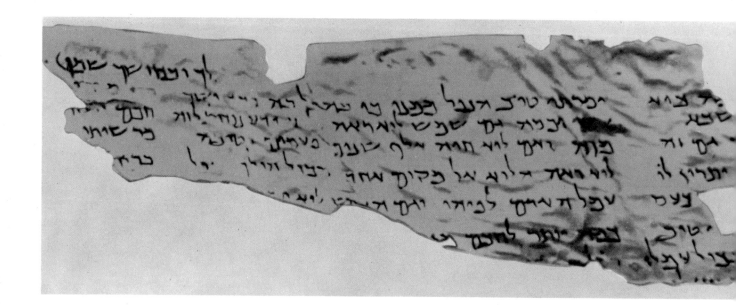

These verses from Ecclesiastes, in which the Preacher maintains that a still-born child that has never known the light and sun is more fortunate than a grown man who can never obtain lasting satisfaction from the pleasures of life (cf. Job 3 : 16), also occur in one of the Dead Sea Scrolls found in Cave D near Khirbet Qumran. Altogether, the following passages from Ecclesiastes are preserved in this fragment of the Dead Sea Scrolls: 5 : 13-17; 6 : 3-8; 7 : 7-9. There are a few textual variants which would seem to indicate that the writer of the Scroll had in front of him a different Hebrew version from that of our Masoretic text. The Scroll is written in one of the most elegant and perfect Hebrew scripts that has come down to us from those ancient times (see the photograph). A comparison of this script with that of other Dead Sea Scrolls, and with other scripts on papyri and ostraca from the time of the Second Temple, strongly suggests that this Scroll was written in the middle of the 2nd cent. B.C. In that case, the Book of Ecclesiastes must be of still earlier date, since copies of it were already in circulation at that time.

For as the crackling of thorns under a pot, so is the laughter
of the fools . . .   (Ecclesiastes 7 : 6)

Himself a prolific writer of maxims (Eccles. 12 : 9), the Preacher was well versed in wisdom literature and quoted
from it apophthegms and parables similar in form to those in the Book of Proverbs, but at the same time bearing
the stamp of his own particular philosophy, mood and style (Eccles. 7 : 1-20). A recurrent theme in these proverbs
is the contrast between the wise man and the fool, the latter being the butt for the author's shafts of sardonic
wit. Fools are always frivolous: "the heart of fools is in the house of mirth" (ibid. 7 : 4). Fools never tire of
praising a man to his face, but "it is better for a man to hear the rebuke of the wise than to hear the song of fools"
(ibid. 7 : 5; for this use of "song" in the sense of "praise" cf. Isa. 42 : 10; Jer. 20 : 13; Ps. 106 : 12; 149 : 1).
There is as little real substance to the panegyric of fools as there is to their laughter and merrymaking.
The Preacher punningly compares the praise and laughter of the fool to "the crackling of thorns (Heb. *sirim*)
under a pot *(sir)*." The reference here is to the thorny burnet (*Poterium spinosum* L.) which is found growing
everywhere in Israel, especially on waste land (see the photograph). This prickly dwarf shrub is still used for fuel
by the Arabs to-day, just as it was by the ancient Israelites. Its branches burn with a muffled snapping sound.
Thus the point of the simile used here is as follows: just as the crackling of thorns (cf. Isa. 34 : 13; Hos. 2 : 6;
Nah. 1 : 10) grates on the ear, so does the fool's fatuous laugh only exasperate those who hear it.

A living dog is better than a dead lion.   (Ecclesiastes 9 : 4)

One of the reasons for the Preacher's profound pessimism is his keen awareness of the inescapability of death and his consequent belief that man's fate
is no better than an animal's: "As one dies, so dies the other . . . and man
has no advantage over the beasts . . . all are from the dust and all turn to
dust again" (Eccles. 3 : 19-20). Therefore, since "the living know that they
will die, but the dead know nothing" (ibid. 9 : 5), the Preacher clings
passionately to life, regarding it as the be-all and end-all of human experi-
ence. This attitude of his finds expression in the telling aphorism at the head
of this page, in which the dog, the biblical symbol of abject degradation
(e.g. 1 Sam. 17 : 43; 24 : 14), is preferred to the lion, the symbol of majestic
courage (e.g. Gen. 49 : 9; Jer. 4 : 7; Amos 3 : 8; and elsewhere).
Even in its death throes, the lion aroused the awed admiration of the
ancients. The picture above — one of the finest achievements of Assyrian
sculpture — is part of a relief of Ashurbanipal at Nineveh showing a lion
which has been mortally wounded in a royal lion-hunt (cf. Vol. III, p. 170).
The arrow has entered its body between its right shoulder and mane and
evidently come to rest in, or close to, its heart. Blood is pouring from the
dying animal's mouth. But it can be seen that, even in face of death, the lion
still keeps its majesty and pride.

LET your garments
be always white; let
not oil be lacking on
your head.

(Ecclesiastes 9 : 8)

For all his deep-seated pessimism and cynicism, the Preacher loves life (see p. 174) and is deeply attached to its pleasures (Eccles. 11 : 7). He therefore advises man, in the style of contemporary wisdom literature, to be happy and enjoy his short span of life (cf. cf. p. 171): "Go, eat your bread with enjoyment, and drink your wine with a merry heart . . . Enjoy life with the wife whom you love . . . because that is your portion in life and in your toil at which you toil under the sun" (ibid. 9 : 7-9). Similar advice had already been given in the ancient Babylonian epic of Gilgamesh whose hero, Gilgamesh king of Uruk, searched everywhere for the secret of immortality: "Gilgamesh, whither rovest thou? The life thou pursuest thou shalt not find . . . Thou, Gilgamesh, let full be thy belly, make thou merry by day and night. Of each day make thou a feast of rejoicing, day and night dance thou and play! Let thy garments be sparkling fresh, thy head be washed; bathe thou in water. Pay heed to the little one that holds on to thy hand, let thy spouse delight in thy bosom! For this is the task of mankind!" Much the same hedonistic philosophy is expressed in one of the ancient Egyptian "Songs of the Harper". This particular song is actually from the 14th cent. B.C., but was ascribed to Intef, one of the Eleventh Dynasty Pharaohs (22nd and 21st cent. B.C.): "In order that thy heart may forget the preparations for thy burial. Follow thy desire while thou livest. Put myrrh upon thy head and clothing of fine linen upon thee . . ." The "sparkling fresh garments" mentioned in the Babylonian epic and the "clothing of fine linen" in the Egyptian song are the exact counterparts of the Preacher's "white garments". All three evidently denote the rich attire that was a mark of nobility or distinction in the ancient world.

In ancient art, white garments and anointing-oil indicate a festive occasion, as can be clearly seen in an Egyptian wall-painting of the 13th cent. B.C. from the tomb of Userhet (see the reproduction). Here the deceased Egyptian nobleman is portrayed, in the company of his family, accepting food and drink from the goddess of the sycamore. His hair is encircled by a gold band studded with gems, his body is clothed in white, and on his head there is a cone of perfumed ointment. His mother and wife, seated beside him, are similarly attired. The whole scene is one of aristocratic refinement and elegance.

DESIRE fails, because man goes to his eternal home . . .　　　(Ecclesiastes 12 : 5)

The Preacher depicts the approach of old age in images taken from both nature and social life. The real purpose of this sombre description is to throw into bright relief the happy days of youth from which man should extract all the joy and pleasure that he can (cf. pp. 171, 175). The onset of old age is marked by the following symptoms: loss of energy, infirmity of body, physical weakness, failing eyesight and feebleness of mind: "and one rises up at the voice of a bird" (Eccles. 12 : 4). Age deprives man of his faculties and dulls his natural emotions. Even physical desire fails.

The Hebrew word used here for desire *(ebyonah)* is also the name of the fruit of the caper-bush *(Capparis spinosa L.)* which grows between rocks and in the fissures of walls (see the photograph). The elongated fruit of the caper is carried on the end of a long stalk. The plant's white flowers with their soft, purple stamens, disclose their full splendour in the evening, remain open all through the night, and then wither the next morning. The buds are picked before they open and pickled in vinegar, to be used as a condiment. In antiquity the fruit (see the detail at the top right) was thought to be an aphrodisiac. The verse from Ecclesiastes may therefore mean that, in old age, this fruit is no longer effective, since man can no longer be roused to sexual desire.

ESTHER

IN the days of Ahasuerus . . .   (Esther 1 : 1)

The Book of Esther is a vividly told romance about the miraculous deliverance of the Jews from extermination in the days of the Persian Empire. The story, which is not lacking in touches of satire, shows us the insecure and wretched position of a people which, being scattered amongst all the other nations, was at the mercy of the arbitrary whims of princes and depended for its very existence on the good offices of influential courtiers. Although no confirmation has yet been found in Persian sources of the historicity of the events related in Esther, the actual setting of the biblical book, and not least its numerous descriptions of court etiquette, accord perfectly with what we know of the imperial court at Susa. There were many Persian monarchs like Ahasuerus, ruling over a far-flung empire, eagerly indulging in sensual pleasures, and deputing some of their royal powers to their ministers.

Ahasuerus is usually identified with Khshayarsha the son of Daryavash, the Xerxes of Greek tradition (486–465 B.C.), famous in history for his wars against Greece. According to the Greek authors, Xerxes was a temperamental emperor, a character which fits that of the king described in the Book of Esther as ruling "over one hundred and twenty seven provinces" (see p. 180). The figure of Ahasuerus-Xerxes is sculptured in stone on many reliefs on the walls of his palaces in his capital city, Persepolis. The relief reproduced here portrays a royal audience. The king is seated on the imperial throne, holding the royal sceptre in his right hand (see p. 191) and, in his left, the lotus flower — a characteristic adjunct of the human figures in the Persepolis reliefs. On the ground in front of him there are two incense-burners. Before the king stands a Median dignitary, with his right hand pressed to his lips in a gesture of veneration for his royal master. Standing behind the king are the holder of his fan, his weapon-bearer, and his bodyguard, the last holding a spear.

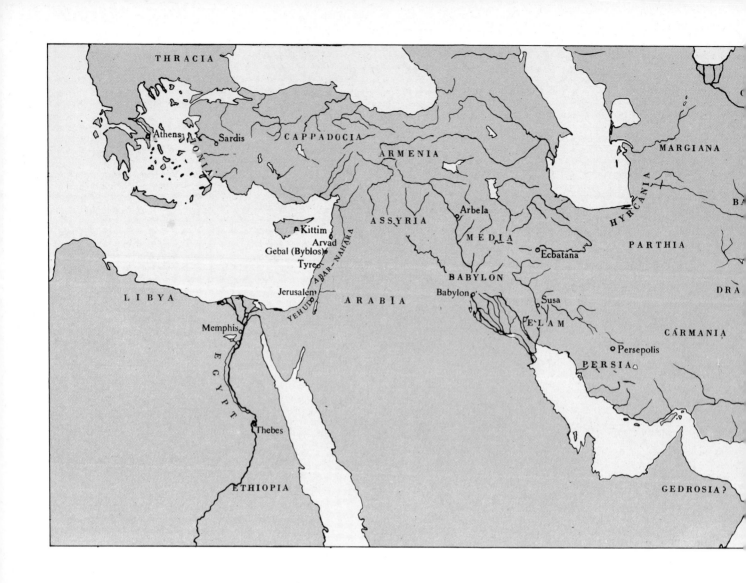

THE Ahasuerus who reigned from India to Ethiopia over one hundred and twenty-seven provinces. (Esther 1 : 1)

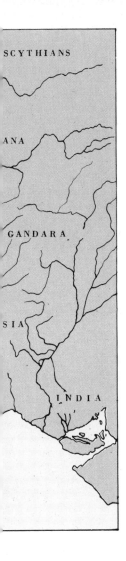

The limits assigned in the Book of Esther to the dominions of Ahasuerus, as including all the lands "from India to Ethiopia", correspond exactly to the historical extent of the Persian Empire. The Hebrew word here translated "India" really referred to the River Indus, and therefore denoted only the north-western part of the great Indian sub-continent; while the term Cush (here translated Ethiopia) was applied to Nubia, beyond the southern borders of Egypt (see the map). Moreover, the Book of Esther's description of Ahasuerus as ruler of the whole known world is in keeping both with the titles assumed by Xerxes in his own inscription — "king of the lands in which dwell many peoples", "king of the whole world" — and also with the tradition mentioned by Herodotus, to the effect that the purpose of Xerxes' attack on Greece was, in the Persian king's own words, to extend the borders of his empire "until the sun shall behold no other land than ours".

The expression "one hundred and twenty-seven provinces" evidently refers to the administrative division of the Persian empire. Herodotus speaks of Persia as being divided into twenty satrapies (see p. 229); and Darius, towards the end of his reign, increased their number from 21 to 29. These satrapies were further sub-divided into smaller administrative units (see p. 224) which are the "provinces" of the Book of Esther.

Contemporary works of art provide us with detailed representations of the payment of taxes by the countries subject to the Persian emperor (see Esth. 6 : 1). Twenty three reliefs from the entrance to the audience-hall of Darius and Xerxes at Persepolis portray deputations of tax-bearers from twenty three satrapies in the Persian empire, two of them from India and Ethiopia. In the upper picture, a Persian prince is seen leading in the head of the Indian deputation, which is bringing gold dust in jars placed in wicker baskets and carried by an Indian attendant on a yoke across his shoulders. Behind him are two more Indians leading a wild-ass(?). The last figure in the row is carrying two war-axes. In the lower picture, a Median prince is bringing the Ethiopian deputation into the royal presence. Its tribute consists of a covered vessel, an elephant tusk (carried on the third man's shoulder) and an okapi — a rare African animal.

IN the third year of his reign he gave a banquet for all his princes and servants, the army chiefs of Persia and Media and the nobles and governors of the provinces being before him.

(Esther 1 : 3)

Behind the wording of this verse about the banquet given by Ahasuerus lie the realities of the court of the Medo-Persian empire, which is often portrayed in ancient Persian art. To this banquet, of which a full and detailed description is given in the Book of Esther (see p. 184), all the principal courtiers were invited, including "the nobles" (the chief members of the ruling aristocracy), "the princes of the provinces" (the governors of the satrapies) and "the army of Persia and Media". This last was, apparently, the royal bodyguard which, in the Persian empire, was regularly composed of both Persian and Median troops. From the time of Cyrus onwards (see Vol. III, p. 75), the Persians gradually absorbed the racially, linguistically and culturally kindred kingdom of Media and made the Medes equal partners with themselves in the administration of their empire. The mixed Medo-Persian character of the imperial court is seen in two reliefs, reproduced here, from the steps leading to the Persepolis council-chamber, the construction of which was begun by Darius and completed by his son Xerxes. Below — Persian princes, each holding a lotus-flower in his right hand and a bow-case in his left; they are preceded by three spear-bearing Persian soldiers of the royal bodyguard. The princes are marked out as Persian by their long robes and tall hats. Above — Median Princes, also with lotus-flowers in their hands, some of them carrying a bow-case fastened to their girdles. They are wearing the characteristic short, tight Median tunic. It is conjectured that such a procession of princes took place in honour of the king's birthday, which was perhaps the same as the Persian New Year.

It was evidently a regular practice of the Persian rulers, at the royal banquets, to put on show the luxurious appointments of the court and the palace treasures. What is stated in the Book of Esther about the silver rods, the couches of gold and silver, the golden goblets, and all the other various lavish appurtenances displayed at the feast given by Ahasuerus (ibid. 1 : 6-7), accords well with the description given by Herodotus (IX. 80) of the booty in gold and silver left behind by the Persians after they had been routed by the Greeks in the time of Xerxes: "The Greeks went all through the camp and found tents decorated with gold and silver, couches overlaid with gold and silver, goblets of gold and cups and other drinking vessels". Herodotus goes on to relate how the Greek commander took possession of Xerxes' own regal equipage, including vessels, beds and tables all of silver and gold, exactly as described in the Book of Esther. Many artistically wrought gold vessels have come down to us from the time of the Persian empire. The gold goblet in the picture above is from the 6th or 5th cent. B.C. The lion which forms its base is a common decorative motif on the gold vessels and jewels of the Persian kings. In the picture below there is a gold cup of the same period, adorned with the figures of winged lions — an originally Assyrian motif that found its way into Persian art. The handles of this particular drinking-vessel are executed in the form of a double-headed ibex. Other vessels of the same period also have goat-shaped handles, but with a single head.

To gather all the beautiful young virgins to the harem in Susa the capital . . . (Esther 2 : 3)

The method by which the new queen was selected after Vashti's fall from grace was apparently a departure from the usual Persian court custom. It is probable that the queen was normally chosen from one of the noble families (of which there were seven in all, according to Herodotus III. 84). In this case, however, the choice was made on the advice of the king's attendants, who suggested that eligible virgins should be collected by special officials from all over the kingdom. These maidens were all placed in the women's house in Susa, the capital city, in the charge of Hege, or Hegai (in Sanskrit *aga* means "eunuch"), the king's eunuch and guardian of the harem, who took great pains with their beauty treatment, supplying them with cosmetics for a whole year to fit them for their appearance before the king (see p. 186). At the end of "her period of beautification", each of the maidens was taken to the king in the evening, and returned the next morning "to the second harem in custody of Shaashgaz the king's eunuch who was in charge of the concubines" (Esth. 2 : 14), since she was now one of the king's concubines. The royal harem occupied a position of considerable importance in the Persian court, and the women of the palace even took part in the various plots and intrigues concerning the throne (see p. 192).

The remains of the palace built by Xerxes at Persepolis for his queen Amestris can give us some idea of the appearance of a "women's house" of this kind. The harem was divided into two sections, each containing a hall with its ceiling supported by four pillars, and a small, narrow room runing off it. The picture is a reconstruction of the facade of the harem. The principal remains of the building still standing are the entrance, the stone window-frames, the bases of the pillars and the pillars of the outer walls; while the walls painted white, the roof, and the pillars and their capitals have been reconstructed from archaeological finds made at Persepolis.

A<small>ND</small> he quickly provided her with her ointments and her portion of food, and with seven chosen maids from the king's palace . . .

(Esther 2 : 9)

Many young maidens, amongst them Esther, were brought to the royal harem and placed in the custody of Hegai, the eunuch of the women (see p. 185). All these elaborate preparations were directed to a single aim — the satisfaction of the king's desires. The course of beauty treatment undergone by the girls consisted of "six months with oil of myrrh and six months with spices and ointments for women". The future concubines were also waited upon by women of the royal household, specially appointed for the purposee.

A very interesting picture of a noble Persian lady of those times has been preserved on a Persian cylinder-seal, dating to the 5th cent. B.C. (see the reproduction above). Resplendent in a robe of fine linen with embroidered hems, this great lady (who may be no other than the queen herself) is seated on a chair, with her feet on a footstool, holding a lotus-flower in her left hand. Before her stands a serving-girl, who is offering her what appears to be a cosmetic container shaped like a bird. To the right of the girl there is an incense-burner from which aromatic smoke is rising; and behind this stands a eunuch wearing a long Persian cloak and a crown, the mark of aristocratic rank, and holding a kind of bucket which apparently contains the incense. The chair, the footstool and even the incense-burner are strikingly similar to the king's chair, footstool and incense burner depicted on the reliefs from Persepolis (see pp. 179, 191).

AND when Esther was
taken to King Ahasuerus
into his royal palace . . .
(Esther 2 : 16)

The royal palace of Ahasuerus, to which Esther was taken at the end of her year's beauty treatment, was apparently the king's private residence, close to the women's house or harem, but separate from it. The palaces of the Persian kings were renowned for their splendour and magnificence. Though practically nothing has survived of the brick-built royal palaces at Susa (see p. 196), at Persepolis archaeologists have unearthed an elaborate complex of stone palaces dating to the reigns of Darius, Xerxes and their successors. Seen in the upper photograph is the "Hall of Pillars" (*apadana* in Persian), the royal throne-room which was the most magnificent and famous of all the palatial structures at Persepolis. In this hall there were 72 gigantic pillars (of which 13 are still standing on their bases), each topped by a capital in the form of two bulls on whose backs the wooden beams of the ceiling rested (cf. p. 196). In shape the hall was a square of about 200 ft. by 200 ft., large enough to hold ten thousand people on a festive occasion. The lower photograph shows the remains of Xerxes' royal palace at Persepolis. The ground-plan of the structure and its main entrances, with various reliefs engraved on the doorposts, are well preserved. In the relief in the centre of the photograph, the king's figure is seen protected by a sunshade carried by an attendant who is walking behind him.

I WILL pay ten thousand talents of silver into the hands of those who have charge of the king's business, that they may put it into the king's treasuries.

(Esther 3 : 9)

Haman promises Ahasuerus the huge sum of ten thousand silver talents in return for the royal assent to the extermination of the Jews. This amount was about two thirds of the total annual revenue of the Persian empire which, according to Herodotus (iii. 95), amounted in Darius' reign to seventeen thousand silver talents. The two great cities of Persia — Susa and Persepolis — were famous for their wealth and for the quantities of silver and gold stored in their treasuries. Greek historians expatiate on the enormous size of the treasures looted by Alexander the Great in these two cities. According to one estimate, he carried off 50,000 talents of silver from Susa alone; while from Persepolis, which according to the same Greek historians was the richest city on the face of the earth, he took the fantastic sum of 120,000 talents of silver.

The money offered by Haman to the king is to be brought to the king's treasuries (Persian *ganza*; Heb. *genazim*) by "those who have charge of the king's business" (i.e. the accountants of the royal exchequer), chief amongst whom were the treasurer (Persian *ganzabara*; Heb. *gizbar*) and his deputy. The treasury of Xerxes has been excavated at Persepolis (see the aerial photograph above). In it were found weapons and hundreds of tablets inscribed in Elamite, containing a record of the revenues of the royal exchequer. The treasury itself is a spacious pillared hall enclosed by narrow corridors. It was surrounded by a high wall in which there was only one gateway. This entrance led into the guard-rooms and thence into the treasury proper. The principal royal treasuries were apparently not in Susa, but in Persepolis, which was a safe and well fortified city lying far from any border, deep in the interior of the country.

EVERY province in its own script and every people in its own language . . . (Esther 3 : 12)

The order for the extermination of the Jews was written by Haman in the name of king Ahasuerus and sent to the governors of the various subject peoples in the appropriate script and language. Such was actually the regular procedure in the Persian empire in those times. The official document was first written out in Persian, and then translated into the languages of the peoples for whom it was intended. Besides Persian, which was the language of the royal court, the princes and the priests, there were several other official languages in use in Persia. First there was Elamite, the language of the country of Elam which had been absorbed by Persia; this was the tongue in which most of the accounts in the royal treasuries were written (see the previous page). Then there was Babylonian, since the Persian emperors regarded themselves as the successors of the Babylonian kings. And there was also Aramaic, which was the language mainly used in writing in the western part of the Persian empire. Aramaic served as a *lingua franca* for the peoples of Babylonia, Syria and Palestine who spoke it or, at least, understood it; and it was also widely used in lands where it was not spoken, such as India, the Caucasus, Egypt, and Asia Minor. In contrast to Persian, Elamite and Babylonian, which were written on clay tablets (see Vol. III, p. 273), Aramaic was usually written on papyrus.

Reproduced here are a few examples of the languages and scripts that were in common use in the Persian empire (from top to bottom):

a — c. Three extracts from a royal decree of Xerxes at Persepolis, written in the following sequence: Persian, Elamite, and Babylonian.

d. An Aramaic papyrus from Elephantine, dating to the 5th cent. B.C., which was written to the Persian governor.

e. Part of the Phoenician inscription on the sarcophagus of Eshmunazar, king of Sidon, apparently from the 4th cent. B.C.

f. An Egyptian papyrus — a deed of sale — in the demotic script, from the fourth year of the reign of Ptolemy III (244-243 B.C.).

g. A section of a Lydian inscription of the 5th cent. B.C., from Sardis (the Hebrew *Sepharad,* see Vol. III, p. 248), the capital city of Lydia in Asia Minor.

h. Part of a Greek inscription from the 5th cent. B.C.

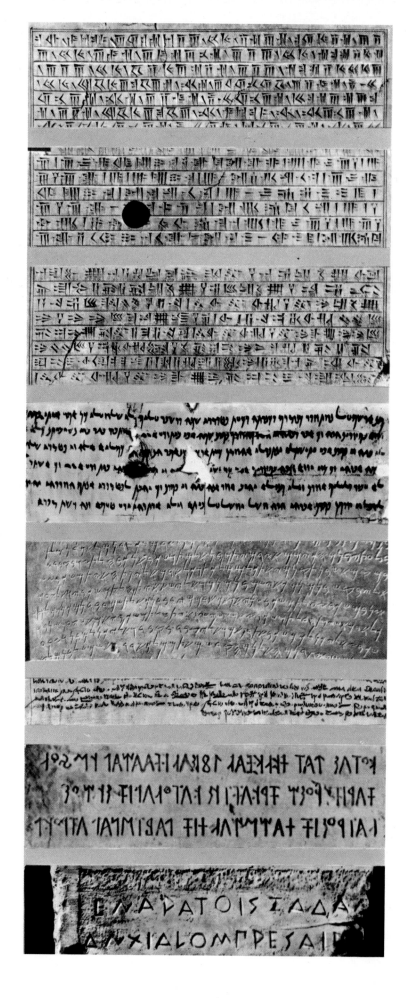

HE went up to the entrance of the king's gate . . .
(Esther 4 : 2)

Mordecai was in the habit of sitting by the king's gate, perhaps because that was the nearest he was permitted to come to the actual royal buildings, and of "walking in front of the harem, to learn how Esther was and how she fared" (Esth. 2 : 11, 19). Another possible explanation is that this was a privilege granted him because of the favour he enjoyed in court circles (ibid. 2 : 12; 3 : 2). In the time of his nation's peril, when he went out into the city "wailing with a loud and bitter cry", he approached no nearer than "the entrance of the king's gate, for no one might enter the king's gate clothed with sackloth" (ibid. 4 : 1-2). No gateways and actual buildings have remained standing on the site of Susa, the Persian capital, but it may be presumed that the royal residences there were built on much the same plan as those at Persepolis, where the imperial palaces stood on an artificial terrace towering high above the surrounding city. Steps led up from the city to the king's gate and from there to the palaces. The gateway of Xerxes at Persepolis (see the photograph above) can help us to form a visual image of the gate of Susa, where the servants of king Ahasuerus "bowed down and did obeisance to Haman" (ibid. 3 : 2). This gateway, with its surrounding wall, is a square structure with two entrances, one on the west side and the other on the east. Each of these entrances is flanked by colossal statues of winged bulls (cf. Vol. III, p. 159), placed there to guard the access to the palace and strike terror into all who approached the gate. There is evidence that the recesses in the bull-crowns were inlaid with brightly glittering gems. Carved into the stone above these guardian genii is an inscription of Xerxes, stating that he built this gate and named it "the Gate of all the Lands", i.e. the gateway through which the envoys of many nations would pass.

THE king was sitting on
his royal throne inside the
palace opposite the entrance
to the palace ... and he held
out to Esther the golden
sceptre that was in his hand.
(Esther 5 : 1-2)

Dressed in her full regal attire, Esther stands in fear and trembling in the inner court, opposite the king's palace, from where she can see Ahasuerus sitting on his throne and holding the golden sceptre in his hand. The queen's life and the fate of her nation now hang upon the movement of that sceptre. Though other ancient sources also repeatedly describe "the splendour and pomp of the majesty" of the mighty Persian king and the great awe which his presence struck into all around him, only the Book of Esther contains the information that such severe restrictions on the right of entry into the inner court applied even to the queen, when she wished to appear before the king (see Esth. 4 : 11). Whether this particular detail is accurate or not, the whole description of Ahasuerus as sitting on his throne, sceptre in hand, corresponds exactly to the portrayal of the Persian kings in the art of the time. Thus, in the relief from Persepolis — reproduced above — the Persian monarch Darius is seen seated on his throne. He is wearing a wide-sleeved robe and holding a royal sceptre, topped by a knob of gold or precious stone, in his right hand, and a lotus-flower with two buds in his left. In this relief, Darius is wearing the customary tall Persian hat, but not the royal insignia — the gold crown and bracelets — such as are worn by Xerxes on his relief (p. 178). The reason for this difference may be that Darius is here not shown on a formal state occasion, but at his regular daily task of receiving his courtiers. The throne without arms on which the king is sitting, and the footstool under his feet, are both made of wood overlaid with gold; and the legs of the throne end in lion's paws. The sceptre in the king's hand is also apparently of gold-covered wood. When placed upright it was as tall as a man, so that the king could easily stretch it out to anyone standing opposite, but at some distance from, him in the inner court, exactly as related in the Book of Esther: "Then Esther approached and touched the top of the sceptre" (ibid. 5 : 2).

THE king's servants who attended him ...
(Esther 6 : 3)

In the Persian empire, court-plots against the ruling monarch were frequent. Xerxes himself was assassinated in his bedchamber by one of his attendants, as the result of a conspiracy that originated in the royal harem (see p. 185). It is, therefore, not at all surprising that the Persian kings should have showered honours upon loyal princes, and especially upon those who saved their lives or the lives of their friends. This was the custom followed by Ahasuerus, when — after an interval of forgetfulness — he decided to give Mordecai the Jew a public reward for his part in revealing the plot formed against the king's life by two of the eunuchs of his palace-guard. In thus honouring Mordecai the king was assisted by his "servants" (ibid. 6 : 3, 5), i.e. the younger members of his entourage.

A visual record of such youthful royal attendants is preserved in Persian art. In the relief from the palace of Darius I (521-486 B.C.), reproduced here, a youth with a completely beardless chin (which some scholars take to be an indication of his being a eunuch) is seen holding a container of perfume in his right hand and a towel in his left. His broad-sleeved upper garment is similar to the robes worn by the Persians in the Persepolis reliefs (see p. 191); while the folds in the garment, which give depth to the relief, are evidence of the Greek motifs introduced into Persian art by the Greek artists who were already at this time employed in the royal palaces of Persia.

THE horse which the king has ridden, and on whose head a royal crown is set. (Esther 6 : 8)

With subtle irony, the Book of Esther describes how Haman advises Ahasuerus to exalt "the man whom the king delights to honour" by having him clothed in royal attire and placed upon the king's own horse, and how this advice of his is punctiliously carried out with regard to Mordecai the Jew (Esth. 6 : 6-12). To ride on the king's horse in public, through the crowded streets of Susa, was thus the greatest honour that an imperial minister who had won the king's special favour could hope to be accorded. The king's horse had a specially important status in the Persian court. These animals were all of the Nesean breed typical of the western Iranian plateau. They were a favourite theme in Persian art, as is illustrated by the reproduction below of a relief from the *apadana* (Hall of Pillars) of Darius and Xerxes at Persepolis, showing three horses being led by attendants. The horsemen are dressed in Median fashion: high, round hat, an upper garment reaching down to the knees, and close-fitting trousers. The most striking feature of these horses was their magnificent ornamental headdress, a form of equine decoration that was popular on the Iranian plateau as early as the Assyrian period (as testified by contemporary reliefs; cf. p. 139). This headdress was made from the horse's own mane, the hairs of which were combed out and then plaited into the form of a lotus-flower. Some scholars hold that the expression used of the king's horse in the Book of Esther "on whose head a royal crown is set", refers to a decoration of this kind, which was indeed like a crown on the horse's head. In Greek tradition the horses of the Persian king were pure white steeds with head-ornaments of gold.

SEAL it with the king's ring . . .   (Esther 8 : 8)

The "king's ring" mentioned here is the signet-ring with which official documents were signed to give them the royal imprimatur. Hence, when Ahasuerus removes his ring from his finger and gives it to Haman, or takes it away from Haman and gives it to Mordecai (Esth. 3 : 10; 8 : 2), he is in fact investing the recipients with sweeping powers. From that moment they are entitled to make use of the king's name and signature as they please (ibid. 8 : 8; cf. Gen. 41 : 42). In ancient Persia, royal documents were sealed in one of two ways: with a signet-ring when they were written on papyrus in Aramaic, Egyptian or Phoenician; or with a cylinder-seal when they were inscribed on clay tablets in Persian, Elamite or Babylonian (cf. p. 189). One of the finds in the excavations at Persepolis is a gold ring engraved with the figure of an antelope of the type known as *Dama mesopotamica* (see the upper picture). It was a ring of this kind that was used for making the impression on the clay seal attached to the papyrus. The sealing was done as follows: the papyrus was tied up with a piece of string or ribbon, then a lump of clay was placed over the knot and stamped with a signet-ring (cf. Vol. III, p. 130). This is how, in the time of Ahasuerus, the "letters" were sealed which decreed the fate of nations and provinces. The lower picture is a reproduction of an impression of a cylinder-seal which belonged to Xerxes and was found on an Elamite tablet in the royal treasury at Persepolis. The king is standing between two winged bulls (a characteristically Persian motif), with the winged emblem of the sun (Ahuramazda) above his head. On the left there is a palm-tree, another typical feature of Persian royal seals of the same period.

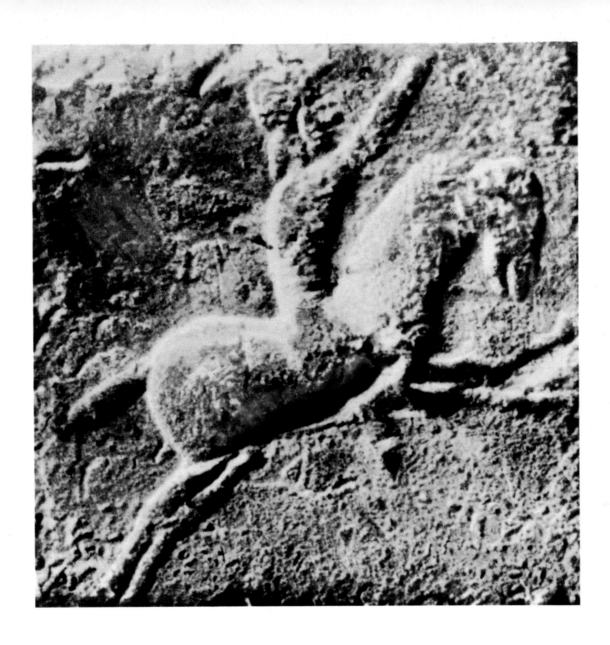

LETTERS were sent by mounted couriers riding on swift horses . . .   (Esther 8 : 10)

There is no question of cancelling Haman's decree outright, "for an edict written in the name of the king and sealed with the king's ring cannot be revoked" (Esth. 8 : 8). But what can be done is to send fresh "letters" to the provinces of the empire, summoning their Jewish inhabitants to take up arms and defend themselves. Since time is short and the edict urgent, it is sent out by "mounted couriers", messengers riding on fast, pedigree royal steeds. The Greek historians confirm that the Persian royal couriers (ibid. 3 : 13, 15) were famous in antiquity for their speed and reliability. The efficient and orderly control of such a far-flung empire depended upon the maintenance of close and constant communication between its various parts. The couriers operated in relays, each riding throughout the day and at dusk reaching the next post, where he handed on his message to a fresh courier mounted on a fresh horse. This Persian "postal service" functioned day and night, at all seasons of the year, and in all sorts of weather. The couriers travelled by the "king's highway", along which there were posting-stations for the change-over of horses and riders and which ran from the Aegean coast to Susa, with offshoots to Syria, Palestine and Egypt. These roads served both administrative and commercial purposes. A fast Persian courier, mounted on a horse at full gallop, is depicted on the impression of a stone seal from Nippur in Babylonia, dating to the 5th cent. B.C. (see the reproduction). The courier is holding the reins in his right hand and a spear in his left. He is wearing a hat fastened under his chin by leather straps, and a tight-fitting cloak.

A DECREE was issued in Susa . . .

(Esther 9 : 14)

In the course of its history the Persian empire had several capital cities: Babylon, Ecbatana (see p. 225), Susa and Persepolis (Parsa). Darius I transferred the capital from Babylon and Ecbatana to Susa, which was near to Babylonia. But, before very long, Persepolis became the first city of the empire. Darius and Xerxes apparently resided in Susa only during the winter, moving to Persepolis for the long summer months when the heat in Susa grew too intense for comfort. In earlier times, Susa had been the capital of the kingdom of Elam. Darius not only restored the palaces of its ancient kings, but also added new royal buildings of his own. The chief glory of the king's palace, the "hall of pillars" (in Persian, *apadana*), was decorated, like all the rest of the structure, with glazed bricks on which a colourful variety of pictures were painted. An echo of the dazzling impression made by the luxurious splendour and artistic brilliance of such a royal residence can probably still be heard in the description of "the king's palace" given in the Book of Esther: "There were white cotton curtains and blue hangings caught up with cords of fine linen and purple to silver rings and marble pillars, and also couches of gold and silver on a mosaic pavement of porphyry, marble, mother-of-pearl and precious stones" (Esth. 1 : 6). To-day, all that remains of Susa is a mound of ruins—see the aerial photograph below. Its palaces, being built of burnt brick, have not withstood the ravages of time. Only the sturdy stone capitals of the pillars, topped by two bulls joined together in the middle (see the detail above, and cf. p. 187), survive as mute testimony to the former greatness and splendour of imperial Susa.

T HESE days of Purim shall never fall into disuse among the Jews . . .　　　(Esther 9 : 28)

The new festival of Purim was not readily accepted into the religious calendar by all the Jews in the Persian empire. First, Mordecai alone wrote letters to his brethren, explaining the reason for the festival and the religious obligation to observe it. But that was not enough: Esther and Mordecai had later jointly to write "this second letter about Purim" (Esth. 9 : 29), in order to enforce its observance. However, once the festival had really taken root in the congregations of the diaspora, it came to be regarded with particular affection on account of its popular character, as is clear not only from the wealth of legend that grew up around the story of Esther and Mordecai, but also from various artistic representations of the theme. An outstanding example of the latter is found in the synagogue-frescoes at Dura-Europos (on the middle Euphrates), from the 3rd cent. A.D. The section from the western wall, reproduced above, portrays Ahasuerus and Esther, the king seated on a magnificent throne and the queen to his left on one of less imposing proportions. Ahasuerus is dressed in Persian fashion, with a royal turban on his head (see Vol. III, p. 288). He is holding his sceptre in his left hand, while with his right he has given a "letter" to one of his attendants. Standing behind the king's throne is a scribe, and, to his left, one of the royal ministers. Esther's head is adorned with a high crown, like "a wall and a tower", and beneath her feet there is a footstool with the word "Esteir" written on it in Aramaic characters. Next to her stands a waiting-woman who is arranging her veil. Ahasuerus' throne is raised up on a dais with five steps, on each of which crouch lions and eagles. There is also a lion on either side of the throne itself. On the third step the word "Hashverosh" is written in Aramaic characters. This throne is similar to the description of Solomon's given in 1 Kings 10 : 18-20; 2 Chron. 9 : 18 (cf. p. 267). In the late Aramaic translation of Esther it is stated that Ahasuerus sat on the actual throne of Solomon. The eagles on the steps, next to the lions, are also an artistic motif from Jewish legend.

197

DANIEL

THIS was the dream; now we will tell the king its interpretation.   (Daniel 2 : 36)

The Book of Daniel falls into two parts: first, Daniel's life-story (chaps. 1-6), followed by his apocalyptic visions of the end of time (chaps. 7-12). It is related that Daniel was one of the young Jewish deportees from Judah who, together with his companions, was brought up at the Babylonian court. All these youths steadfastly remained true to the God of Israel and His Law, despite the constant danger in which they placed themselves by so doing. Daniel, like Joseph before him, rose to a position of high authority (Dan. 2 : 48-49), after he had successfully described and interpreted a dream dreamt by the Babylonian king. In his dream the king saw a large statue with a head of gold, chest and arms of silver, stomach and thighs of bronze, legs of iron, and feet partly of iron and partly of clay. Suddenly, this image was pounded into fine dust by a stone and became "like the chaff of the summer threshing-floors", while the stone grew into a huge mountain which filled the whole earth (ibid. 2 : 31-36). This dream was interpreted by Daniel as follows: the head of gold was Babylon, which was to be followed by a succession of three different empires, until finally God raised up an empire which should destroy these three and endure for ever (ibid. verses 36-45). There is considerable uncertainty about the identity of the empires alluded to in the interpretation of the dream. According to one view, the silver empire is Media, the bronze one Persia, and the iron one the empire founded by Alexander the Great, while the statue's mixed iron and clay feet are the Diadochi, some of whom were strong rulers and some weak. On the other hand, the dream may embody the widely held ancient belief in the division of human history into four ages of varying duration and quality: the golden age, the silver age, the bronze age, and the iron age. Even in ancient art, the Persian and Greek empires were treated symbolically no less than realistically, as can be seen in the pictures reproduced here.

On p. 200, right, the Persian god Ahuramazda is seen standing inside the winged ring which was the official emblem of the Persian empire. The god is raising his right hand in blessing and holding a goblet-shaped lotus-flower in his left. The illustration on p. 201 shows a head of Alexander the Great (on a coin of Ptolemy). The king is here portrayed as a god, with a covering of elephants' hide over his head and "horns" protruding from his forehead, as from the foreheads of Babylonian gods. (Cf. the horns on the foreheads of the gods and kings of ancient Mesopotamia, p. 50 above). On p. 200, left, is a coin from the reign of Antiochus IV, showing the god Apollo seated on the earth's omphalos (navel-stone) at Delphi, with an arrow in his right hand and a bow in his left. Apollo was, at that time, the symbol of the Seleucid empire.

WHEN you hear the sound of the horn, pipe, lyre, trigon, harp, bag-pipe, and every kind of music, you are to fall down and worship the golden image that King Nebuchadnezzar has set up.

(Daniel 3 : 5)

Daniel's companions heroically refuse to join in the idolatrous rites of the Babylonians, and, even when about to be thrown into the fiery furnace, they do not bow down to the image erected by Nebuchadnezzar with such ceremonial splendour in the plain of Dura, outside Babylon (Dan. 3 : 1-4). The worship of this statue, made of solid gold, is described in the Book of Daniel as a cultic innovation which was imposed by royal decree upon the "peoples, nations, and languages" of the Babylonian empire. There may be allusion here to the gods of Assyria and Babylon at the height of their power. Or perhaps this is an echo of the "heresy" of the Babylonian king Nabonidus, whose religious innovations were bitterly opposed by the priests of Marduk (cf. Vol. III, p. 75). The image described in Daniel is inaugurated with great public pomp and mass obeisances, to the accompaniment of music played by three kinds of wind-instrument (the horn, the pipe, and the bagpipe) and three kinds of string-instrument (the lyre, the trigon, and the harp). The horn (Heb. *qeren,* cf. Josh. 6 : 5) is the same as the ram's horn (*shofar;* see Vol. II, p. 30); the pipe (Heb. *mashroqith,* rendered by the Greek translators as *syrinx*) is the Greek shepherd's pipe with a double stem; the lyre (Heb. *kaithros* = Greek *kitharis*) was a seven-stringed instrument, very popular in Greece and the emblem of Apollo, the god of music; the trigon (Heb. *sabkha* = Greek *sambuca*) was a triangular shaped instrument with four strings; the harp (Heb. *psanterin* = Greek *psalterion*) was another stringed instrument; while the bagpipe (Heb. *sumponia*) was a wind-instrument consisting of a wind-bag with tubes attached to it. Four of these six instruments are illustrated in the pictures here which are all painted on Attic vases of the 5th cent. B.C. On the right of p. 202 — a youth playing a "lyre"; on the left — a bearded man plucking a "harp". On p. 203 — a youth playing on a "double-pipe".

AND this is the writing that was inscribed: Mene, Mene, Tekel and Parsin.

(Daniel 5 : 25)

At a great banquet given in the royal halls, Belshazzar, the king of Babylon, desecrated the vessels carried off from God's Temple in Jerusalem. Suddenly, in the midst of the revelling, the king was struck dumb with fear by the sight of a hand which wrote four words on the palace wall. After all the wise men of Babylon had been unable to decipher the words, Daniel interpreted them as a prophecy of the city's impending doom (Babylon did indeed fall to Cyrus, the Persian king, in 539 B.C.; see below p. 219; and Vol. III, p. 75). The writing interpreted by Daniel has a double meaning. On the one hand, the Aramaic words "*Mene, mene, tekel upharsin* (= and *parsin*)" may symbolically point to the fast approaching end of the Babylonian empire: God has counted out (Heb. *manah* = Aramaic *mene*) its days, weighed (Heb. *shakal* = Aram. *tekel*) its king in the scales and found him wanting, and divided up (Heb. *paras*) his dominions and apportioned them to Media and Persia. At the same time, taken literally, these words simply denote the weights called *maneh, shekel* and *peres,* which were employed as units of exchange before the introduction of coinage and subsequently gave their names to the coins themselves. The Babylonian *mina* (Heb. *maneh*) was made up of sixty *shekels.* The *shekel* continued to be both a weight and a coin. *Peres* apparently meant half of any previously mentioned weight; thus, in our verse here it would be half a *shekel.* The upper picture is a Babylonian *mina* from the reign of Nebuchadnezzar II. At the bottom right there is a Persian *shekel* (cf. below, p. 222). At the bottom left — a weight from the time of the Divided Monarchy inscribed with the word *beka* (i.e. half a *shekel*), enlarged eight times.

THEN the king commanded, and Daniel was brought and cast into the den of lions . . .

(Daniel 6 : 16)

After the Persian conquest of Babylon, Daniel rose to a position of such importance at the court of Darius that "the king planned to set him over the whole kingdom" (Dan. 6 : 3). For all that, Daniel still remained true to the faith of his fathers and, despite the king's stern interdiction, regularly turned to Jerusalem three times a day in prayer, going down on his knees and giving thanks to his God (ibid. verse 10). This provided the other courtiers with their opportunity to denounce Daniel to the king and thus have him thrown to the wild beasts, as decreed in the royal interdiction. The king tried hard to save Daniel, but the courtiers reminded him that he himself had signed this law and that "no interdict or ordinance which the king establishes can be changed". So Daniel was cast into the lion's den. But "God sent His angel and shut the lions' mouths" (Dan. 6 : 22), so that Daniel emerged from his ordeal without so much as a scratch upon him. The deliverance of Daniel in the lion's den became, for later generations of Jews, a symbol of God's miraculous intervention in time of trouble. It is referred to in prayers and liturgical poems — "He who answered Daniel in the lions' den will answer me too" (the Penitential Prayers); and it also appears as one of the motifs of later Jewish art (as in the synagogue mosaic at Naaran, near Jericho). The motif is ultimately derived from an ancient artistic tradition in which the lion was a symbol of supernatural forces.

The picture above is a reproduction of a bronze support in the form of three lions. This unique object was found at Persepolis and belongs to the time of Darius' successors (5th cent. B.C.). Assyrian influence is evident in the modelling of the individual animals, but the functional nature of the whole design is something that was rare in Assyrian art. (On the lion in Assyrian art cf. Vol. II, p. 101; Vol. III, p. 235; and this volume, p. 174).

CONCERNING the ten horns that were on its head, and the other horn which came up and before which three of them fell, the horn which had eyes and a mouth that spoke great things . . .

(Daniel 7 : 20)

This part of Daniel's vision apparently refers to the persecutions of the Jews by the Seleucid kings (Dan. chaps. 7-12). The Seleucid empire is represented as a "terrible, dreadful and exceedingly strong" beast (the fourth beast, ibid. 7 : 7) which devours everything and tramples down the whole earth (ibid. 7 : 19-24). From it ten kings shall arise, of whom the last shall be more wicked than all the rest: "he shall speak words against the Most High and shall wear out the saints of the Most High, and shall think to change the times and the law; and they shall be given into his hand for a time, two times, and half a time" (ibid. verse 25). This is apparently an allusion to Antiochus IV Epiphanes (175-164 B.C.), who appears in Daniel's vision as the tenth horn with human eyes and a vainglorious mouth.

As part of his attempt to unite the Hellenistic kingdoms against the growing power of Rome, Antiochus IV sought to bring together the various peoples of his empire by establishing a single official cult for all of them — that of Olympian Zeus (see below, p. 215). When he tried to enforce this policy in Judah, he touched off an outburst of violent popular resentment which culminated in the Hasmonean revolt. The horrors of Antiochus' persecutions are indelibly imprinted upon the annals of Jewish history. Antiochus was a bold and tyrannical ruler, much given to lavish display and visionary political schemes. His enemies regarded these qualities as evidence of megalomania, and accordingly changed his honorific title Epiphanes (the god revealed) to the derogatory epithet Epimanes (the madman). The bronze mask reproduced above, which was found in the village of Shami in the Persian province of Khuzistan (near Susa, the capital), is considered by most scholars to be a likeness of Antiochus IV.

I RAISED my eyes and saw, and behold, a ram standing on the bank of the river. It had two horns; and both horns were high, but one was higher than the other, and the higher one came up last. (Daniel 8 : 3)

On the river Ulai in Elam (not far from the capital, Susa) Daniel had a vision of the struggle between Persia and Greece. Persia is symbolically represented as a ram with two horns, one of which stands for Media, and the other, "higher" one, for Persia: "and the higher one came up last" (Dan. 8 : 3). The ram had once been vigorous and strong, "charging westward and northward and southward; no beast could stand before him, and there was no one who could rescue from his power" (ibid. verse 4). But now its valorous days are past and it is no longer a match for the he-goat (an allusion to Alexander the Great) which comes furiously charging at it.

The ram was apparently, in antiquity, a well-known symbol for the Persian empire. It is mentioned as such in a literary work about astrological geography from the Persian period. In this work the various countries are symbolically represented by animals: Persia appears as a ram, while Syria (meaning the Seleucid kingdom) is described as a he-goat. The symbolism of Daniel's vision is thus seen to be based on established ancient patterns.

Reproduced above is a ram's head, made of gold, from the Persian period. The ram was a favourite subject of Persian art, so much so that its shape often adorns purely functional objects such as jar-handles.

As I was considering, behold, a he-goat came from the west across the face of the whole earth . . .

(Daniel 8 : 5)

The he-goat (see p. 207) charged furiously at the ram "and cast him down to the ground and trampled upon him; and there was no one who could rescue the ram from his power" (Dan. 8 : 7). The he-goat stands for Greece, which is about to overthrow Persia. The conspicuous horn between the he-goat's eyes is, of course, Alexander the Great, who defeated the army of Darius III on various battlefields in Asia. The engagement which decided the mastery of the ancient world was fought near Issus in 333 B.C. Above is a scene from the battle, as depicted in a mosaic (from the 1st cent. A.D.) which is a copy found at Pompeii of a Hellenistic original. At the left, Alexander is seen forcing his way through the ruck of fighting men to the chariot of Darius which is at the right of the picture. A mounted Persian nobleman bars Alexander's way; the Macedonian king thrusts him through with his spear and he falls to the ground. Another Persian belonging to the entourage of Darius dismounts from his horse to aid the wounded man, but he is too late. Meanwhile, many Persians come rushing to their king's defence, and the driver of his chariot manages to extricate him from danger. However, at this critical moment the Persian king has no thought for his personal safety, but is stretching out his hand, in a gesture of deep compassion, to the mortally wounded nobleman. The latter's sacrifice was not in vain: the king and his entourage escaped from the disaster that threatened them.

In his vision (chaps. 11-12), Daniel foretells the later history of the Hellenistic empires. Alexander the Great's empire will be broken up "and divided toward the four winds of heaven" (Dan. 11 : 4). After him, "the king of the south" will be supreme, until one of his princes, whose "dominion shall be a great dominion", becomes more powerful than he (ibid. verse 5). "The king of the south" is Ptolemy I Lagos, one of Alexander's generals, who, after his royal master's death (323 B.C.), seized control of Egypt and Palestine and founded the empire of the Ptolemaic dynasty. The prince who, according to Daniel's vision, "shall be stronger" than Ptolemy, is Seleucus I, another of Alexander's generals. Seleucus conquered Mesopotamia and made himself master of the greater part of Alexander's empire, so that his was indeed "a great dominion": it stretched from the Aegean Sea to India, and was stronger and larger than the empire of the Ptolemies. The picture on the left is a bronze bust of Seleucus I which was found at Herculaneum, near Pompeii. Below is a marble head of Ptolemy I which was found in Egypt.

THEN the king of the south shall be strong, but one of his princes shall be stronger than he and his dominion shall be a great dominion. (Daniel 11 : 5)

THE daughter of the king of the south shall come to the king of the north to make peace ... a branch from her roots shall arise in his place; he shall come against the army and enter the fortress of the king of the north ...

(Daniel 11 : 6-7)

The next scene beheld by Daniel in his vision (see p. 210) is the daughter of the king of the south coming to the king of the north "to make peace" (i.e. to conclude a peace-treaty). But this treaty is soon broken, when one of this daughter's offspring takes up arms against the king of the north and makes himself master of his country (Dan. 11 : 6-8). The allusion here is most probably to Berenice, the sister of the Egyptian king Ptolemy III Euergetes, who was given in marriage to the Seleucid king Antiochus II, after he had divorced his first wife Laodice. When Berenice was subsequently murdered, at Laodice's instigation, her brother Ptolemy marched on Syria to avenge her death. In the war which followed between Ptolemy III and Seleucus II (Kallinikos), the son of Antiochus II, Ptolemy III at first (246 B.C.) captured "the stronghold" (Seleucia, the port of Antioch) and "the fortress of the king of the north" (Antioch), and gained control of large areas of Syria. "He shall also carry off to Egypt their gods with their molten images and with their precious vessels of silver and gold" (ibid. 11 : 8). Eventually, however, the royal forces of "the king of the south" were compelled to withdraw from the whole of Syria, except Seleucia.

Reproduced above is a coin bearing the likeness of Ptolemy III represented as a god. On his head he is wearing a crown formed of the sun's rays, and on his chest the "golden breastplate" of Zeus and Athena (the "aegis"). The trident behind his back is the symbol of his dominion on the sea.

THEN the king of the north shall come and throw up siegeworks, and take a well-fortified city. And the forces of the south shall not stand . . . and he shall stand in the glorious land . . .   (Daniel 11 : 15-16)

Daniel next sees in his vision two great battles that were fought between the Seleucids and the Ptolemies for the control of Palestine (Dan. 11 : 10-15). From the moment of the break-up of Alexander the Great's empire, the kings of Syria continually claimed possession of Palestine, "the glorious land", but were for a long time unable to enforce this claim. When Antiochus III, called "the Great" (223-187 B.C.), tried to conquer Palestine at the battle of Raphiah (217 B.C.), his large army was defeated by the Egyptian king (ibid. 11 : 12). However, in 198 B.C., Antiochus made another attempt and this time defeated the Egyptian general, Scopas, near Panias: "and the forces of the south shall not stand, or even his picked troops, for there shall be no strength to stand" (ibid. 11 : 15). The rule of the Ptolemies in Palestine was now further weakened by revolts which broke out inside the country, and in which some of the Jews apparently also took part: "In those times many shall rise against the king of the south; and the men of violence among your own people shall lift themselves up in order to fulfil the vision; but they shall fail" (ibid. verse 14). Palestine passed under Seleucid control.

Above is a reproduction of a marble head of Antiochus III which was found in Syria.

AFTERWARD he shall turn his face to the coastlands, and shall take many of them; but a commander shall put an end to his insolence . . .

(Daniel 11 : 18)

In his attempt to re-establish the empire of Alexander the Great, Antiochus III came into conflict with the growing power of Rome, which had recently become a decisive political force in the Mediterranean area. Daniel's vision contains a description of the defeats inflicted on Antiochus by the Romans who had now penetrated as far as Asia Minor. The meaning of the verse above is: Antiochus attacked "the coastlands" and conquered many peoples, till he was eventually opposed and defeated by "a commander", in punishment for his insolence to Rome (Dan. 11 : 18). "The commander" alluded to here is apparently the Roman consul Lucius Cornelius Scipio Asiaticus, who advanced deep into Asia Minor and destroyed the army of Antiochus near Magnesia. Antiochus was obliged to sign a peace-treaty (188 B.C.) and to agree to the partial disarmament of his forces and the payment of an enormous fine. Lacking the means to meet his obligations, he resorted perforce to confiscating the treasures of his country's temples and was killed while doing so. This event appears to be referred to in the following words of the vision: "Then he shall turn his face back towards the fortresses of his own land; but he shall stumble and fall, and shall not be found" (ibid. 11 : 19).

In the illustration above, a bearded Roman general, wearing a breastplate, is seen making an offering to three gods: Mars (helmeted), Venus-Aphrodite, and Vulcan. Behind the general stands the goddess of victory who is placing a crown upon his head. This relief (from the 1st cent. B.C.), which was found on the base of an altar in Italy, gives us a picture of a Roman conqueror in the East.

F ORCES from him shall appear and profane the temple and
fortress . . .   (Daniel 11 : 31)

Antiochus IV Epiphanes (see p. 206) marched into Jerusalem and proceeded
to punish its rebellious inhabitants by desecrating the Temple and "fortress",
forbidding the perpetual burnt offering, and setting up "the abomination
that makes desolate" in the Sanctuary (Dan. 11 : 31; cf. p. 215). The
"fortress" (Heb. *maoz*) may be used here simply as a descriptive term for the
Temple. Many scholars, however, are of the opinion that it is the same as the
"castle" (*birah*) of Neh. 7 : 2, i. e. the citadel that was erected on the northern
side of the Temple. The Bible mentions two towers in Jerusalem — the
Tower of Hananel (or Hananiah) and the Tower of the Hundred (Zech.
14 : 10; Neh. 7 : 2; 12 : 39)—which guarded the narrow saddle connecting
the Temple Mount with the ridge to the north of it. In Nehemiah's day
these two towers were made into a citadel to protect the Temple, and placed
under the command of a special officer (Neh. 7 : 2). Antiochus IV captured
this "fortress", which gave him control of the Temple, and maintained a
garrison in it. In the time of the Hasmoneans, Simon strengthened the
defences of the citadel and made it his residence. Herod replaced it by a
powerful fortress which he called the "Antonia". In the Jewish war against
the Romans, the Antonia was occupied by the Zealots who held out there
until the Romans forced their way into it.
Photographed below are the remains of the walls of the Antonia fortress (at
the right) in the old City of Jerusalem, in the street leading to the Lions'
Gate (St. Stephen's Gate).

HE shall honour the god of fortresses instead of these; a god whom his father did not know he shall honour with gold and silver, with precious stones and costly gifts.

(Daniel 11 : 38)

The verse above is apparently a character-sketch of Antiochus IV Epiphanes, who greatly increased the power of his kingdom and was vaingloriously boastful of his own might (p. 206), even to the extent of attributing divine powers to himself: "He shall exalt himself and magnify himself above every god and speak astonishing things against the God of gods" (Dan. 11 : 36). This self-aggrandizement had a primarily political purpose: the unification of the medley of peoples comprising the Seleucid empire. Antiochus wanted to introduce a degree of uniformity into the multiplicity of faiths existing throughout his empire by establishing the cult of Olympian Zeus as the central feature of them all. Accordingly, in his reign the likeness of Apollo (p. 201), who had till then been the dynasty's emblem, was replaced on Seleucid coins by that of Zeus, "a god whom his fathers did not know" (ibid. 11 : 38). Like the Semitic deities "Baal of the Heavens" and "Hadad", the similar "Zeus of Fortresses" was well suited to the task of binding the Semitic peoples of the Seleucid empire together in a single, uniform belief. Since Antiochus was an avid imitator of Roman customs, it was probably his ambition to identify this god with the Roman Jupiter Capitolinus (who was also "the god of fortresses"), and thereby gain for his empire a strength and stability rivalling those of contemporary Rome.

Above is the head of Olympian Zeus, as it appears on coins of the city of Olympia from the 4th cent. B.C.

EZRA

AND
NEHEMIAH

EZRA

IN the first year of Cyrus king of Persia ... the LORD stirred up the spirit of Cyrus king of Persia so that he made a proclamation throughout all his kingdom and also put it in writing ... "The LORD the God of Heaven, has given me all the kingdoms of the earth, and he has charged me to build him a house at Jerusalem, which is in Judah."

(Ezra 1 : 1-2)

The proclamation of Cyrus, the Persian king, permitting the exiles from Judah to return to Jerusalem, was promulgated in 538 B.C., after Cyrus' conquest of Babylon (cf. Vol. III, p. 75). The verse at the head of this page probably contains the wording of the proclamation as it was publicly announced by heralds and then despatched to the various parts of the empire in letters carried by royal messengers. The official version of the decree — the "record" (Ezra 6 : 2) which was written in Aramaic — was no doubt deposited in the imperial archives (see below, p. 225). This proclamation extols Cyrus as having been charged by God with the rebuilding of the Temple, and describes him as the ruler to whom the Lord, the God of the heavens, has given "all the kingdoms of the earth".

Similar terms to these are used by Cyrus of himself in an inscription on a cylinder (see the reproduction), where he presents himself as the emissary of Marduk, the god of Babylon: "He (Marduk) searched and looked and observed in all the lands, seeking for an upright ruler after his own heart ... He called Cyrus by name ... to be the ruler of the world ... charged him to advance upon Babylon, his city. He led him by the direct way to Babylon, going at his side like a friend and companion ... I am Cyrus, king of the world ... I have taken care for the well-being of Babylon and of all its (sacred) cities. Marduk the great lord rejoiced in my deeds and blessed me, Cyrus the king ... that worships him, with abundance of good things ...".

The inscription goes on to describe the rejoicing of all the peoples "from the Upper Sea to the Lower Sea", when they heard of Cyrus' victory over Babylon. And indeed, Cyrus continues, for all those "whose temples had been in ruins for many days, I restored to their place the images of the gods that had formerly stood inside them and erected (for them) everlasting shrines. I gathered together all the inhabitants and restored to them their dwelling-places". In the light of this clear portrayal of Cyrus as rebuilding destroyed temples, fostering their cults, and restoring scattered populations (and the exiles as a whole) to their native lands, his proclamation concerning the Jews, with the consequent Return to Zion, is seen to be part and parcel of the general policy followed by the Persian ruler in the lands conquered by him.

A ND all who were about them aided them with vessels of silver, with gold, with goods, with beasts . . .

(Ezra 1 : 6)

Immediately after Cyrus' proclamation, the heads of the clans of Judah and Benjamin in the Babylonian exile set about organizing the Return to Zion and collecting volunteers for the rebuilding of the Temple in Jerusalem. Those that decided to remain in exile helped those that were returning home, in the spirit of the proclamation which stipulated that "each survivor . . . be assisted by the men of his place with silver and gold, with goods and with beasts . . ." (Ezra 1 : 4).

The Book of Ezra then goes on to give a list of the various kinds of gifts that were customarily presented in those times as "freewill offerings for the house of God" (ibid.), or as tribute to the king or his officials. Concrete illustrations of such gifts can be found in Persian art of the same period.

In the reproduction below — part of a relief from the Hall of Pillars built by Darius and Xerxes at Persepolis (see p. 187) — Babylonians, wearing caps and festive cloaks, are seen presenting tribute to the king. The first two have bowls of silver or gold in their hands, while the third is carrying a piece of woven material with tassels at its ends. The last two Babylonians are leading in a bullock. The picture above is of a Persian silver bowl which was discovered in one of the Palestinian tells, and which is very similar to the bowls carried by the tribute-bearers in the lower illustration.

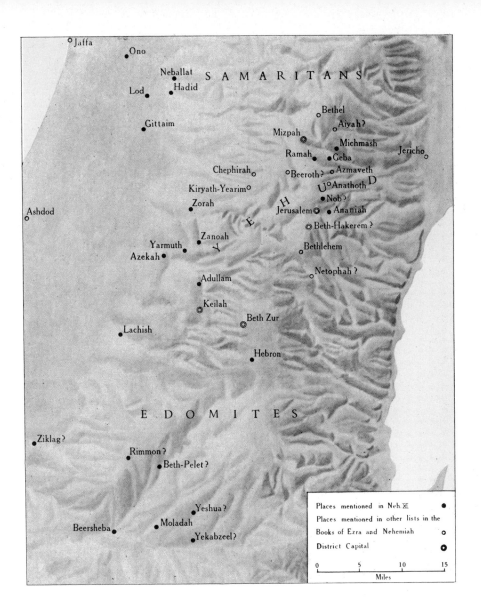

Places mentioned in Neh. XI   ●
Places mentioned in other lists in the
Books of Ezra and Nehemiah   ○
District Capital   ◉

0   5   10   15

Miles

Now these were the people of the province who came up out of the captivity... they returned to Jerusalem and Judah, each to his own town. (Ezra 2 : 1)

The list of those Jews who returned from the exile and made their way back, each to his own city, in a series of waves from the time of Zerubbabel and Jeshua onwards (Ezra 2 : 2-35; Neh. 7 : 6-36), provides us with information about the settlements of Judah in that period and also about the boundaries of the province. While some of the returning exiles are identified by their clan-relationship, others are listed according to their places of residence in Judah which stretch from Bethel in the north to beyond Bethlehem in the south, and from Jericho on the east up to Ono in the north-west (see the map).

From these biblical lists it is evident that the territory of Judah had been greatly reduced: the area occupied by the returned exiles measured no more than about 24 miles from north to south and about 30 miles from east to west. All the rest of the war-ravaged settlements of the pre-destruction kingdom of Judah remained outside the reconstituted province. Some of these places were re-settled in Nehemiah's day and later (see p. 238), while others were occupied by Judah's immediate neighbours: the Samaritans to the north, the Edomites to the south (from Hebron southwards, see Vol. III, pp. 246-247, 296), and the inhabitants of northern Philistia (who are apparently the Ashdodites of Neh. 13 : 23-24) to the south-west.

S IXTY-ONE thousand darics of gold . . .
(Ezra 2 : 69)

The Temple in Jerusalem had still to be restored and only voluntary contributions on a large scale could provide the means for this great undertaking. The heads of families set the people a good example: "according to their ability they gave to the treasury of the work sixty one thousand darics of gold, five thousand minas of silver, and one hundred priests' garments" (Ezra 2 : 69).

The darics mentioned in this verse (Heb. *darkhemonim*; in 1 Chron. 29 : 7 *adarkhonim*) were coins issued by the Persian king Darius I (521–486 B.C.), in order to establish a uniform shape and weight for the metal ingots (silver, gold, copper and bronze) which served as currency in the ancient East in the second and first millennia B.C. The first coins in antiquity were those minted by the Lydians, whose currency contained 40-60% pure gold, as early as the 7th cent. B.C. The Lydians were followed by the Persians and Greeks, who issued silver and gold coins of the same type.

Reproduced above is a Persian daric from the reign of Darius or his son, Xerxes. It is stamped with the likeness of the bearded monarch clad in royal robes and wearing a Persian crown. He is holding a spear in his right hand and a bow in his left. The fully bent right knee is meant to indicate that he is running swiftly.

THEY will not pay tribute, custom, or toll ...
(Ezra 4 : 13)

The anti-Jewish letter sent to the Persian king, which is quoted in Aramaic in the Book of Ezra 4 : 7-16, lists the various categories of taxes demanded from the subject peoples of the Persian empire in the various satrapies. While permitting its population complete freedom in matters of religious worship and local administration, the imperial government was most strict in its exaction of the regular payment of taxes. Three classes of these are mentioned in our verse here: the "tribute" (Heb. *mindah,* from Akkadian *mandattu*), also called "the king's tax" (Neh. 5 : 4), a fixed tax paid to the king by his subjects in the satrapies; the "custom" (Heb. *belo,* perhaps from the Persian *beli* = "tax", or, as others think, from the Akkadian *biltu* = "tax" or "tribute"); and the "toll" (Heb. *halakh,* from the Akkadian *ilku* = a tax in the form of forced labour for public works). Imperial taxes consisting of these kinds of tribute are illustrated above on reliefs from the Hall of Pillars of Darius and Xerxes at Persepolis (see pp. 180-181). At the top: a deputation of Ionians presenting (to the king?) two cups, four bowls, and rolls of material. In the centre: a deputation of Scythians presenting a horse, two bracelets and clothing. At the bottom: a deputation of Bactrians bringing with them two cups, two bowls, and a Bactrian camel (with two humps).

THE province of Judah . . .

(Ezra 5 : 8)

In consequence of the anti-Jewish letter which was sent to the Persian king (see p. 233), Tattenai, "the governor of the province beyond the River", and his associates came to "the province of Judah (Yehud)" and, on seeing the work being done on the restoration of the Temple, addressed the following question to the elders of Judah: "Who gave you a decree to build this house?" (Ezra 5 : 3, 9).

What is here called "the province of Judah" was subject to the satrap of the satrapy known as *Eber-nahara* (Beyond the River: — see p. 229), which also included Phoenicia, Syria and Cyprus. Judah, (or rather Yehud, as it was than called), enjoyed local autonomy within the wider framework of the satrapy and was ruled by a governor ("the governor of the Jews") appointed directly by the Persian king. The official representative and acknowledged leader of the population of Judah was the High Priest, supported, apparently, by a council of elders consisting of the heads of the various clans ("the elders of the Jews" of Ezra 6 : 7). Evidence as to the status of Judah in the Persian period and the position occupied by the Temple and its priests is provided by contemporary coins and seal-impressions found in the territory of Judah. At the top: a coin bearing the legend *yhd*, from the end of the Persian period. In its shape and emblems (the owl of Athena, with olive leaves beside it) the coin is simply a copy of the Attic drachma which was common currency in the countries of the Mediterranean in the 4th cent. B.C. In the centre: a seal-impression of the letters *yhd* on a jar-handle from the beginning of the Persian period, which was excavated at Ramat Rahel. This impression was the official emblem of the province and proof of the collection of taxes by the authorities of Yehud. In the bottom picture: a seal-impression reading "*Yehud/Urio*", from Jericho. Urio is apparently none other than Uriah son of Hakkoz, the father of the Meremoth mentioned in Neh. 3 : 4, 21. Meremoth, the son of Uriah the priest, was, in Ezra's day, the Temple treasurer and had charge of the silver and gold donated by the returning exiles to the House of God (Ezra 8 : 33). The seal shows that Meremoth's father, Uriah, had also held a similar position of responsibility in charge of the revenue of the Temple or its treasury. The seal, which was stamped on jars of oil and wine, served as evidence of the tithes and other offerings that were brought to the house of God (cf. Neh. 13 : 12-13).

Aɴᴅ in Ecbatana, the capital which is in the province of Media . . .

(Ezra 6 : 2)

In the reign of Darius I, Tattenai, the governor of the satrapy Beyond the River, wrote a letter to the king, raising the question of the royal sanction for the rebuilding of the Temple (see p. 224). The elders of Judah claimed that this sanction had been granted them by Cyrus, and Tattenai therefore requested that the royal archives be searched for evidence for such a decree. Eventually a scroll from the first year of Cyrus' reign was discovered in Ecbatana, containing what was apparently the official copy of the decree which had been deposited for safe keeping in the imperial archives (see pp. 219 and 226). Ecbatana, where this scroll was found, was the summer capital of the Achaemenid kings, and Cyrus was residing there in the summer months of the first year of his reign over Babylonia, i.e. 538 B.C., at the time when he promulgated his decree concerning Judah. Ecbatana (the Greek form of the Persian *Hangmatana,* in Hebrew *Ahmeta)* was the chief city of upper Media and lay at the junction of several main highways running from Persia to central Asia, the countries bordering on the Caspian Sea, and Mesopotamia. Above is an aerial photograph of the modern town of Hamadan, which occupies the site of Ecbatana. In the middle of the picture is the tell of the ancient city, with the remains of ancient buildings clearly visible.

WITH three courses of great stones and one course of timber ...   (Ezra 6 : 4)

In the scroll which was found at Ecbatana (see p. 225) Darius I not only categorically ordered that "the house be rebuilt, the place where sacrifices are offered and burnt-offerings are brought" (Ezra 6 : 3), but even went so far as to specify the measurements of the new Temple, the vessels that were to be restored to Jerusalem, and the source from which the work was to be financed: "let the cost be paid from the royal treasury" (ibid. 6 : 4). The scroll also lays down the method to be followed in the construction of the Temple — one course of wood to every three courses of heavy stone. This is probably a reference to the beams (usually of cedar of Lebanon) which were inserted at intervals horizontally into the stone walls, to reinforce the whole structure and give it greater stability. Excavation has shown that this method of bulding was practised at Ugarit and in Crete — both of them close to well-wooded areas — as early as the middle of the second millennium B.C. It was also known in Palestine: traces of it have been discovered at Beth-Shan in a building from the end of the Late Bronze Age, and at Megiddo in various structures from the time of Solomon. Some scholars hold that there is a reference to this method of building in the description of Solomon's Temple: "three courses of hewn stone and one course of cedar beams" (1 Kings 6 : 36). This architectural design evidently continued in vogue at the time of the return from the Babylonian captivity, and throughout the period of the Second Temple.
The picture above is a photograph of the remains of Herod's palace at Masada. Charred remnants of wood were found in the space at the bottom of the stones forming the palace-wall, showing that it had once contained courses of timber. The exceptional preservation of these pieces of wood down the centuries is due to the dry climate of the Judean desert.

WITH this money, then, you shall with all diligence buy bulls, rams, and lambs . . . and you shall offer them upon the altar of the house of your God which is in Jerusalem.

(Ezra 7 : 17)

In the "copy of the letter" given by Artaxerxes I, in the seventh year of his reign (458 B.C.), to Ezra the priest and scribe (Ezra 7 : 11), the Persian king lists, amongst other things, the kind of animals that Ezra is to sacrifice on the altar of the House of God in Jerusalem. The Persian kings, who were greatly concerned to win the favour of the gods of other nations, looked upon the performance of the cult of those gods and the accompanying prayer for the well-being of the king and his family as guaranteeing the security of their empire. Darius states this explicitly in his letter to the satrap of the province Beyond the River, dealing with the decree about the rebuilding of the temple: "that they may offer pleasing sacrifices to the God of heaven, and pray for the life of the king and his sons" (ibid. 6 : 10). Rams and sheep are frequently mentioned in the sacrificial passages of the Pentateuch (see Vol. I, pp. 181-182). The ram commonly used for food and sacrifice in those days in Mesopotamia was of the kind known as *Ovis vignei* which is a native of the Asian steppes. The picture above of two rams being brought as tribute to the Persian king is reproduced from the relief adorning the Hall of Pillars of Darius and Xerxes at Persepolis. The two tribute-bearers are inhabitants of Cilicia in Asia Minor. Thick-fleeced rams of this type are still bred to-day in the countries of the East, from central Asia to Palestine.

FOR I was ashamed to ask the king for a band of soldiers
and horsemen to protect us against the enemy on our way . . .
(Ezra 8 : 22)

Since Ezra was setting out from Babylon with the official sanction of king Artaxerxes and his advisors and ministers (Ezra 7 : 27-28), he had every right to request a royal escort on his journey to Judah. This is what was done later by Nehemiah, who made his way from Susa to Jerusalem with the assistance of the satrap of Beyond the River and with an escort of officers and horsemen provided by the king (Neh. 2 : 7-10). Ezra, however, refused to ask for foot-soldiers and cavalry as a demonstration to the king of his trust in God (see Ezra 8 : 22).

Of the various tasks performed by the Persian army none was more important than that of enforcing the king's rule in the satrapies and patrolling the vital lines of communication on which the security of the far-flung empire depended. Since conspiracies and court-intrigues were of frequent occurrence in Persia, the organization and arming of the king's bodyguard were matters of supreme political significance. Median soldiers of the royal guard are seen in the picture above, which is a relief made of glazed bricks on a frieze from the palace of the Persian kings at Susa. The arms that they are carrying were used both in actual fighting and on formal parades. They consist of a bow slung over the shoulder, a quiver of arrows strapped to the back, and a long spear (characteristic of the period) held ceremonially upright in the hand. The bow is of the composite type (see Vol. I. p. 75; Vol. II p. 142) which was perfected into a highly efficient weapon in the Persian period, as can be clearly seen in the illustration. With its ends bent right back towards its central bulge, the composite quality and technical perfection of the bow is evident also in its small size, which made it extremely flexible and easy to handle.

T HEY also delivered the king's commissions to the king's satraps and to the governors of the province Beyond the River . . .   (Ezra 8 : 36)

On their journey from Babylon to Judah, Ezra and his companions carried with them the king's orders to his satraps and provincial governors concerning the donations to the Temple and Ezra's political status (see p. 226). The explicit distinction made here between a Persian satrapy (*ahashdarpana*) and a province *(pahvah)* is historically accurate: the satrapy was the largest single administrative unit of the Persian empire, while the provinces were the smaller districts into which it was subdivided. In Cyrus' reign there were already 20 satrapies. Changes and improvements in this method of imperial administration were made in the time of Darius I (see p. 182). Judah, like Samaria, was part of the fifth satrapy comprising a wide area extending from the river Euphrates to Egypt which had already been called by the Assyrians and Babylonians *ebir nari* — Heb. *eber hanahar* (Beyond the River, i.e. west of the Euphrates). Each satrapy was governed by a satrap (a Greek corruption of the Persian *khshatrapavan*, meaning "protector of the realm"). The satraps had jurisdiction over territories that had formerly been independent kingdoms and in fact behaved, to all intents and purposes, as rulers in their own right. They kept a close watch on the provincial governors, were responsible for law and order within their satrapies, commanded the armies recruited from the inhabitants of the various districts under their rule, kept the roads in good repair, enforced the payment of taxes, and were the supreme judges in the territories under their control. They had the special privilege of being allowed to issue coins in their own name, as is proved by the silver tetradrachm of the satrap Orontas (see the reproduction), the son-in-law of Artaxerxes II, which was minted about the year 360 B.C. at Colophon.

THEN Ezra withdrew from before the house of God, and went to the chamber of Jehohanan the son of Eliashib ...

(Ezra 10 : 6)

Ezra's first act in Jerusalem was to take a firm stand against the prevalent practice of inter-marriage with foreign women and the consequent mingling of "the holy race with the peoples of the land" (Ezra 9 : 2). After a prayer for God's help, he made the people solemnly undertake "to put away these wives and their children" (ibid. 10 : 3). He then issued a proclamation throughout Judah calling on all the returned exiles to gather in Jerusalem to resolve on their complete segregation from the other peoples of the country and the divorce of their foreign wives. Johanan (Jehohanan) the son of Eliashib (who is also mentioned in Neh. 12 : 23) was presumably one of Ezra's assistants and loyal supporters. In Ezra's time (c. 458-456 B.C.) Johanan may not yet have been High Priest, and probably lived in the chamber of his father Eliashib the High Priest in the Temple (cf. Neh. 13 : 28). Johanan is referred to as the High Priest many years later, in the letter sent by the Jews of Elephantine to Bagoas, the governor of Judah, in 408 B.C. (see the reproduction of the papyrus above), requesting him to intervene on their behalf in the matter of the rebuilding of the temple at Elephantine which had been destroyed by Egyptian priests. The writers mention that they had previously sent a letter to Johanan "the High Priest" and his colleagues in Jerusalem, and another to Delaiah and Shelemiah, the sons of Sanballat the governor of Samaria, but had received no reply: "To this day we have been wearing sack-cloth and fasting, making our wives as widows, not anointing ourselves with oil or drinking wine". If, as seems probable, Johanan was appointed High Priest in Nehemiah's day, he must have been a very old man with a long record of service at the time when the Jews of Elephantine appealed to the governor of Judah.

NEHEMIAH

WHY should not my face be sad, when the city, the place of my fathers' sepulchres, lies waste...

(Nehemiah 2 : 3)

In the twentieth year of the reign of Artaxerxes I (445 B.C.), Nehemiah the son of Hacaliah, the king's Jewish cupbearer, asked his brother Hanani and other men who had just come from Judah about the condition of "the Jews that survived, who had escaped exile, and concerning Jerusalem" (Neh. 1 : 1-2). From them he learnt that "the survivors there in the province who escaped exile are in great trouble and shame; the wall of Jerusalem is broken down, and its gates are destroyed by fire" (ibid. verse 3). On hearing this, Nehemiah was at first overcome with grief. Then, as he prayed to God (ibid. verses 5-11), he resolved to rebuild the ruins of Judah and Jerusalem. He found a favourable opportunity of bringing his anxiety and distress to the king's notice and thus obtaining the royal permission to go to Jerusalem and restore it with full official support. Nehemiah did not reveal the full extent of his plans to the Persian king, but contented himself with a modest request: "If it pleases the king ... that you send me to Judah, to the city of my fathers' sepulchres, that I may rebuild it" (Neh. 2 : 5). Nehemiah here purposely stresses the closeness of the ties that bind him to the city in which his ancestors are buried. When the First Temple was still standing, the burial ground in Jerusalem apparently already stretched along the sides of the Kidron Valley, next to the village of Siloam. In Second Temple times it covered a wide area outside the city walls, extending from Sanhedria, across Mount Scopus and the Mount of Olives, to the Kidron Valley on the south-east.

Photographed above is part of the ancient cemetery in the Kidron Valley. In the left centre stands the tomb of the Hezir family (from the 2nd cent. B.C.), and on the right the monument from Herodian times which is popularly known as Zechariah's tomb. Both are hewn out of the natural rock. The tomb of the Hezir family was the burial place of "the priests of the family of Hezir" (in the words of the inscription found on the facade of the tomb); whereas Zechariah's tomb was merely a cenotaph belonging to one of the nearby burial caves, or, according to another view, to the tomb of the Hezir family. The ground at the base of Zechariah's tomb is covered with flat tomb-stones of later date, since in subsequent generations it was considered a special honour to be buried there.

THEN I went up in the night by the valley and inspected the wall; and I turned back and entered by the Valley Gate, and so returned.

(Nehemiah 2 : 15)

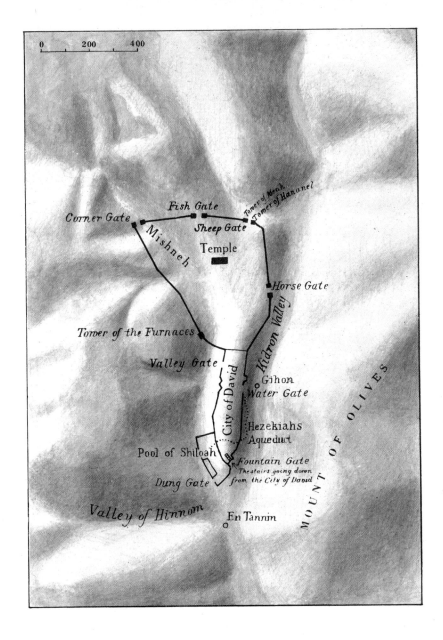

Nehemiah stole out secretly by night, with a few of his followers, to examine the broken wall of Jerusalem and its fire-damaged gates at close quarters. After this reconnaissance, he disclosed his real intentions to the priests, nobles and officials: "You see the trouble we are in, how Jerusalem lies in ruins with its gates burned. Come, let us build the wall of Jerusalem, that we may no longer suffer disgrace" (Neh. 2 : 17). The people responded eagerly to his words, all the more readily as he no doubt told them of the king's favourable attitude to the undertaking. The work of rebuilding the wall began forthwith. As a matter of fact, Nehemiah did not construct an entirely new wall, but merely repaired and strengthened the already existing wall from the time of the First Temple. The descriptions in the Book of Nehemiah thus provide us with a basis on which to reconstruct the course of the pre-destruction wall of Jerusalem (Neh. 2 : 14–17; chap. 3; 12 : 31–41). The city is conjectured (cf. Vol. II, p. 220) to have extended over the area of the eastern hill and the central valley, being bounded on the east by the Kidron Valley, on the south by the valley of Hinnom, on the west by the Tyropoeon valley, and on the north by the wall encircling the Temple. Seven city gates are mentioned in the Book of Nehemiah (see the diagram). The location of these gates makes it possible to reconstruct the line followed by Nehemiah in his reconnaissance of the ruined city. Setting out from the Valley Gate, on the west, he travelled in the direction of the Jackal's Well (apparently En-Rogel) and the Dung Gate; i.e. he skirted round the south-western and southern sides of the city, then climbed south-eastwards to the Fountain Gate and up the sloping bed of the Kidron as far as the King's Pool, on the other side of the King's Garden. From this point onwards the debris lay so thick that the animal on which he was riding could not advance any further (Neh. 2 : 14), so Nehemiah continued on foot along the watercourse, made his way through the ruins of the wall, crossed the City of David from one side to the other, and returned to the point from which he had started.

As far as the stairs that go down from the city of David.
(Nehemiah 3 : 15)

The means for the rebuilding of the wall of Jerusalem, together with its towers and gates, were provided by the leading families in the city and by inhabitants of both the nearby and more distant places in Judah. Priests, nobles, and heads of communities made themselves responsible for erecting different parts of the capital's wall and its gates. One of them, Shallum, the ruler of the district of Mizpah, repaired the Fountain Gate and also rebuilt the wall of the Pool of Shelah, probably the Pool of Siloam (Neh. 3 : 15), which was near "the stairs that go down from the city of David". This description has been strikingly confirmed by the discovery of just such a flight of steps at the south-eastern end of the city of David, next to "the wall of the Pool of Shelah". The steps are cut into the rock at a very steep angle and run diagonally downwards from the city. The whole flight, which is 43 ft. long and approximately 6 ft. wide, leads from the upper part of the city to a gate in the wall, which is apparently the ancient "gate between the two walls" mentioned elsewhere in the Bible (2 Kings 25 : 4; Jer. 39 : 4; 52 : 7; cf. Vol. III, p. 137).

In the photograph above, the remains of the steps can be clearly seen, partly built and partly hewn out of the rock.

Now that which was prepared for one day was one ox and six choice sheep . . . and
every ten days skins of wine in abundance . . .   (Nehemiah 5 : 18)

Nehemiah sharply contrasts his own exemplary probity during his twelve years as governor of Judah with the
extortionate practices of the other nobles and officials (Neh. 5 : 1-13), and also of the former governors who
"laid heavy burdens upon the people" (ibid. verse 15), and declares that, during his whole term of office, "neither
I nor my brethren ate the food of allowance of the governor" (ibid. verse 14). The governors who preceded
him had, as usual with officials appointed by the Persian government, imposed heavy taxes on the people, and
their underlings too had lorded it over the populace, feeding themselves at the latter's expense. Nehemiah's
subordinates, on the contrary, were devoted public servants; and Nehemiah himself defrayed the cost of
entertaining nobles and officials at his table, quite apart from visitors from beyond the borders of Judah
(ibid. verse 17). In a manner reminiscent of the description of "Solomon's provision for one day" (1 Kings
4 : 22-23), Nehemiah enumerates the quantities of food consumed daily at his residence: one bull, six choice
sheep, fowls (see Vol. II, p. 210), and wine. It has been calculated that the meat was sufficient to feed eight hundred
men, and all at Nehemiah's own expense: "Yet with all this I did not demand the food allowance of the governor,
because the servitude was heavy upon this people" (Neh. 5 : 18). The kinds of food mentioned in the verse
above were also served at the table of the Persian emperors. Reproduced above is a relief from the palace of
Artaxerxes II (404-358 B.C.) at Persepolis in which Median and Persian court-attendants are seen bringing a
sheep and wine to the king's table. The last of the group is carrying a wine-skin.

IN it was written, "It is reported among the nations, and Geshem also says it . . ."
(Nehemiah 6 : 6)

The enemies of Judah, led by Sanballat the Horonite, Tobiah the Ammonite, and Geshem (or Gashmu) the Arab (see Neh. 2 : 10, 19; 4 : 1; 6 : 1) joined forces in a concerted effort to interfere with the rebuilding of the wall, and even plotted to assassinate Nehemiah himself. In an "open letter" (perhaps to gain greater publicity) to Nehemiah, they charged him with encouraging the Jews to revolt against the Persian monarch so that he could realize his ambition of making himself king of Judah (Neh. 6 : 5-6). The name Geshem is found in Arabic inscriptions and also appears in a Nabatean inscription in the form Gashmu, as in the Hebrew of our verse here. The reference is apparently to Geshem, the king of Qedar, who ruled at that time over the Arab tribes in the south of Palestine and Trans-Jordan. Since his kingdom extended as far as Wadi Tumilat and was contiguous with the southern border of Judah, he tried to intervene in the internal affairs of the neighbouring country and tilt the balance of power in Jerusalem in his favour. The identity of Geshem the Arab has been settled beyond any shadow of doubt by the discovery of an object dating to the period in question. His name is explicitly mentioned on the inner rim of a silver dish which was found at Tell el-Maskhuta, twelve miles from Ismailia in Egypt (see the reproduction). The inscription on the dish reads as follows: "Which Qainu the son of Geshem the king of Qedar brought as an offering to Han-Ilat". The dish is from the end of the 5th, or the beginning of the 4th cent. B.C. Qainu therefore ruled in about the year 400, which would mean that his father was on the throne in the second half of the fifth century, i.e. in the time of Nehemiah.

MOREOVER in those days the nobles of Judah sent many letters to Tobiah...
(Nehemiah 6 : 17)

Tobiah the Ammonite allied himself with Sanballat the Samaritan and Geshem the Arab (see p. 236) in an effort to undermine Nehemiah's position, and was even ready to resort to actual warfare (Neh. 4 : 7-8). He apparently had great influence in Jerusalem in Nehemiah's time and was supported by many of the nobles of Judah, including his own relatives (Neh. 6 : 18). Tobiah himself belonged to one of the leading families in Judah: he was related to the High Priest and had a chamber in the Temple (Neh. 13 : 4-8). He was probably descended from the Tobiads who were one of the wealthy and distinguished Jewish families that returned from the Babylonian exile in the reign of Darius (Zech. 6 : 10).

Some scholars hold that the Tobiads were an aristocratic family in Gilead already in the time of the First Temple. In Nehemiah's day the family was permanently established in Trans-Jordan from where its influence extended to Jerusalem. The Tobiah of that time may have been a high official in the Persian empire, possibly even the provincial governor of the territory of Ammon (hence perhaps the appellative given him by Nehemiah — "the Ammonite servant", i.e. the king's servant in Ammon; or simply "the Ammonite", Neh. 2 : 10, 19).

Under the rule of the Ptolemies and Seleucids, the Tobiad family played an important part in the social and political life of Judah, and its descendants were amongst the leading Jewish Hellenizers. It controlled an entire principality extending over a large area of southern Gilead in Trans-Jordan, and had officials and mercenary troops at its disposal. The centre of Tobiad power was Tyros (Heb. *Zor* or *Zur*), a fortress on the height of Iraq el-Amir above Wadi es-Sir. Here are the remains of the palace of Tobiah, known to the Arabs as Qasr el-Abd. Close to the palace is the Tobiad tomb, with the name "Tobiah" cut in the rock in Aramaic letters above its entrance (see above). Some scholars date the inscription to the 3rd or 2nd cent. B.C., but others as early as the year 400 or even at the end of the 6th cent. B.C., i.e. in the time of Nehemiah or even in the days of the Return to Zion.

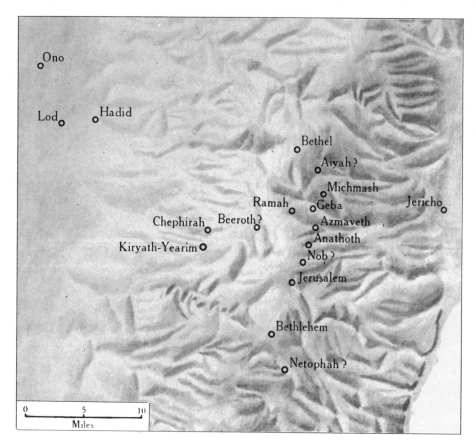

THESE are the chiefs of the province who lived in Jerusalem; but in the towns of Judah every one lived on his property in their towns . . .

(Nehemiah 11 : 3)

From the time of the Return to Zion until Nehemiah's day, the population of Judah steadily increased and more places in the hill country and on the coastal plain were resettled. Indeed, this Jewish resettlement eventually burst the narrow limits of the Persian province to which the first exiles had returned (see this volume, p. 221) and overflowed into other parts of Palestine — into the hill-country of Ephraim, Trans-Jordan, the mountains of Hebron, and even into the Negeb (Neh. 11 : 25-36). Some scholars maintain that, as a result of this expansion, Nehemiah annexed to Judah some regions of the neighbouring provinces. Jerusalem too, which had been a desolate ruin at the time of the Return, now became a well-fortified and well-defended walled city. As part of his efforts to repopulate Jerusalem, Nehemiah transferred one out of every ten of the inhabitants of the outlying settlements, chosen by lot, to the capital (Neh. 7 : 4; 11 : 1). In the generation following Nehemiah, Jerusalem enjoyed considerable economic prosperity and rose to be an administrative and cultic centre. Handles of clay vessels stamped with the letters *YRShLM*, that is, Yerushalem, dating to the beginning of the Hellenistic period and already showing the influence of the Greek *polis*, bear witness to Jerusalem's special status (cf. p. 224).

The map above, on the left, shows the extent of Jewish-occupied territory in Nehemiah's day. The detail on the right is a photograph of a seal-impression which was found in the excavations at Ramat Rahel, just outside Jerusalem. On it can be seen a five-pointed star with five letters, Y-R-Sh-L-M, between the points, together making up the word Yerushalem = Jerusalem.

LACHISH and its fields...
(Nehemiah 11 : 30)

Amongst the cities of the coastal plain resettled in Nehemiah's day were Lachish and its fields, and Azekah and its villages. Lachish occupied a strategic position at the approaches to the Hebron hills, south-west of Beth Govrin, and controlled the main highways running from the hill-country of Judah down to the Mediterranean coast and the south. In the latter part of the Canaanite period, Lachish was a royal city and an important fortress. Later, in the time of the kingdom of Judah, it repeatedly suffered the ordeal of attack, siege and destruction, first in the reign of the Assyrian king, Sennacherib, and then in the days of the Babylonian monarch, Nebuchadnezzar (see Vol. II, pp. 39, 286-287; Vol. III, p. 131). It was finally razed to the ground when the First Temple was destroyed and remained a heap of ruins for about a hundred and fifty years, till it was resettled, together with the other cities of the coastal plain and the Negeb, in Nehemiah's day. Preserved on the site are the remains of a public building of this period, which may have been the residence of the Persian governor. The temple of the sun excavated at Lachish — complete with its square court, small cells, steps and corridors — apparently also belongs to the Persian period. Apart from these two structures, only a few mean houses were uncovered at Lachish dating to the time of the Persian empire.

In the upper photograph — Tell ed-Duweir, the site of Lachish. Below — part of the front of the Persian building discovered in the excavation of the tell, with the steps leading up to it.

MEN of Tyre also, who lived in the city, brought in fish and all kinds of wares and sold them on the Sabbath to the people of Judah, and in Jerusalem.   (Nehemiah 13 : 16)

One of the many problems that Nehemiah had to grapple with, in the territory re-occupied by the returned exiles, was the desecration of the Sabbath by the brisk trade plied, with total disregard for the holiness of the day, by both the inhabitants of Judah and the Tyrians (Neh. 13 : 15-16). These latter, because of their close business connections with the Phoenician coastal cities, were in a position to supply the population of Judah with many of its requirements, and had thus made themselves an influential factor in the country's economy.

The Phoenicians, i.e. the people of Tyre and Sidon, reached the height of their power under the Persian empire. Phoenicia was one of the most important provinces in the satrapy Beyond the River and its chief cities — Tyre, Sidon, and Arvad — then enjoyed greater prosperity than ever before. Granted possession of the coastal cities of Palestine, from Acre to the borders of Gaza, by their Persian overlords, the Phoenicians proceeded to establish commercial colonies all along the Sharon plain and in Philistia. From these cities they conducted a flourishing international barter-trade between the Orient, on the one hand, and Greece and the Aegean islands, on the other. The physical appearance of the Phoenicians, with their characteristic Syrian caps, has been preserved in the art of the Persian period. In the reproduction on the left, a relief from the reign of Darius or Xerxes, found at Persepolis, Phoenicians are seen presenting tribute to the Persian king. The tribute consists of two jars, two bowls and two bracelets. On the right is the head of a Phoenician clay figurine from the Persian period, found in a temple close to Michmash (on the coast near modern Herzliya), which apparently was a Phoenician colony in those times.

ND one of the sons of
Jehoiada, the son of Eliashib
the high priest, was the son-
in-law of Sanballat the
Horonite; therefore I chased
him from me.

(Nehemiah 13 : 28)

In Nehemiah's day, the schism between the Jews and the Samaritans, the first signs of which had appeared
right at the beginning of the Return to Zion, grew wider and deeper. The leaders of the returning exiles —
from Zerubbabel and Jeshua down to Ezra and Nehemiah — refused to have anything at all to do with the
numerically, politically and economically superior Samaritans, let alone agree to unite themselves with them
by alliance or intermarriage. Sanballat, the governor of Samaria, had influentaial connections in Jerusalem,
and the grandson of the High Priest Eliashib was his son-in-law. According to Josephus, the son-in-law was
called Menasseh and Sanballat's daughter Nikaso. In his efforts to root out foreign influences from the household
of the High Priest, which was also related by blood to Tobiah the Ammonite (Neh. 13 : 4-7), Nehemiah
expelled Sanballat's son-in-law from Jerusalem. By this expulsion Nehemiah intended to set up a barrier between
Jews and Samaritans and thus prevent their intermarriage.

From this point onwards the antagonism between the two communities rapidly increased until the Samaritans
repudiated the sanctity of Jerusalem and built their own temple on Mount Gerizim outside Shechem. This
act marked the complete and irrevocable sundering of the two communities: The temple on Mount Gerizim
enjoyed the favour of foreign suzerains from Antiochus Epiphanes onwards and continued in existence long
after its Jerusalem counterpart, being finally destroyed only in the 5th cent. A.D.

The first detailed representation of Mount Gerizim and the temple on it (from Hadrian's time) occurs on a
coin from the reign of Antoninus Pius (86-161 A.D.; see the reproduction). The mount is shown with its two
peaks: the temple is on the left peak and the altar on the right. At the foot of the wooded mount there can be
seen a row of pillars and a sanctuary. A long line of steps (about 1500 of them, according to a Byzantine tradition
from the 4th cent. A.D.) leads right up to the temple, while there is a road for vehicles running up to both peaks.
Part of the row of steps was discovered some years ago.

CHRONICLES

I.

The genealogical lists in the opening chapters of the First Book of Chronicles (chaps. 1-9) record the descent of the leading families, and above all of the priesthood and royal house which were both closely connected with the Temple. The largest amount of space is devoted to the genealogies of Judah (ibid. chaps. 2-4). The author's sole purpose in tracing the family-tree of Judah at such length — see the diagram on the right — was to show the growth and ramification of the tribe and thereby add to the glory of the royal family descended from it. The list of David's descendants enumerates all the kings of Judah and ends with the sixth generation after Zerubbabel the son of Shealtiel, the grandson of King Jehoiakim. This interval of six generations, i.e. roughly 150 years, between Zerubbabel the son of Shealtiel, who was the national leader when the second Temple was being built (520-516 B.C.), and the seven sons of Elioenai listed in 1 Chron. 3 : 24, may be taken to indicate that the Books of Chronicles were edited at the beginning of the 4th cent. B.C. — about one or two generations later than Nehemiah's time.

The Genealogy of David and his Descendants

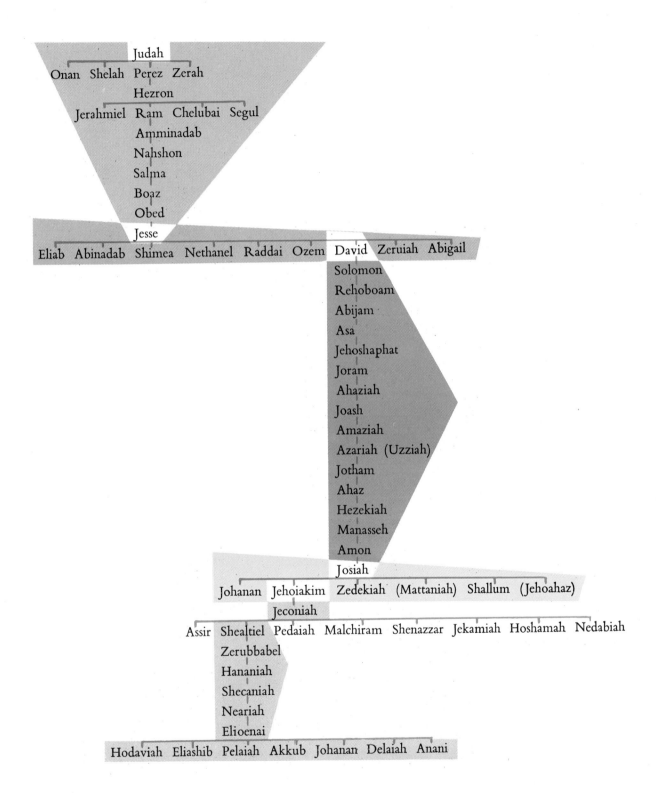

A ND the families of the house of linen workers of Beth-Ashbea.　　　　(1 Chron. 4 : 21)

It may be inferred from this verse that there were in Judah family-guilds of weavers and dyers who traced their descent back to distinguished clan-leaders.

Some scholars hold that Beth-Ashbea is the name, not of a clan-leader, but of a place where families of artisans lived. Other passages in 1 Chron. also tell of families of craftsmen living in special settlements or in special quarters of the various cities. Thus, scribes dwelt at Jabez (ibid. 2 : 55), smiths in Ge-Harashim ("Smiths' Valley") (ibid. 4 : 14), and potters at Netaim and Gederah (see p. 247). Since, therefore, the professional and economic organization of Judah was based mainly on family inheritance, the craftsmen's guilds did not disappear at the beginning of the Second Temple either (Neh. 3 : 8, 31). The archaeological evidence from Tell Beit Mirsim (the biblical Debir?), where a number of dyeing workshops from the 8th cent. B.C., were discovered, confirms what is stated in the Bible about families of craftsmen living in the hill-country of Judah. Reproduced here is a dye-works containing two cylindrical stone vats with, beside them, two oblong storage tanks. At the top of each vat there is a round hole giving access to the inside. From the narrowness of this opening it may be assumed that, in the linen-works at Tell Beit Mirsim, only threads or strands of woven stuff were dyed.

THESE were the potters and inhabitants of Netaim and Gederah; they dwelt there with the king for his work.

(1 Chron. 4 : 23)

Amongst the craftsmen in Judah who were organized in family-guilds (see p. 246), special mention is made of the potters, i.e. the makers of clay vessels. It is expressly stated that they were royal employees and lived in settlements specially established for such: "they dwelt there with the king for his work". Archaeological excavations have confirmed that there were families of potters living in the hill-country of Judah in the time of the Monarchy.

In many Judean tells jar-handles have been found stamped with an emblem above which are inscribed the letters *lammelekh* ("belonging to the king"), and underneath the name of a city in Judah: Hebron, Ziph, Socoh, or Memshat (identification still uncertain). The seal-impressions on these handles are of two different kinds: on some of them the emblem is a four-winged creature like a beetle, whereas on others it has only two wings and is similar to the Assyrian sun-emblem (cf. this volume, p. 25). The former of the two versions appears to be more ancient — from the 8th cent. B.C. —, the latter dating to the end of the Judean Monarchy. As regards the word *lammelekh,* scholarly opinion in divided: one view is that it refers to a measure authorized by the king and that the jars stamped with the word were therefore used as officially sanctioned royal containers; while other scholars hold that the word is the stamp of the royal pottery-works, and that the cities whose names appear on the seal-impressions were centres of the royal pottery industry where potters, such as those mentioned in the verse above, lived.

Reproduced here is a seal, inscribed "belonging to the king, Socoh", which was found in the excavation of one of the Palestinian tells.

So the God of Israel stirred up the spirit of Pul king of Assyria . . .
and he carried them away, namely, the Reubenites, the Gadites,
and the half-tribe of Manasseh . . .   (1 Chron. 5 : 26)

In the reign of Pekah, king of Israel, in the year 733-732 B.C., Pul — i.e. the
Assyrian monarch Tiglath-Pileser III — swept down upon the Northern
Kingdom and conquered the bulk of its territory on both sides of the Jordan,
leaving only the hill-country of Ephraim in the possession of the Israelite
ruler (see Vol. II, pp. 279-281). The purpose of this Assyrian campaign was to
suppress the revolt led by Rezin, the king of Aram, and Pekah (Isa. 7 : 1-9).
Pekah's chief allies in this war were evidently the Gileadites (2 Kings 15 : 25)
and the other inhabitants of Trans-Jordan — the tribes of Reuben and Gad,
and half the tribe of Manasseh — who were renowned from of old as "valiant
men who carried shield and sword, and drew the bow, expert in war" (1 Chron.
5 : 18), and whose genealogy is given in the chapter from which the verse at the
head of this page is taken. These tribes were the first to feel the weight of Tiglath-
Pileser's punitive measures. They were deported, together with their notables
(ibid. verse 6), and the conquered Trans-Jordanian territories were divided up into
three Assyrian provinces: Gilead, which comprised only the northern part of
the region known by that name; Karnaim, with its administrative centre
apparently at the city of Karnaim (to-day Sheikh Saad), near to the ancient
capital Ashtaroth which was destroyed in the fighting; and the Hauran.
An Assyrian relief of Tiglath-Pileser III's time from Calah, part of which is
reproduced below, gives a contemporary picture of this deportation. Prisoners-
of-war from the city of Ashtaroth are here seen being marched off into captivity,
carrying their "exile's baggage" on their backs (cf. Vol. III, p. 167). They are
being hustled along by an Assyrian soldier with a raised cudgel in his hand.
The deportees are wearing long fringed robes and, on their heads, the turban
which was the characteristic headgear of Syria and Palestine in the Assyrian
period. (For the continuation of the relief, showing the city of Ashtaroth, see
Vol. II, p. 49).

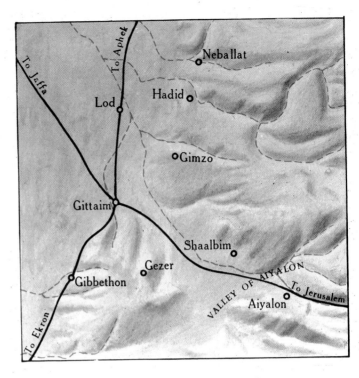

THE sons of Ephraim . . . whom the men of Gath who were born in the land slew, because
they came down to raid their cattle.

(1 Chron. 7 : 20-21)

In the genealogical table of Ephraim, reference is made to the killing of Ephraimites by the men of Gath. The
Gath mentioned here is most probably the same as Gittaim (2 Sam. 4 : 3; Neh. 11 : 33) which lay on the south-
western edge of the territory occupied by the Joseph tribes (see the map). This Gath, or Gittaim, must be
carefully distinguished from the Philistine city of Gath to the south-west of Judah. Gittaim became an important
centre of population on the northern borders of Philistia (1 Sam. 7 : 14) and would seem to have had a non-
Israelite population even in Saul's day (2 Sam. 4 : 3). This is the Gath that was captured by Hazael, king of
Aram, before he began his advance on Jerusalem (2 Kings 12 : 17); and it is also apparently the city whose
fortifications were destroyed by Uzziah, king of Judah (2 Chron. 26 : 6, cf. p. 281). This Gath subsequently
became part of the kingdom of Ashdod and was reduced by the army of Sargon, the Assyrian monarch, in
711-712 B.C.
It seems likely that the site of Gath-Gittaim is to be identified with Tell Ras Abu Hamid, not far from Ramleh
(see the photograph). The tell extends over an area of approximately 50 acres. The sherds found on it testify to
the continuous occupation of the site from the begining of the Iron Age down to the early Arab period, when
it was superseded by the new city of Ramleh. It is of interest to note that, in the Middle Ages, Jewish tradition
identified Ramleh with the biblical Gath-Gittaim.

THESE Gadites were officers of the army ... who crossed the Jordan
in the first month, when it was over-flowing all its banks ...

(1 Chron. 12 : 14-15)

The Book of Chronicles is lavish in its praise of the Gadites who crossed the Jordan in order to join the fugitive
David's roving bands in the wilderness of Judah. With their lion-hearted courage and gazelle-like fleetness of
foot (1 Chron. 12 : 8), they crossed the Jordan at the hardest and most dangerous time of the year, in the first
month, when the river was in flood.

In spring, the Jordan overflows its banks and is particularly difficult to cross (Josh. 3 : 15). The melting of the
snows on the Hermon at the end of winter replenishes the sources of the Jordan, which rise at the foot of the
mountain, and the river begins to rush in spate down its tortuous course. It is still further swollen by torrents of
water that come racing down into it from its numerous tributaries in the mountains to the east and west, the
chief of which is the largest of them all — the Yarmuk river. At the beginning of spring the Jordan overflows
and floods "the pride of the Jordan", i. e. the strip of wooded land on either side of it (see Vol. I, p. 244;
Vol. II, p. 24).

The photograph above shows the twisting course of the Jordan in the valley of Beth-Shan. Stretching out on
either side of the river is the plain of the Jordan. On the left bank can be seen clumps of trees, the surviving
remnants of "the pride of the Jordan". The right bank has been cleared of trees. In the background are the
mountains of Gilead.

AND David and all Israel went up to Baalah, that is, to
Kiryath-Yearim . . .   (1 Chron. 13 : 6)

One of David's first acts, after he had established his capital in Jerusalem, was to instal the ark of God there, in order to invest the royal city with a special sanctity and thus make it a religious and cultic centre for all the Israelite tribes (see Vol. II, p. 171). Prior to its transference to Jerusalem, the ark had rested in the house of Abinadab on the hill *(gibeah)* of Kiryath-Yearim, on the road leading up to Jerusalem (Josh. 18 : 28). Kiryath-Yearim (the modern village of Abu Ghosh) lay on the border of the territory allotted to the tribe of Judah (ibid. 15 : 9-10), close to a fertile valley and at the junction of roads to Benjamin and Judah. The city was already known as an important Canaanite centre before the Israelite conquest of the country. Then, it was sacred to the cult of Baal, as is indicated by its various alternative names: Baalah (Josh. 15 : 10), Kiryath-Baal (Josh. 18 : 14), Baale-Judah (2 Sam. 6 : 2). At the time of the Israelite conquest, it was part of the confederation of Hivvite cities which offered no resistance to Joshua (Josh. 9 : 17). The name Kiryath-Yearim was presumably given it with reference to the surrounding landscape which was famous for its woods.
The site of the ancient city of "the hill of Kiryath-Yearim" is Tell Deir el-Azhar, north of the modern village of Abu Ghosh. The wooded tell is seen in the centre distance of the photograph above.

THE singers, Heman, Asaph, and Ethan, were to sound bronze cymbals.   (1 Chron. 15 : 19)

According to this verse from the Book of Chronicles, King David appointed the Levites to serve as singers and musicians in the Temple (1 Chron. 15 : 16-19; ibid. chap. 25). Included in their number were the families of Asaph, Heman and Ethan, from whom the psalmists were descended.
Vocal and instrumental music were an integral part of the Temple service. The usual instruments employed were the harp, the lyre, the trumpet and the cymbals. The cymbalists probably led the processions of worshippers round the Temple courts, beating out the step. That is why this task was entrusted to the most distinguished of the Levitical singers who belonged to the families of Asaph, Ethan, and Heman (1 Chron. 6 : 16-32 : 15 : 16-17; 16 : 4-7; 2 Chron. 5 : 12).
Ancient cymbals consisted of a pair of round bronze plates. Because of its flexibility, bronze can produce a high, ringing note of sustained reverberation. The cymbals were fastened to the player's fingers by threads or straps. In the small cymbals reproduced above, which date to the time of the kings of Judah, the holes through which the retaining threads or straps were threaded are clearly visible.

W<small>HO</small> came and encamped before Medeba . . .　　　　　(1 Chron. 19 : 7)

The Ammonites' allies in their battle against David's forces at the approaches to Medeba were the three kingdoms of Aram Zoba, Aram Naharaim and Maacah. The Arameans hurried to the aid of the Ammonites, in order to bring Trans-Jordan within their own sphere of influence and check the expansion of David's kingdom. The wide plain near Medeba, which lies south of Rabbath-Ammon (see the map in Vol. II, p. 175), was evidently deliberately chosen by the Ammonites as the scene of the main engagement, since it enabled them to throw their numerous chariot force and large masses of foot-soldiers into the battle (1 Chron. 19 : 7; cf. Vol. II, p. 176). Medeba, one of the most important cities of Moab, had been conquered by the Amorites before the time of Moses and Joshua (Num. 21 : 30), and was then wrested from the Amorites by the Israelites. After the Israelite conquest, the city was included in the territory allotted to the tribe of Reuben. On the death of David, it reverted to Moabite sovereignty, until Omri reconquered it, together with the surrounding region, as related in the inscription of the Moabite king, Mesha: "And Omri took possession of the land of Medeba". However, after the death of Ahab, Mesha succeeded in regaining the whole area for Moab. Because of the fertility of the surrounding district and the position occupied by the city on the main highway in Trans-Jordan — the "King's Highway" — Medeba retained its importance throughout the time of the Second Temple and the Roman and Byzantine periods. Above is a general view of the modern town of Madaba which occupies the site of the biblical Medeba.

THERE arose war with the Philistines at Gezer . . .   (1 Chron. 20 : 4)

In a series of battles fought out in the Valley of Rephaim near Bethlehem, in the approaches to the central hill-region, and in the coastal plain, David established his superiority over the Philistines and "smote them from Geba to Gezer" (2 Sam. 5 : 25; cf. 1 Chron. 14 : 16). Founded in the fourth millennium B.C., Gezer was one of the most important of the royal cities in Canaan. In the Late Canaanite period it controlled an extensive territory in the northern Shephelah. This fortified city, which stood at the junction of the main highways running from south to north of the country and from the coast to the central hills, was not conquered by the Israelite tribes during their occupation of Canaan, even though its king, Horam, suffered a crushing defeat at Joshua's hands (Josh. 10 : 33). Since it was the key strategic point in the coastal plain on the borders of Philistia, it is hardly surprising that one of the decisive engagements between David and the Philistines was fought there.

In Solomon's time, Gezer was captured by the Pharaoh of the day and presented by him "as dowry to his daughter, Solomon's wife" (1 Kings 9 : 16). The city was re-fortified, on account of the strategic position that it occupied on the highway to Jerusalem (ibid. verse 17). After Solomon's death, Gezer was laid waste by the Egyptian Pharaoh Shishak and seems never to have recovered its former importance throughout the period of the Israelite Monarchy. The archaeological finds made on the site indicate that the city achieved a degree of renewed prosperity in the Persian period; and in Hasmonean times it was the second most important fortified centre in the country, after Jerusalem.

Photographed above is Tell Jezar (Gezer) in the northern Shephelah, the site of the biblical Gezer, as is proved not only by the similarity of the names, but also by the bi-lingual inscriptions from the time of the Second Temple found incised on stones in various places in the vicinity of the ancient settlement. From the wording of these inscriptions — *tehum gezer* — it is clear that they mark the limits of the area within which the carrying of objects was permitted on the Sabbath. The excavations carried out on the site confirm the biblical evidence about the city's greatness in the Canaanite period and in the time of Solomon.

Now Ornan was threshing wheat ... (1 Chron. 21 : 20)

According to the story told in 1 Chron. 21 and 2 Sam. 24, the plague afflicting the Israelites was stayed, after David had built an altar on the threshing-floor of Araunah (Ornan) the Jebusite in Jerusalem and sacrificed burnt-offerings and peace-offerings on it (see Vol. II, p. 198). When David came to the threshing-floor, Ornan "was threshing wheat", an expression which may mean either that he was actually taking part in the work or merely supervising the labourers.

In antiquity threshing was done in two stages. First, the grains were extracted from the ears of corn by one of two methods — either by beating them, or by treading them out under human feet or animals' hooves. Then, the chaff was separated from the grain by winnowing it in the wind (cf. Vol. III, p. 220; and this volume, p. 21)

The picture reproduced below — a painting from the tomb of Menna in Egypt, from the Eighteenth Dynasty — illustrates the ancient method of threshing by the treading out of the grain under the hooves of animals. The two men standing on the ricks are raking the corn with their forks under the hooves of four oxen whose necks are yoked together. A third labourer is guiding the oxen and urging them on.

H E set stonecutters to prepare dressed stones ...   （1 Chron. 22 : 2）

The Book of Chronicles has a great deal to say about the preparations made by David, towards the end of his life, for the building of the Temple (see p. 259). He assembled the building materials (1 Chron. 22 : 2-3), chose the special craftsmen (ibid. verse 15), and took on stonecutters from amongst the resident aliens (meaning, apparently, the Canaanites living within the confines of his kingdom). Archaeological finds in Palestine have shown that Solomon subsequently used dressed stones or ashlars not only in the construction of the Temple, but for other public buildings of his as well.

This use of carefully shaped and well dressed stone in the latter days of David's reign and in the time of Solomon was a definite innovation in Israel. The distinguishing feature of ancient Israelite stone-work was the wide margin cut by the masons along three edges of the block, leaving an undressed boss in the centre (cf. Vol. II, p. 237).

Reproduced above is part of the city-gate of Megiddo from Solomon's time. It is built of dressed stone.

THE first lot fell to Jehoiarib, the second to Jedaiah, the third to Harim, the fourth to Seorim ... The twenty-fourth to Maaziah.

(1 Chron. 24 : 7-8, 18)

According to the Book of Chronicles, the priests were, in David's time, divided up into twenty four families, each of which in turn officiated at the service of the Temple for one week — from Sabbath to Sabbath. When the rota was completed, it began again from the beginning. Thus every family officiated for two weeks (but not consecutively) in the course of a year. On the three pilgrim festivals (Passover, Pentecost and Tabernacles) all the priests were on duty together.

This priestly rota of duty was a permanent institution in Second Temple times, and is also one of the basic elements in the doctrine of the Qumran sectaries whose writings have recently been discovered in the Judean desert. One of these fragments contains a list of the main festivals of the year, together with the names of the courses of priests officiating at them. The priestly families mentioned are those of Joiarib, Jedaiah, Maoziah, Seorim, Jeshua; and, altogether, the list, fragmentary though it is, appears to be identical with that in the chapter of Chronicles from which the verse at the head of this page is taken. The only difference is that, instead of the twenty four courses of priests known to us from the Bible and Rabbinical literature, the writings of the Judean sect refer to twenty six such courses, in accordance with the sect's own peculiar calendar. There are grounds for believing that such priestly rota-schedules were in use in other circles, besides the sectaries of the Judean desert. On a fragment of an inscription (see the reproduction) discovered at Caesarea, the following numerical sequence is preserved: "the fif[teenth cour]se, the sixtee[nth co]urse, the seve[nteenth c]ourse". It may plausibly be conjectured that the missing parts of the inscription listed the names of the priestly courses in the order of their officiation. The organization of the priesthood in courses continued for hundreds of years after the destruction of the Second Temple. Indeed, the allegiance of the priests to their particular courses was so strong that each course settled separately in its own special district in Galilee. The list of these settlements has been preserved in several liturgical poems from the 6th and 7th cents. A.D.

THESE divisions of the
gatekeepers . . .
(1 Chron. 26 : 12)

Besides the singers and musicians appointed by David (see above, p. 252), mention is also made of divisions of gate keepers. According to the Book of Chronicles, the various gates of the Temple were assigned to the various families of gatekeepers by lot. Twenty four watchmen a day, each standing at his appointed station, were required to guard the entrances to the House of the Lord: six on the east side, six on the west (four on the road and two on the *parbar*), four on the north, and four on the south, with the remaining four outside the treasury or "storehouse" (1 Chron. 26 : 12-19).

According to this passage (ibid. verse 1), the gatekeepers were Levites entrusted with the special office of guarding the entrances to the Temple. This office was handed down from father to son. In the time of the First Temple, by contrast, there is mention of priests "who guarded the threshold" (2 Kings 12 : 9). Their duty was also, apparently, to guard the entrances to the Temple, and it too was passed on by inheritance from father to son. Gatekeepers of this kind were a regular institution in the ancient East. The picture reproduced above — part of a tomb-painting of Neferrompet from the time of Ramses II (13th cent. B.C.) — illustrates the functions of the gatekeeper in an Egyptian temple. Two men with yokes on their shoulders are standing waiting outside the gate of the temple of Amon. The gatekeeper is walking towards them. In his hand he holds a whip as the sign of his authority.

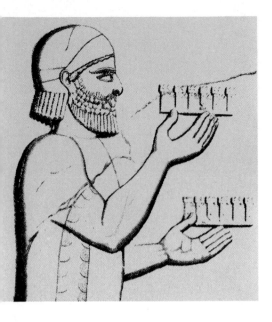

THEN David gave Solomon his son the plan of the vestibule of the temple, and of its houses...

(1 Chron. 28 : 11)

The Temple building, the foundations of which were laid in the fourth year of Solomon's reign (1 Kings 6 : 1), had been planned, according to the Book of Chronicles, down to the last detail by King David towards the end of his life. The plan given by David to Solomon included the various structures comprising the Temple: the vestibule, the upper rooms, the treasuries, the courts, the inner chambers, the room for the mercy seat, and also the proposed design for the cherubim (1 Chron. 28 : 11-18). In our verse here, so far from boasting that the plan is his own handiwork, David expressly tells his son: "All this... by the writing from the hand of the Lord concerning it, all the work to be done according to the plan" (ibid. verse 19).

The ancient kings of Mesopotamia were accustomed to glorying in the temples erected by them in honour of the gods. Thus Gudea, the ruler of the city of Lagash (21st cent. B.C.), proudly recounts in one of his inscriptions how, in his great wisdom, he built the temple of Ningirsu, the god of Lagash, how he collected materials for the structure from the four corners of the earth, and how he took part in the work of building with his own hands. This temple, so Gudea states, was erected at the express bidding of Ningirsu, who actually showed him the plan of it incised on a tablet made of precious stone. It is actually this plan of the temple, engraved on the knees of a statue of Gudea, which bears witness to the king's achievement (see the illustration below). Another form of architectural planning is known to us from the relief of the Assyrian monarch Sargon II. The upper picture shows two models of a fortified city, apparently made of silver or gold, being presented to the king as tribute.

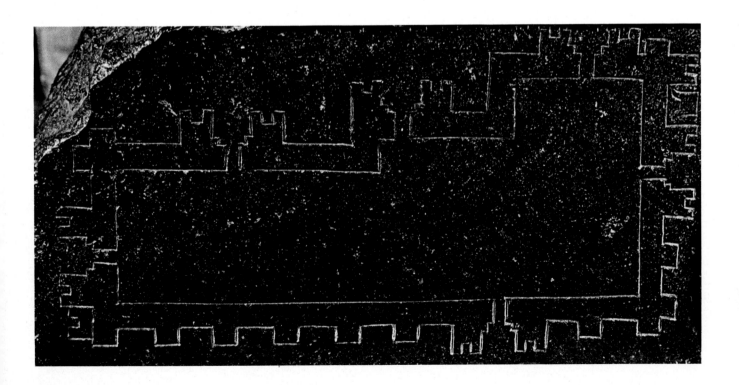

THREE thousand talents of gold, of the gold of Ophir . . .   (1 Chron. 29 : 4)

According to the Book of Chronicles, the leaders of the people had already in David's lifetime donated such varied materials as gold, silver, bronze, iron and precious stones for the Temple that was to be built in Jerusalem (1 Chron. 29 : 1-8). Gold of Ophir, of which the talents contributed to the Temple were made, was particularly high-quality gold, so called from its place of origin (Isa. 13 : 12; Ps. 45 : 9; Job 28 : 16). The various Hebrew words used for gold in the Old Testament — *zahab, paz, haruz, ketem* — like their counterparts in other ancient languages, indicate different grades of the metal, according to its purity, the extent to which it had been refined, its colour, and its various admixtures. The origin of the gold, as an indication of its quality, is also occasionally specified in Egyptian documents, in a manner similar to its designation in our verse here as "gold of Ophir". The location of the land of Ophir, from which King Solomon imported gold and precious stones (1 Kings 9 : 23; 10 : 11; 2 Chron. 8 : 18; 9 : 10) is uncertain. Some scholars would place it somewhere in India or in East African Somaliland, while others identify it with the country of Punt which is mentioned in Egyptian sources. (cf. Vol. II, p. 224).

Reproduced above is an inscription on a potsherd of the 8th or 7th cent. B.C., found at Tell Qasileh on the bank of the Yarkon river, in which gold of Ophir is explicitly mentioned. The translation of the Hebrew wording runs as follows: "Gold of Ophir to Beth Horon, thirty shekels", which is evidently a reference to a sum of thirty shekels of gold of Ophir sent to Beth Horon, the well known ancient settlement on the road to Jerusalem.

II. CHRONICLES

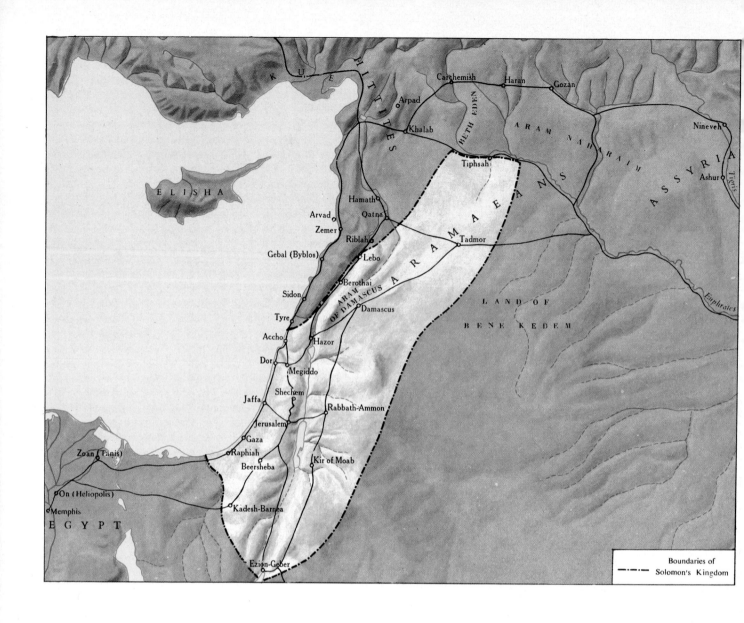

A ND Solomon's import of horses was from Egypt and Kue, and the king's traders received them from Kue for a price. They imported a chariot from Egypt for six hundred shekels of silver, and a horse for a hundred and fifty; likewise through them these were exported to all the kings of the Hittites and the kings of Syria. (2 Chron. 1 : 16-17)

As ruler of an empire extending "from the Euphrates... to the border of Egypt" (1 Kings 4 : 21) King Solomon controlled the main roads leading from the land of the Nile to Mesopotamia and Anatolia (see map on the left). He entered into commercial relations with the Aramean kingdoms and neo-Hittite states, with Tyre and Sidon, and with Egypt and the countries of the Arabian peninsula (cf. Vol, II, p. 227). Our verse here (cf. 1 Kings 10 : 28) indicates that, in his reign, Palestine, as the land-bridge between Africa and Asia, became an important centre on the international trade routes. Solomon's merchants bought horses in Kue (i.e. Cilicia in Asia Minor) and transported them to Egypt; while from Egypt they bought chariots to be sold in the lands of the north. Our verse has even preserved the contemporary prices: six hundred shekels of silver for a chariot, and one hundred and fifty for a horse. In this way, Solomon was able to build up an imposing chariot force, such as was usual in the armies of antiquity, and to make Palestine a factor of international importance in the trade in horses and chariots. The animals in question were, apparently, the famous war-horses of Asia Minor which was the breeding-ground of pedigree steeds. As for chariots, the highly developed chariot-making industry of Egypt, in the second millennium B.C., was renowned throughout the ancient world for the quality of its products (see Vol. II, p. 122).

The upper picture is a relief of a typical Anatolian horse, with short legs and long tail and mane, from the 8th or 7th cent. B.C. Below it is an Egyptian chariot, made of wood and gilded leather (beginning of the 14th cent. B.C.). This type of chariot was fast and easy to manoeuvre.

AND we will cut whatever timber you need from Lebanon, and bring it to you in rafts to the sea of Joppa . . .

(2 Chron. 2 : 16)

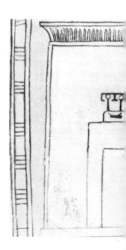

With the help of the workmen sent him by Hiram, king of Tyre, Solomon obtained cedar and cypress from Lebanon for the building of the Temple (see Vol. II, p. 212). The timber was transported in the form of rafts which were tied together and towed by ships to "the sea of Joppa". However, since Joppa and its port were at that time in Philistine hands, the rafts were apparently propelled into the estuary of the Yarkon, anchored in deep water, and then unloaded on the river bank near the important city which in antiquity occupied the site of Tell Qasileh. This city, the ancient name of which is unknown, lay on the northern bank of the Yarkon, just over one mile inland from the sea. From there Solomon's workmen brought the logs overland to Jerusalem.

Rafts of the kind used by Solomon are illustrated in a relief from Khorsabad dating to the reign of the Assyrian king, Sargon II (see the reproduction above). The boats seen here are of the same type as the rounded Phoenician merchant vessels which were dubbed by the Greeks "horse-ships", on account of their horse-headed prow (cf. Vol. II, p. 222; and see also Vol. III, p. 228) The six merchant vessels in the picture are being propelled by oars pulled by slaves sitting in rows, one behind the other, on either side of the ship. Two of the vessels are sailing-ships, as is clearly indicated by the mast in their centre. They are all towing rafts of logs. The water between the rafts is alive with fishes and other sea-creatures.

AND he stored the silver, the gold, and all the vessels in the treasuries of the house of God.

(2 Chron. 5 : 1)

When the work of building the Temple was completed, Solomon brought "the things which David his father had dedicated" into the treasuries of the house of God (2 Chron. 5 : 1). The objects referred to here may have consisted of spoils taken in war and also of tribute from vassal states, like that paid by Toi, king of Hamath — vessels of silver, gold and copper — all of which David dedicated to his God. The Israelite kings were in the habit of storing silver, gold and vessels in the Temple treasuries to be used for national needs in time of emergency, and even for payment of bribes or tribute to other kingdoms (cf. 1 Kings 14 : 26; 15 : 18-20; 2 Kings 16 : 7-9; 18 : 14-17) These reserves were kept in special deposit-rooms. David's plan of the Temple (see p. 259) already made provision for chambers "for the treasuries of the house of God, and the treasuries for dedicated gifrs" (1 Chron. 28 : 12).

Treasuries of this kind were a common feature of temples in the ancient East. Seen in the picture below — a tomb-painting of Rekhmire at Thebes in Egypt, from the 15th cent. B.C. — is the treasury of provisions of the temple of Amon, where the offerings brought by the god's worshippers, and also by representatives of subject peoples, were deposited. The offerings, which are stored in three sets of shelves, consist of the following articles (from right to left, and from top to bottom): in the first set — baskets of grapes, sandals, woven materials sacks of fruit, jars of wine; in the second set — products of Nubia: ostrich-feathers, leather shields, ivory tusks, silver, gold-dust and rings of gold; in the third set — precious stones (in two rounded heaps), linen, incense and spices in jars, and, to the left of them, rings of silver and gold. At the bottom of the pile there are ingots of copper.

In his prayer on the completion of the Temple in Jerusalem, Solomon dwells on its function as a place of supplication to God, alike for the single individual and the whole community, in such ordeals as war, drought, famine, plague, captivity and deportation (see Vol. II, p. 218). Included in this list of tribulations is the locust, one of the most terrible natural disasters of antiquity, against which no human agency was of any avail and from which man could hope to be delivered only by divine mercy (see Vol. III, pp. 224-225).

It was customary in antiquity to try to forestall the locust menace by prayer and entreaty to the gods. Reproduced above is a painting on a glazed brick, which was found in a private house in the city of Ashur (from the 9th cent. B.C.), showing a nobleman standing before the god Ashur and entreating him to ward off the depredations of the locust from his land. To the right of the head of the god, who is standing on a small podium, can be seen the emblems of three other deities: Shamash, Sin and Ishtar. The locust painted above the head of the nobleman, whose hands are raised in supplication, indicates the content and meaning of his prayer.

THE king also made a great ivory throne, and overlaid it with pure gold.   (2 Chron. 9 : 17)

In the course of its detailed inventory of King Solomon's great wealth in gold, silver, ivory and precious stones (2 Chron. 9 : 9-20), the Book of Chronicles here (ibid. verse 18) describes the construction of the ivory throne, overlaid with gold. This throne had six steps, a footstool, and an arm-rest on either side, each supported by a lion couchant (cf. the throne of a Canaanite king depicted on the ivory tablet from Megiddo which is reproduced in Vol. II, p. 45). The term "ivory throne" apparently refers to the ivory carvings with which it was inlaid, in the usual manner of Syrian art (cf. Vol. II, p. 251). Royal thrones of this kind were well known in antiquity. Ashurnasirpal II, king of Assyria, received ivory thrones overlaid with gold as a gift from the king of Aram; and Hezekiah, king of Judah, according to the evidence of Sennacherib's prism, also sent ivory thrones as tribute to the king of Assyria (see p. 285). It is, therefore, not surprising that Solomon should have followed the practice of other ancient monarchs and made himself a magnificent throne after the Syro-Phoenician manner. Solomon's throne occupies a place of unique importance in the later Jewish legend glorifying the splendour of his court and the grandeur of his achievements.

Reproduced above is an ornamental throne on a stone relief from the palace of Sargon II at Khorsabad (721-705 B.C.). This particular relief is one of a long series portraying a royal procession, in which various regal appurtenances were borne aloft on display. Two court-attendants are here carrying the king's throne which is adorned with the figures of four gods under the left arm-rest and a larger figure, perhaps representing the god Ashur, on the back.

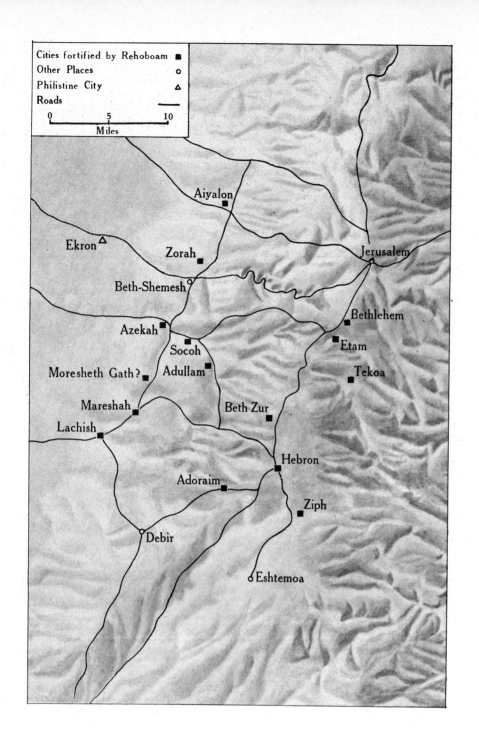

Cities fortified by Rehoboam ■
Other Places ○
Philistine City △
Roads ▬

0   5   10
Miles

Aiyalon

Ekron △

Zorah

Jerusalem

Beth-Shemesh ○

Bethlehem

Azekah

Etam

Socoh

Moresheth Gath? Adullam

Tekoa

Mareshah

Beth Zur

Lachish

Hebron

Adoraim

Ziph

Debir ○

Eshtemoa ○

Rᴇʜᴏʙᴏᴀᴍ dwelt in Jerusalem, and he built cities for defence in Judah. (2 Chron. 11 : 5)

With the division of the Monarchy (see Vol. II, p. 229), the sovereignty of the Davidic dynasty was restricted to the territory of the two tribes, Judah and Benjamin, which remained loyal to it. The first kings of Judah, Rehoboam and his son Abijah, refused to accept the defection of the Northern Kingdom as a fait accompli; indeed, at the end of Rehoboam's reign, the Judeans actually invaded the realm of Jeroboam king of Israel, in an attempt to regain the southern part of the hills of Ephraim by force (see below, p. 270). When Rehoboam set about organizing the defence of his kingdom, he did not build any fortifications on its northern border but only on the west and south, the directions from which Judah was open to attack from Egypt (see p. 269). Thus, the Book of Chronicles refers to the strengthening of many cities in the hill-country and the Shephelah (the "cities for defence" or "fortified cities" of 2 Chron. 11 : 5, 10) : Bethlehem, Etam, Tekoa, Beth-Zur, Hebron, Socoh, Adullam, Adoraim, Ziph, Lachish, Azekah, Mareshah, Zorah, and Aiyalon (see the map). Rehoboam placed these cities under the command of special officers, equipped them with weapons ("shields and spears"), and saw to it that they were supplied with "stores of food, oil, and wine" (2 Chron. 11 : 11). At the same time, apparently in order to ensure the cities' loyalty, he followed the customary ancient practice of placing his sons in important positions in them: "And he dealt wisely, and distributed some of his sons through all the districts of Judah and Benjamin, in all the fortified cities" (ibid. verse 23).

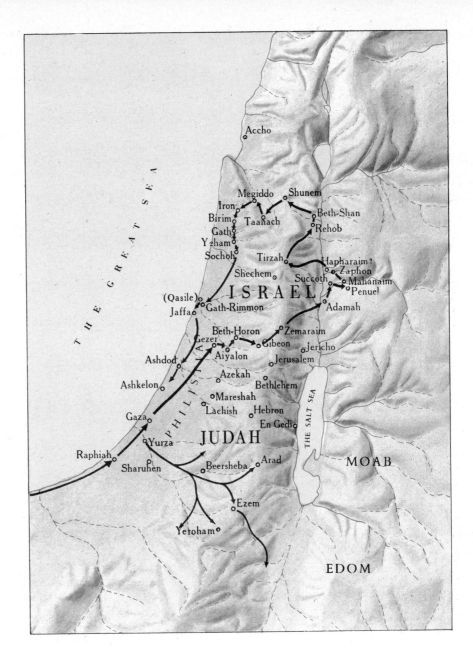

IN the fifth year of King
Rehoboam ... Shishak
king of Egypt came up
against Jerusalem with
twelve hundred chariots
and sixty thousand horse-
men. And the people
were without number
who came with him from
Egypt — Libyans, Sukki-
im, and Ethiopians.

(2 Chron. 12 : 2-3)

Shishak advanced on Jerusalem in the fifth year of Rehoboam's reign, after reducing "the fortified cities of Judah". The capital was saved the ordeal of siege and subsequent destruction by Rehoboam's submission to the Egyptian king and the heavy tribute that he paid to his overlord. In his own inscription, Shishak (see Vol. II, p. 232), the Pharaoh of the Libyan (Twenty Second) Dynasty, makes no mention of his battles, but the list of cities given there indicates the extent of the havoc and destruction which Palestine suffered at the time. From this list it transpires that Shishak penetrated into the country along the coastal strip, the brunt of his attack being directed against the key-cities in the kingdom of Jeroboam the son of Nebat. The direction of his advance is clearly shown on the map above: from the Shephelah, by way of Gezer — Aiyalon — Beth-Horon — Gibeon, to the hill-country of Benjamin and Ephraim; thence to Adamah on the Jordan, and from there on to the main centres of Trans-Jordan — Succoth (Tell Deir Alla), Penuel (Tell el-Hammah), and Mahanaim (Tulul edh-Dhahab on the river Jabbok). Shishak then turned back to the hill-country of Ephraim, to Tirzah, one of the main centres of population in Jeroboam's time (Tell el-Farah?); and from there continued his advance to the cities of the Jordan Valley and the Jezreel Valley which straddled international lines of communication — Rehob, Beth-Shan, Shunem, Taanach, Megiddo — returning thence to Philistia and Egypt by way of Iron and the Sharon and Shephelah costal plains. The archaeological evidence from such important cities of ancient Palestine as Gezer, Megiddo, Beth-Shan, Gath-Rimmon (Tell Jerisheh?), Tell Qasileh on the Yarkon and others, confirms that they were partially or completely destroyed at this time. During Shishak's advance into the kingdom of Israel his forces made a lightning descent upon the Negeb, where they captured some of the principal fortified settlements, in order to secure the southern flank of the main army in its invasion of Judah and Israel (see the map).

AND the priests blew the trumpets.   (2 Chron. 13 : 14)

At one point during the fighting between Jeroboam, king of Israel, and Abijah, king of Judah when the Judean forces were in great danger "for behold, the battle was before and behind them" (2 Chron. 13 : 14), they "cried to the Lord" while the priests blew on the trumpets. The trumpet (Heb. *hazozrah*) was one of the musical instruments used in the Temple (see, e.g. 2 Chron. 5 : 13) and played an important role in the ceremonial celebration of festivals and solemn occasions. In war-time, its function was to rouse the nation's fighting spirit and to proclaim God's deliverance of His people from their foes: "And when you go to war in your land against the adversary who oppresses you, then you shall sound an alarm with the trumpets" (Num. 10 : 9).

Trumpets were similarly employed throughout the ancient East, especially in Egypt (see Vol. I, p. 206). They were valuable instruments made of metal, usually silver, and were kept in a special wooden case. Two of these instruments were found intact in the tomb of Tutankhamon in Egypt. They consist of a long, straight tube which widens out into a funnel-shaped opening at the end.

Reproduced above is a relief from the temple of Ramses III at Medinet Habu in Egypt, dating to the 12th cent. B.C. It shows two trumpeters blowing on their trumpets at the head of a procession of army officers or government officials, and at the same time bending forwards in respectful greeting of the Pharaoh who is marching out to war.

AND Abijah pursued Jeroboam, and took cities from him, Bethel with its villages and Jeshanah with its villages and Ephron with its villages. (2 Chron. 13 : 19)

Abijah the son of Rehoboam, who became virtual ruler of Judah still in his father's lifetime (2 Chron. 11 : 22), waged constant war against the kingdom of Israel and succeeded in defeating its king, Jeroboam, and extending the frontiers of Judah to the north. Mentioned amongst the cities taken by Abijah from Jeroboam is Bethel, which stood close to the border between Judah and Israel, on the site now occupied by the Arab village of Beitin, about 10 miles north of Jerusalem on the main road into the hills of Ephraim (see Vol. I, p. 79). The other two cities listed amongst Abijah's conquests lay to the north of Bethel: Jeshanah, to-day Burj el-Isaneh, just over five miles away; and Ephron, or Ophrah (1 Sam. 13 : 17), to-day et-Tayibeh, a little more than four miles north-east of Bethel. Abijah's conquests thus comprised the southern part of the hill-country of Ephraim which, according to Josh. 18 : 21-24, was considered part of the tribal territory of Benjamin.

Bethel had an ancient tradition of sanctity going back to the days of the Patriarchs and the Judges. Under Jeroboam it became the main religious centre of the Northern Kingdom, rivalling Jerusalem. Abijah's conquest of Bethel thus had the effect of restoring Jerusalem's former supremacy as the one and only holy city. This conquest, however, was of short duration: in Baasha's reign Bethel was recovered by Israel. In the following generations, during the reigns of the dynasties of Omri and Jehu, the city retained its specially holy status, and in the time of Jeroboam II it is called by the priest Amaziah "the king's sanctuary" and "a temple of the kingdom" (Amos. 7 : 13). After the destruction of Samaria, Bethel continued to serve as a sanctuary (2 Kings 17 : 28), till Josiah, king of Judah, gained control of it and pulled down its high places (ibid. 23 : 15). Bethel shared in the general destruction of Judah by the Babylonians, but was subsequently rebuilt at the time of the Return to Zion.

Above is a general view of the Arab village of Beitin which stands on the site of ancient Bethel.

AND the Ethiopians fell until none remained alive . . .   (2 Chron. 14 : 13)

According to the Book of Chronicles, Zerah the Cushite (the Ethiopian) advanced on Asa, king of Judah, "with an army of a million men and three hundred chariots" (2 Chron. 14 : 9) and penetrated into Judah as far as Mareshah. The narrative continues: "And Asa cried to the Lord his God . . . So the Lord defeated the Ethiopians . . . Asa and the people that were with him pursued them as far as Gerar . . . And they smote all the cities round about Gerar, for the fear of the Lord was upon them . . . And they smote the tents of those who had cattle, and carried away sheep in abundance and camels. Then they returned to Jerusalem" (ibid. 14 : 11-15). The details of this historical event are obscure. One explanation is that the biblical text refers here to a Nubian prince who ruled over the region around Gerar, perhaps with Egyptian protection, and from this base tried to conquer areas of the kingdom of Judah. On the other hand, Zerah may have been no more than the leader of semi-nomad Negeb tribes who are referred to as Cushites in Egyptian documents from as early as the 19th cent. B.C. These tribes were racially akin to the Midianites (see Num. 12 : 1; and cf. Ex. 2 : 15-21); and there may also be an allusion to them in Habbakuk 3 : 7: "the tents of Cushan . . . the curtains of the land of Midian", and in 2 Chron. 21 : 16: "And the Lord stirred up . . . the anger of the Philistines and of the Arabs who are near the Ethiopians". However that may be, the tradition about Zerah's possession of a strong chariot-force testifies to his political connections with Egypt, since mere nomads were too poor to be able to purchase war-chariots.

Reproduced above is a relief from Khorsabad, belonging to the reign of Sargon II, which is the only Assyrian relief so far discovered portraying warfare against Nubians. This battle of Sargon's was fought in 720 B.C., in the vicinity of Raphiah on the Egyptian border. At the right two Assyrian cavalrymen are seen at full gallop, with spears poised for action, trampling on the body of a prostrate negro and striking down another negro who is falling, spear in hand. Standing erect to face their charge is a third negro, with his spear raised. At the left an Assyrian soldier, resting on one knee, is shooting an arrow as his foe. The Nubian soldiers can be recognized as such by their crinkly hair and by their garments, which were characteristic of the inhabitants of Egypt and the neighbouring regions.

EVEN Maacah, his mother, King Asa removed from being queen mother...
(2 Chron. 15 : 16)

Asa, king of Judah, was highly esteemed by the biblical historian, because he did away with the foreign altars and the high places, smashed the sacred pillars, cut down the *asherim,* and in general cleared the whole of Judah and Benjamin, as well as the cities captured by him in the Ephraim hills, of idolatrous abominations (1 Kings 15 : 11-14; 2 Chron. 14 : 1-5; 15 : 8-10). As part of this drive against idol-worship, Asa deposed Maacah from her position as queen-mother, on account of the statue ("the abominable image") that she had erected to Asherah. The reference here is apparently not to the king's own mother, but to his grandmother, the mother of his father, Abijah, and the wife of Rehoboam (1 Kings 15 : 2, 10; 2 Chron. 11 : 20).

The queen-mother, i.e. the mother of the reigning monarch, occupied a position of special importance and influence in the political life of ancient Israel. She was highly respected in court circles and was publicly honoured and deferred to by the king himself (1 Kings 2 : 18-19; Jer. 13: 18; cf. Vol. II, p. 270). Particularly well known for their influence were Jezebel (2 Kings 9 : 22) and Nehushta, the mother of Jehoiachin (ibid. 24 : 8-12; Jer. 29 : 2).

In Assyria too, the king's mother was a political personage of great importance. Two Assyrian queen-mothers have gone down in history because of the decisive part played by them in the management of imperial affairs: Sammuramat, the mother of Adad-Nirari III (810-783 B.C.), and Nakia, the wife of Sennacherib (705-691). Both these women feature in the narratives of the classical historians about the Babylonian empires as Semiramis and Nitocris. Nakia, the more important of the two, was apparently an Aramean or Babylonian (Chaldean) by birth, and her Assyrian name was Zakutu. In the reign of her son Esarhaddon (680-669), Nakia was appointed governor of Babylon and superintended the city's restoration. She also played an influential part in getting her grandson, Ashurbanipal, placed on the Assyrian throne.

Seen behind Esarhaddon in the reproduction above — a bronze relief from the beginning of Esarhaddon's reign which perhaps comes from the temple of Marduk — is his queen-mother. She has a mirror in her right hand while, with her left, she is holding a lotus-flower to her nose.

AND Ben-Hadad hearkened to King Asa, and sent the commanders of his armies against the cities of Israel, and they conquered Iyon . . .   (2 Chron. 16 : 4)

Ben-Hadad I, king of Aram, was first an ally of Baasha, king of Israel. But he was prevailed upon by Asa, king of Judah, to break this alliance and attack the Northern Kingdom. In the course of this armed incursion, he reduced many of Baasha's northern cities (see Vol. II, pp. 233–234), including such important centres as Iyon, Dan, and Abel-Maim (in 1 Kings 15 : 20 Abel Beth-Maacah), thus gaining himself a foothold in the northern part of the kingdom of Israel.

Dan, Abel and Iyon were all fortified cities in the region round the headwaters of the Jordan where they controlled the main lines of communication running into the heart of the Northern Kingdom. Of special strategic importance was Iyon, which is identified with the present-day Tell Dibin, to the north of Merj Ayun (north of Metulla). This tell, which rises to a height of 2300 ft. above sea-level and approximately 1970 ft. above the Hulah Valley, dominates the fertile plain of the Valley of Iyon. Through the narrow defile leading into the valley close by the tell there ran, in ancient times, two important highways : one from the Lebanon valley to the Jordan rift; and the other the road from Phoenicia to Aram Damascus, which skirted round the southern fringe of Mt. Hermon and continued thence to Damascus across the Golan plateau. It is, therefore, not at all surprising that Iyon was, from the earliest times, the key to the control of the northern frontier of Canaan. It is already mentioned in the Egyptian execration texts of the 19th cent. B.C.; and it appears in the list of the campaigns of Thutmose III, from the 15th cent. B.C. It was annexed by David to his kingdom. After the division of the Monarchy, it became a frontier post on the border with Aram and was therefore fated to be one of the first cities conquered by Israel's northern enemies — first Ben-Hadad I of Aram, and later, not long before the destruction of the kingdom of Israel, the Assyrian king Tiglath-Pileser III, (2 Kings 15 : 29).

The photograph below shows the Valley of Iyon (Merj Ayun), with the Lebanon range in the distance.

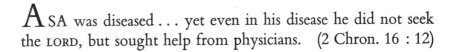

Asa was diseased ... yet even in his disease he did not seek the LORD, but sought help from physicians.   (2 Chron. 16 : 12)

The Book of Chronicles, which portrays King Asa at the beginning of his reign as a pious ruler who "did what was good and right in the eyes of the Lord" (2 Chron. 14 : 2; cf. above, p. 274), is much more critical of his later acts. After a bitter quarrel with the seer Hanani, who came to rebuke him for placing his trust in the king of Aram rather than in the God of Israel, Asa actually began to persecute and oppress some of his subjects (ibid. 16 : 10). The text counts it a further sin on Asa's part that he consulted physicians in his illness. Perhaps Asa sought the treatment of foreign doctors and was thereby obliged to participate in idolatrous rites (see above, p. 115). Ahaziah had, in his day, similarly aroused the wrath of the prophet Elijah by enquiring of Baal-Zebub, the god of Ekron, about his sickness (2 Kings 1 : 2-17). Evidently, in the biblical historian's opinion, Asa should have trusted in the Lord and sought the advice of a prophet, as was done some time later by Hezekiah, king of Judah (ibid. 20 : 11), who displayed exemplary piety in this matter.

Medecine was quite a well developed science in antiquity. Together with magical and ritual measures, the doctors of Mesopotamia and Egypt also made use of healing drugs extracted mainly from plants. The doctors carefully guarded the secrets of their art and usually passed them on only to their sons. The chief progress in medical science was made in Egypt, where the doctors had a long tradition to draw on, and even learnt to perform complicated operations. In the picture above — a tomb-painting of Nebamon from the reign of Amenhotep II (15th cent. B.C.) — a doctor is shown handing medicines from an elongated jar to a prince who is seated on his throne. The doctor is an Egyptian, whereas the prince is Syrian, as is evident from his clothes and those of his entourage.

H<small>E</small> built in Judah
fortresses . . .
(2 Chron. 17 : 12)

The "fortresses" (Heb. *biraniyyoth*) built by Jehoshaphat, king of Judah (871-849 B.C.) were simply strong-points erected at various strategic points in the country, to protect the main highways and safeguard communications between the unwalled villages and the walled cities. Strong-points of this kind have been excavated in our day in Judah and the Negeb, particularly close to the principal ancient roads to Elath and Kadesh-Barnea. The photograph below is of one such fortress in Nahal Raviv, about 30 miles south of Beersheba. The fortress was built on a high hill and is still fairly well preserved. It is encircled by a casemate wall, consisting of two parallel walls with rooms built in between them which were used as stores and living-quarters (see the picture above). The outer wall of the fortress was made of large stones and still rises to a height of 9 ft.

HE appointed judges in the land . . . (2 Chron. 19 : 5)

According to the Book of Chronicles, Jehoshaphat instituted many administrative reforms in the collection of taxes, the organization of the army, and the purification of religious worship. He also completely re-organized the juridical system of the kingdom (2 Chron. 17 : 7-10), appointing judges in all the walled cities of Judah, and setting up in Jerusalem a court of law in which sat certain priests, Levites and heads of clans, presided over by "the chief priest . . . in all matters of the Lord", and by "the governor of the house of Judah in all the king's matters" (ibid. 19 : 5-11). This machinery of justice, supported by officials and Levites, was a powerful instrument in maintaining social order and ensuring the purity of the religious ritual.

A similar legal reform was carried out by the Egyptian king Horemheb at the end of the 14th cent. B.C. In the section of his ordinances reproduced on the right, Horemheb states that he has chosen ordinary citizens and ministers, all well versed in the law, "that they may give judgement in the two Lands of Egypt both the Upper and the Lower, for the good of the population." He too placed these judges in the large cities of his country, gave them laws and statutes, instructed them in their judicial functions, and admonished them against taking bribes and perverting justice. The judges appointed by Horemheb — temple prophets and priests of the gods — became, from then onwards, royal officials whose duty it was to dispense justice to the people wherever they dwelt. This juridical reform strengthened the position of the priests of the god Amon who now became an integral part of the Egyptian legal system.

A</sub>ND she put him and his nurse in a bedchamber . . .   (2 Chron. 22 : 11)

When Athaliah, the daughter of Ahab, wiped out the whole royal dynasty of Judah, Jehoshabeath, the daughter of King Jehoram and wife of the priest Jehoiada, managed to steal the little Joash the son of Ahaziah away from the king's sons as they were awaiting execution (cf. 2 Kings 11 : 1-3). In this way the last descendant of the ruling house was saved. Some time later, Joash was anointed king in a popular revolution led by the priests, the heads of the clans, and the officers of the army (see Vol. II, p. 271). When rescued from Athaliah's murderous clutches, Joash was still an infant. Jehoshabeath hid him with his wet-nurse for six whole years in the bedchamber of the Temple, to which apparently only the priests had access. The nurse evidently became a kind of foster-mother to Joash (cf. above, p. 75), rearing him and giving him his early upbringing. It may be deduced from this that the royal families of antiquity were in the habit of placing their infants in the care of special wet-nurses, as is implied also by the story about the infancy of Moses (Ex. 2 : 7-10).

Reproduced above is a relief from a royal palace at Carchemish, from the first half of the 8th cent. B.C., showing a woman with a child in her arms clasped close to her heart. This woman may be a foster-mother or a wet-nurse at the court of the local ruler. The inscription (written in the Hittite hieroglyphic script) identifies her as a woman of the court named Tuvarsas. The infant in her arms is one of the sons of Araras, king of Carchemish.

THEN he brought out the king's son, and put the crown upon him . . . and they said "Long live the king." (2 Chron. 23 : 11)

After Joash had been kept hidden away in the Temple from the queen, Athaliah, for six years (see p. 278), the moment came for him to be crowned. This was actually the culmination of a carefully planned and executed plot against Athaliah, the leading spirit of which was Jehoiada the priest, secretly supported by the Levites, the heads of the clans, and the captains of hundreds (2 Chron. 23 : 2-3, 8-9; cf. Vol. II p. 271). The conspiracy had a religious and dynastic character (ibid., verse 3). When all the preparations were complete, Jehoiada and his aides presented the king's son to the people, publicly crowned him, and proclaimed him king (ibid. verse 11). Then "Jehoiada made a covenant between himself and all the people and the king that they should be the Lord's people" (ibid., verse 16). As customary in the coronation ceremonies of the ancient East, Joash's crowning was also given the sanction of religious ritual. The ceremony was accompanied by song, hymns of praise, instrumental music, the playing of pipes and the blowing of trumpets (ibid. verses 12-14; 1 Kings 1:40). The traditional shout of "Long live the king" was a sign of the people's loyal support of its sovereign (1 Kings 1 : 39). In the picture above, Egyptian courtiers are greeting their king Horemheb, the founder of the Nineteenth Dynasty in Egypt (14th cent. B.C.). The courtiers are rendering homage to their new sovereign, with their hands raised and their faces uplifted in a gesture of reverent submission.

ABLE to handle spear and shield. (2 Chron. 25 : 5)

On ascending the throne after his father Joash had been assassinated in his bed by his attendants (2 Chron. 24 : 25), Amaziah immediately devoted his energies to placing his kingdom in a state of military preparedness (see Vol. II, p. 275). Like other kings of Judah, he organized the army on a clan-basis "and he mustered those twenty years old and upward, and found that they were three hundred thousand picked men, fit for war, able to handle spear and shield". It was, no doubt, with this new force that Amaziah fought his wars against Edom and Joash, king of Israel. Whereas the small shield (Heb. *magen*) covered only part of the ancient warrior's body, the large shield *(zinah)*, protected him entirely. Being cumbersome and heavy, it was held in front of the warrior by a special shield-bearer (1 Sam. 17 : 41; cf. above, p. 60). The picture reproduced above — a relief from Nineveh dating to the reign of Sennacherib (704-681 B.C.) — illustrates the employment of the large shield on the battle-field. Three pairs of Assyrian soldiers are seen engaged in the siege of an enemy city, each of them protected by a large screen made of plaited rushes which is the *zinah*. One of each pair is steadying the shield with one hand and holding a spear in the other, just as described in the expression in our verse here: "able to handle spear and shield". The second of each of the pair of soldiers is shooting an arrow at the beleaguered enemy. The great advantage of the large shield was that the warrior could stand upright behind it and thus fire his arrows with greater accuracy, even at long range. This relief also clearly demonstrates the construction of the large shield from bulrushes stitched to each other, with their heads bound tightly together at the top.

HE went out and made war against the Philistines, and broke down the wall of Gath and the wall of Yabneh and the wall of Ashdod ...

(2 Chron. 26 : 6)

King Uzziah created a large, well organized and well equipped army (see p. 277) with which he extended the borders of his kingdom to the south and west, in the direction of Philistia, the Negeb and the Arabah: "And his fame spread far, for he was marvellously helped, till he was strong" (2 Chron. 26 : 15; cf. Vol. II, p. 276). In the course of his incursion into Philistia, he took Gath (i.e. Gittaim; see p. 249) and Yabneh (i.e. Yabneel, Josh. 15 : 11), both of which lay north of Ashdod, and annexed the northern part of the country to Judah. He then set up fortifications in the conquered areas: "And he built cities in the territory of Ashdod and elsewhere among the Philistines" (ibid. verse 6). He also strengthened the defences of Ashdod, the capital city of the kingdom of Ashdod, which rose to political power and importance in the time of the Judean Monarchy.

However, Uzziah's triumphs were short-lived. Ashdod not only quickly regained its independence, in the reign of his grandson Ahaz, but even began to expand into the territory of Judah. In the time of Sargon II, Ashdod is mentioned in Assyrian inscriptions as having risen in revolt in an attempt to throw off the Assyrian yoke. The city was then governed by a ruler named Yamani who, after being swept into power by a revolution, allied himself with Egypt and fortified Ashdod against Assyria. Sargon reduced the city, turned it in 712-711 into an Assyrian province, and deported many of its inhabitants, replacing them by people from other lands. (Isa. 20 : 1; cf. Zech. 9 : 6). Under Sennacherib, Ashdod once more recovered its freedom and, with Assyrian help, again expanded its frontiers at the expense of Judah. The city suffered again during the transition from Assyrian to Babylonian rule and the struggle between these two empires for control of the road to Egypt. In Nebuchadnezzar's day it was the capital of a kingdom subject to Babylon; and, at the end of the Babylonian period, it was made the chief city of a province.

Photographed below is Tell Isdud (Ashdod), about 10 miles north of Ashkelon and 3 miles from the sea.

AND he built towers in the wilderness and hewed out many cisterns...

(2 Chron. 26 : 10)

The kingdom of Judah reached the height of its political and economic power in the reign of Uzziah (see the previous page). This monarch, who was famed for his initiative and drive (cf. Vol. II, p. 276), excuted a programme of large constructional works, ranging from the erection of strongpoints and defensive towers to the establishment of new settlements in Judah and the south, particularly in the frontier regions. He brought prosperity to the Negeb and the Judean wilderness by developing agriculture in the marginal districts on the edge of the desert, and especially by his encouragement of vine-growing and sheep-rearing: "For he had large herds, both in the Shephelah and in the plain, and he had farmers and vinedressers in the hills and in the fertile lands, for he loved the soil" (2 Chron. 26 : 10). Merchants' caravans now passed once more along the roads of the Negeb and the Arabah, as they had done in the days of Solomon and Jehoshaphat: to Edom and Elath and Kadesh-Barnea, to Sinai and Egypt.

Archaeological survey has shown that, in Uzziah's reign (8th cent. B.C.), there were many settlements in the Negeb guarding the lines of communication. These are the "fastnesses" (Heb. *mezadim*) or "towers" (*migdalim*) mentioned in the Bible. On the site of many of these settlements the remains of houses and sheep-pens have been discovered. The local population apparently lived by trade, sheep-rearing, and also agriculture. Near the fortresses water-cisterns were found hewn out of the natural rock, for the collection of flood-water from the winter rains. These cisterns provided sufficient water for the needs of the local inhabitants and of travellers throughout the year, and were even used for irrigating the cultivated plots of the Negeb. Such a Negeb cistern is seen in the picture here. As in the later Nabatean and Roman periods, so in Uzziah's time too the settlements in the arid expanses of the Negeb were triumphs of organization, industry and resourcefulness, made possible by proper military security and the maintenance of an intricate network of roads.

IN Jerusalem he made engines, invented by skilful men, to be on the towers and the corners, to shoot arrows and great stones ...

(2 Chron. 26 : 15)

One of Uzziah's great achievements was the organization of the army. In addition to "the mighty men of valour", he created a regular fighting force "to help the king against the enemy", and fitted it out with a variety of military equipment — shields, spears, helmets, coats of mail, bows, and slingstones. Amongst the measures taken by the king to strengthen this army, mention is made of "engines invented by skilful men". These were wood-and-iron structures mounted on top of the towers of the defence-works, to provide protection for the bowmen and slingers who fired their arrows and stones from behind them. A visual illustration of such an "engine" is found on the relief from the palace of Sennacherib portraying the capture of Lachish in the year 701 B.C. (see the reproduction). Above the city's wall and towers peculiar structures can be seen, with round objects like shields on them. There is no means of knowing whether these shields were an integral part of the original design, or whether they belonged to the marksmen and had been hung there by them. Behind these structures stand soldiers, mostly archers singly or in pairs, interspersed with an occasional group of three slingers. Thus protected from the enemy's arrows, they are able to stand fully upright and shoot their weapons to the maximum range. Uzziah's military innovation is here faithfully and accurately depicted by an Assyrian sculptor who lived several decades after the Judean king's death.

לכה הבת כה
עטמי עוזיה
מלך יהודה
ולא למפתח

AND they buried
him with his fathers in
the burial field which
belonged to the kings,
for they said, "He is a
leper." . . .
(2 Chron. 26 : 23)

It is related in the Book of Chronicles that King Uzziah was afflicted with leprosy because he presumed to burn incense in the Temple of the Lord in place of the Aaronite priests: "And leprosy broke out on his forehead, in the presence of the priests in the house of the Lord, by the altar of incense" (2 Chron. 26 : 19). According to the verse at the head of this page, Uzziah, as a leper, was buried, not in the City of David like the other kings of Judah, but in a special burial-ground near the graves of his ancestors (cf., however, 2 Kings 15 : 7). The body was apparently disinterred later and the bones transferred to another place. This is evident from an Aramaic inscription (see the reproduction) on a plaque of hard, light-coloured limestone, now in the collection of antiquities of the Russian Church on the Mount of Olives, which reads as follows:

Hither were brought
The bones of Uzziah
King of Judah
Not to be opened.

From the language and from the script, which is characteristic of epitaphs carved on ossuaries, the inscription may be dated to the end of the Second Temple. As it is not known where this inscription was originally discovered, it cannot be of any assistance to us in tracing the location of Uzziah's reinterment which was still known in the time of Benjamin of Tudela and in that of the Karaite Judah Hadassi.

AFTER these things and these acts of faithfulness Sennacherib king of Assyria came and invaded Judah and encamped against the fortified cities, thinking to win them for himself.   (2 Chron. 32 : 1)

Jerusalem's successful resistance to the assaults of the forces of the Assyrian king Sennacherib, in the year 701 B.C. (see Vol. III, p. 63), is described in the Bible as one of God's great marvels (2 Kings chaps. 18-19; Isa. chaps. 36-37). It was this resistance that saved Judah from destruction and its population from exile.

This particular Assyrian campaign is described in detail on one of the few of Sennacherib's prisms recording the king's battles in chronological sequence that has been preserved intact (see the reproduction on the right). Sennacherib boasts of his victory in the following terms: "As to Hezekiah the Jew, who did not submit to my yoke, I laid siege to 46 of his strong cities, walled forts and to the countless small villages in their vicinity, and conquered (them) by means of well-stamped (earth-)ramps, and battering-rams brought near (to the walls combined with) the attack by foot-soldiers (using) mines, breeches, as well as by storming the walls with the help of ladders. I drove out (of them) 200,150 people, young and old, male and female, horses, mules, donkeys, camels, big and small cattle beyond counting, and considered (them) booty. Himself I made a prisoner in Jerusalem his royal residence, like a bird in a cage. I surrounded him with earthwork. I made utterly repugnant to him the going out through his city-gate".

The inscription ends with a list of the tribute paid by Hezekiah to Assyria. The first part of this list accords in detail with that given in the biblical narrative (2 Kings 18 : 14-16): "30 talents of gold and 800 talents of silver" (a figure which apparently includes, in addition to the 300 talents mentioned in the Bible, the weight of the silver stripped off the Temple doors by Hezekiah). Sennacherib then adds: "precious stones, the best antimony, large cuts of red stones, couches and arm-chairs inlaid with ivory, elephant-hides, ivories, ebony-wood, box-wood, and all kinds of treasures; as well as his own daughters and concubines, male and female singers. And his (personal) messenger he sent to me to deliver the tribute and to do obeisance".

A great many people were gathered, and they stopped all the springs and the brook that flowed through the land . . .

(2 Chron. 32 : 4)

One of the most difficult problems that faced Hezekiah after his revolt against his Assyrian overlord, Sennacherib, was the provision of water for the capital in time of siege. Jerusalem had always drawn its water from the Gihon spring which lay outside the city walls. From the end of the Late Canaanite period onwards, repeated attempts were made to cut subterranean channels to this spring, so as to make its waters available even when the city was closely beleaguered. Hezekiah too, when preparing for his revolt, ordered a tunnel to be cut through the rock, to bring the water of the spring into the city (2 Kings 20 : 20; cf. Vol. II, p. 291). In order to ensure a constant flow from the spring for the inhabitants, while at the same time denying its use to the enemy ("Why should the kings of Assyria come and find much water?"), Hezekiah had the mouth of the Gihon and its old surface conduit ("the brook that flowed through the land") blocked, and its waters diverted into the new tunnel (or "conduit").

The cutting of this tunnel was done simultaneously from both ends. Owing to technical problems presented by the nature of the rock, the shaft had to follow a winding course. Thus, although its distance from end to end is only 1050 ft. in a straight line, its actual length is 1683 ft. The tunnel is symmetrical in shape and the stone-work well finished (see the photograph above), but its height varies on account of the difficulties encountered in the cutting. An inscription incised into the wall of the tunnel, not far from its outlet (reproduced in Vol. II, p. 291), records the manner in which this remarkable feat of engineering was accomplished and how the water flowed "from the spring to the pool". The new pool (Heb. *berekhah*), which served as a reservoir for the water, was apparently the pool in the Valley of Hinnom to-day called el-Birkeh.

He practiced soothsaying and augury and sorcery, and dealt with mediums and with wizards . . .

(2 Chron. 33 : 6)

In the reign of Manasseh, king of Judah, the growing political and cultural pressure exercised by the Assyrian empire on its subject peoples in Syria and Palestine led to the spread of idolatry in Jerusalem, on the Assyrian and Tyrian pattern. Manasseh erected altars to Baal and "the host of heaven", made an Asherah-image which he placed in the Temple, and even sacrificed his own son as a burnt-offering (2 Chron. 33 : 3-6; 2 Kings 21 : 3-6). In addition to these sins, the biblical historian charges him with soothsaying, augury, and having dealings with mediums and wizards. Acts of sorcery like these usually involved the uttering of spells designed to nullify the baleful influence of demons and evil spirits.

Reproduced above is an amulet in the form of a small gypsum plaque which was found at Til Barsip (now Arslan Tash in Syria, on the Euphrates) and is from the 7th cent. B.C. On it is inscribed, in Aramaic characters, a spell to ward off night-demons. Also engraved on the amulet is the figure of a god wearing a short Syrian tunic, with an Assyrian-style headdress, and holding an axe in his right hand. The hole at the top of the charm was evidently made to take the thread by which it was attached to the wearer's body. On the front (other) side of the amulet are engraved the figures of a winged sphinx and a she-wolf in the act of devouring a man (see Vol. I, p. 120).

THEREFORE the LORD brought upon them the commanders of the army of the king of Assyria, who took Manasseh with hooks and bound him with fetters of bronze and brought him to Babylon.　(2 Chron. 33 : 11)

The Book of Chronicles relates that Manasseh was taken captive and that, while a prisoner in Babylon, he repented of his evil ways and returned to God (2 Chron. 33 : 12-13). From the account which follows of the fortification of Judah (ibid. verse 14), it appears that Manasseh had tried to throw off the Assyrian yoke. Some scholars hold that the king against whom he revolted was Ashurbanipal (668-630 B.C.); others that it was the latter's father, Esarhaddon (680-669 B.C.). According to the second theory, Manasseh was supported in his insurrection by Tirhaka, king of Ethiopia, Assyria's great enemy (see Vol. II, p. 288). When the revolt failed, Manasseh was taken captive and carried off in fetters and hooks to imprisonment in Babylon.

The "hook" (Heb. *hoah*, or *hah*, cf. Isa. 37 : 29) was originally a ring inserted into the nostrils of a bull to which the animal's halter was attached. The Assyrians were in the habit of putting such rings through the noses of the kings captured by them in war. This practice is clearly illustrated on the relief from Zenjirli, in northern Syria, which is reproduced here: two captive princes, portrayed as dwarfs beside the gigantic figure of their conqueror, are being led by ropes passed through "hooks" in their noses and their ends held by the Assyrian king, Esarhaddon. The taller of the two captives is Baal, king of Tyre, or perhaps Tirhaka, king of Ethiopia, himself.

AND they boiled the holy offerings in
pots, in cauldrons, and in pans ...
                    (2 Chron. 35 : 13)

This verse lists three kinds of utensil used in boiling the offerings at the great celebration of the Passover that was
held in the eighteenth year of Josiah's reign in Judah. Since the utensils specified — pots, cauldrons and pans —
were not set apart only for sacred purposes, it may be assumed that those used in the sacrifices were made of
superior material, perhaps metal in place of the everyday pottery.
The pot (Heb. *sir*), though an all-purpose cooking utensil (2 Kings 4 : 39), was especially employed in the preparation of meat (Ex. 16 : 3), as was the cauldron *(dud)* (1 Sam. 2 : 14; Ezek. 24 : 5). The pan, or dish *(zalahath)*, on the other hand, was generally used, in biblical times, for serving food (2 Kings 21 : 13)and only rarely,
it would seem, for cooking it (see Vol. II, p. 292; and this volume, p. 83).
Reproduced above are two cooking utensils which were in common use in the period of the Israelite Monarchy.
The more elongated of the two (below) is identified by some scholars as a biblical "pot", and the round one (above)
as a "cauldron".

NEVERTHELESS Josiah would not turn away from him ... but joined battle in the plain of Megiddo. (2 Chron. 35 : 22)

One of the great battles that decided the fate of the kingdom of Judah was fought near Megiddo, at the entrance to the Valley of Jezreel, in the year 609 B.C. In this engagement King Josiah, who had regained complete independence for his country, tried to bar the way to the forces of Pharaoh Neco which were advancing to the aid of the tottering Assyrian empire (see Vol. II, p. 296), According to our verse here, Neco sought to avoid a head-on clash with Josiah: "But he sent envoys to him saying, 'What have we to do with each other, king of Judah? I am not coming against you this day, but against the house with which I am at war; and God has commanded me to make haste'..." (2 Chron. 35 : 21). Neco was evidently anxious to press onwards without fighting, since he was hurrying to the assistance of the Assyrian army which was at that time engaged in northern Syria against the combined forces of Babylonia and Media. But Josiah, fearing Egyptian domination of his kingdom, rejected the Pharaoh's peace-feelers and marched out to do battle with him. The fate of the engagement was decided when Josiah, mortally wounded, was carried off the field by his attendants and brought to Jerusalem, were he died (2 Chron. 24-25).

The scene of the battle between the armies of Josiah and the Pharaoh, described in our verse as "the plain of Megiddo", was the south-western part of the valley near the ancient city (see the photograph on the left), where the *Via Maris* from Egypt to Syria ran past the foot of the city-mound. Close to Megiddo this road split into two lines: one to the plain of Acre and thence northwards to Phoenicia; and the other, by way of the valley of Ginossar, to Damascus or the Lebanon. The plain of Megiddo, lying thus at the junction of important international highways, had from time immemorial been the scene of battles against invading armies. It was thus natural that Josiah should have taken up his position there to oppose Neco's advance.

The untimely death of Josiah, the greatest of the last Davidic kings, brought to an end Judah's brief period of independence. Only twenty four years later, the First Temple was destroyed and the people of Judah carried off captive to Babylon. Seventy years were to pass from the battle of Megiddo before hope dawned for the restoration of the fallen kingdom, when, in the first year of his reign (538 B.C.), Cyrus, the Persian king, opened the gates for the Return to Zion (see above, p. 219). The latest of the books in the Old Testament canon ends on this hopeful note of return and revival.

עמוד ימני (דברי הימים ב לו · תהלים א–ב)

וַיֶּגֶל הַשְּׁאֵרִית מִן הַחֶרֶב אֶל בָּבֶל וַיִּהְיוּ
לוֹ וּלְבָנָיו לַעֲבָדִים עַד מְלֹךְ מַלְכוּת פָּרַס ‭·‬ לְמַלֹּאות
דְּבַר יְהֹוָה בְּפִי יִרְמְיָהוּ עַד רָצְתָה הָאָרֶץ ‭·‬ אֶת
שַׁבְּתוֹתֶיהָ כָּל יְמֵי הָשַּׁמָּה שָׁבָתָה לְמַלֹּאות שִׁבְעִים
שָׁנָה ‭·‬ וּבִשְׁנַת אַחַת לְכוֹרֶשׁ מֶלֶךְ
פָּרַס לִכְלוֹת דְּבַר יְהֹוָה בְּפִי יִרְמְיָהוּ הֵעִיר יְהֹוָה
אֶת רוּחַ כֹּרֶשׁ מֶלֶךְ פָּרַס וַיַּעֲבֶר קוֹל בְּכָל
מַלְכוּתוֹ וְגַם בְּמִכְתָּב לֵאמֹר ‭·‬ כֹּה אָמַר
כֹּרֶשׁ מֶלֶךְ פָּרַס כָּל מַמְלְכוֹת הָאָרֶץ נָתַן לִי
יְהֹוָה אֱלֹהֵי הַשָּׁמַיִם וְהוּא פָקַד עָלַי לִבְנוֹת לוֹ
בַיִת בִּירוּשָׁלַם אֲשֶׁר בִּיהוּדָה מִי בָכֶם מִכָּל עַמּוֹ
יְהֹוָה אֱלֹהָיו עִמּוֹ וְיָעַל ‭·‬

— סכום הפסוקים אלף ושבע
מאות וששים וחמשה ‭·‬

אַשְׁרֵי הָאִישׁ אֲשֶׁר לֹא הָלַךְ בַּעֲצַת רְשָׁעִים
וּבְדֶרֶךְ חַטָּאִים לֹא עָמָד וּבְמוֹשַׁב לֵצִים לֹא יָשָׁב ‭·‬
כִּי אִם בְּתוֹרַת יְהֹוָה חֶפְצוֹ וּבְתוֹרָתוֹ יֶהְגֶּה יוֹמָם וָלָיְלָה ‭·‬
וְהָיָה כְּעֵץ שָׁתוּל עַל פַּלְגֵי מָיִם אֲשֶׁר פִּרְיוֹ
יִתֵּן בְּעִתּוֹ וְעָלֵהוּ לֹא יִבּוֹל וְכֹל אֲשֶׁר יַעֲשֶׂה יַצְלִיחַ ‭·‬
לֹא כֵן הָרְשָׁעִים כִּי אִם כַּמֹּץ אֲשֶׁר תִּדְּפֶנּוּ רוּחַ ‭·‬
עַל כֵּן לֹא יָקֻמוּ רְשָׁעִים בַּמִּשְׁפָּט וְחַטָּאִים בַּעֲדַת צַדִּיקִים ‭·‬
כִּי יוֹדֵעַ יְהֹוָה דֶּרֶךְ צַדִּיקִים וְדֶרֶךְ רְשָׁעִים תֹּאבֵד ‭·‬

לָמָּה רָגְשׁוּ גוֹיִם וּלְאֻמִּים יֶהְגּוּ רִיק ‭·‬
יִתְיַצְּבוּ מַלְכֵי אֶרֶץ וְרוֹזְנִים נוֹסְדוּ יָחַד
עַל יְהֹוָה וְעַל מְשִׁיחוֹ ‭·‬ נְנַתְּקָה אֶת מוֹסְרוֹתֵימוֹ
וְנַשְׁלִיכָה מִמֶּנּוּ עֲבֹתֵימוֹ ‭·‬ יוֹשֵׁב בַּשָּׁמַיִם יִשְׂחָק
אֲדֹנָי יִלְעַג לָמוֹ ‭·‬ אָז יְדַבֵּר אֵלֵימוֹ בְאַפּוֹ

עמוד שמאלי (תהלים ב–ד)

וּבַחֲרוֹנוֹ יְבַהֲלֵמוֹ ‭·‬ וַאֲנִי נָסַכְתִּי מַלְכִּי
עַל צִיּוֹן הַר קָדְשִׁי ‭·‬ אֲסַפְּרָה אֶל חֹק יְהֹוָה
אָמַר אֵלַי בְּנִי אַתָּה אֲנִי הַיּוֹם יְלִדְתִּיךָ ‭·‬
שְׁאַל מִמֶּנִּי וְאֶתְּנָה גוֹיִם נַחֲלָתֶךָ וַאֲחֻזָּתְךָ אַפְסֵי אָרֶץ ‭·‬
תְּרֹעֵם בְּשֵׁבֶט בַּרְזֶל כִּכְלִי יוֹצֵר תְּנַפְּצֵם ‭·‬
וְעַתָּה מְלָכִים הַשְׂכִּילוּ הִוָּסְרוּ שֹׁפְטֵי אָרֶץ ‭·‬
עִבְדוּ אֶת יְהֹוָה בְּיִרְאָה וְגִילוּ בִּרְעָדָה ‭·‬
נַשְּׁקוּ בַר פֶּן יֶאֱנַף וְתֹאבְדוּ דֶרֶךְ
כִּי יִבְעַר כִּמְעַט אַפּוֹ אַשְׁרֵי כָּל חוֹסֵי בוֹ ‭·‬

מִזְמוֹר לְדָוִד בְּבָרְחוֹ מִפְּנֵי אַבְשָׁלוֹם בְּנוֹ ‭·‬
יְהֹוָה מָה רַבּוּ צָרָי רַבִּים קָמִים עָלָי ‭·‬
רַבִּים אֹמְרִים לְנַפְשִׁי אֵין יְשׁוּעָתָה לּוֹ בֵאלֹהִים סֶלָה ‭·‬
וְאַתָּה יְהֹוָה מָגֵן בַּעֲדִי כְּבוֹדִי וּמֵרִים רֹאשִׁי ‭·‬
קוֹלִי אֶל יְהֹוָה אֶקְרָא וַיַּעֲנֵנִי מֵהַר קָדְשׁוֹ סֶלָה ‭·‬
אֲנִי שָׁכַבְתִּי וָאִישָׁנָה הֱקִיצוֹתִי כִּי יְהֹוָה יִסְמְכֵנִי ‭·‬
לֹא אִירָא מֵרִבְבוֹת עָם אֲשֶׁר סָבִיב שָׁתוּ עָלָי ‭·‬
קוּמָה יְהֹוָה הוֹשִׁיעֵנִי אֱלֹהַי כִּי הִכִּיתָ
אֶת כָּל אֹיְבַי לֶחִי שִׁנֵּי רְשָׁעִים שִׁבַּרְתָּ ‭·‬
לַיהֹוָה הַיְשׁוּעָה עַל עַמְּךָ בִרְכָתֶךָ סֶּלָה ‭·‬

לַמְנַצֵּחַ בִּנְגִינוֹת מִזְמוֹר לְדָוִד ‭·‬
בְּקָרְאִי עֲנֵנִי אֱלֹהֵי צִדְקִי בַּצָּר הִרְחַבְתָּ לִּי
חָנֵּנִי וּשְׁמַע תְּפִלָּתִי ‭·‬ בְּנֵי אִישׁ
עַד מֶה כְבוֹדִי לִכְלִמָּה תֶּאֱהָבוּן רִיק תְּבַקְשׁוּ כָזָב סֶלָה ‭·‬
וּדְעוּ כִּי הִפְלָה יְהֹוָה חָסִיד לוֹ
יְהֹוָה יִשְׁמַע בְּקָרְאִי אֵלָיו ‭·‬ רִגְזוּ וְאַל תֶּחֱטָאוּ
אִמְרוּ בִלְבַבְכֶם עַל מִשְׁכַּבְכֶם וְדֹמּוּ סֶלָה ‭·‬

דִּישׁוּעָר ‭ג‬ אֲשֶׁר עֶשֶׂר יִישׁוּעָה תְּוָרֵירֵהּ וְשַׁבְּכֶם מִיט לְהוֹרָה וְהֵשׁוּעָה ‭·‬
חָזַסֵר ‭ב‬ בְּטֶע וְמִיהַנֵזוּ חֹושְׁעָנִי בְּאֵפֶר ‭·‬

The plate is a photograph of the concluding section of the Books of Chronicles from the Bible Codex *(Kether Torah)* of Aharon ben Asher (a Massorete who lived at the end of the 9th or beginning of the 10th cent. A.D.). In this manuscript, as usual in the texts written by the Massoretes and in Sephardic manuscripts, the Books of Chronicles are placed before the Psalms.

INDEXES

OBJECTS AND MONUMENTS

PHOTOGRAPHS